Football

For Mum and Dad

Football

A Sociology of the Global Game

Richard Giulianotti

Polity Press

First published in 1999 by Polity Press in association with Blackwell Publishers Ltd.

Editorial office:
Polity Press
65 Bridge Street
Cambridge CB2 1UR, UK

Marketing and production:
Blackwell Publishers Ltd
108 Cowley Road
Oxford OX4 1JF, UK

Published in the USA by
Blackwell Publishers Inc.
Commerce Place
350 Main Street
Malden, MA 02148, USA

ISBN 0-7456-1768-9
ISBN 0-7456-1769-7 (pbk)

A catalogue record for this book is available from the British Library.

Library of Congress Cataloging-in-Publication Data
Giulianotti, Richard, 1966-
    Football: a sociology of the global game / Richard Giulianotti.
        p.   cm.
    Includes bibliographical references (p.) and index.
    ISBN 0-7456-1768-9 (hb : alk. paper). — ISBN 0-7456-1769-7 (pb :
alk. paper)
        1. Soccer—Social aspects.   2. Soccer—History.   3. Sports—
Sociological aspects.   I. Title.
    GV943. 9. S64G576   1999
    306.4′83—dc21   99-11069
                                                                          CIP

Typeset in 10½ on 12 pt Times
by Ace Filmsetting Ltd, Frome, Somerset
Printed in Great Britain by TJ International Ltd, Padstow, Cornwall

This book is printed on acid-free paper.

Contents

Acknowledgements   vii

Glossary   ix

Foreword   xi

1   The Essence of Football: the Historical and Social Bases of the
    Global Game   1

2   The Twentieth-century Sport: Football, Class and Nation   23

3   Spectator Cultures: Passion at Play in Europe and Latin America   39

4   Football Grounds: Emotional Attachments and Social Control   66

5   The Price of Victory: Football Finance and the Television
    Revolution   86

6   Football's Players: from Local Heroes to International Stars   107

7   The Goal of Winning? Football, Science, Tactics and Aesthetics   127

8   The Cultural Politics of Play: Ethnicity, Gender and the
    'Post-fan' Mentality   146

Afterword   166

Notes   174

References   185

Index   208

Acknowledgements

I have many people to thank for their help with my research over the years. My colleagues in the Sociology Department at the University of Aberdeen have always provided sound assistance with my research. Generous research funding came, in turn, from the University's Grants Committee, the Economic and Social Research Council (ESRC), and the Carnegie Trust for the Universities of Scotland. Greetings go to the football and general sports research groupings at the following universities: Strathclyde, De Montfort, Manchester Metropolitan, Leicester, Salford, Liverpool, London (Birkbeck College), Brighton and Goldsmiths. Special thanks to Gary Armstrong for years of joint work, discussion and free accommodation.

Overseas, I owe debts of gratitude to: Alessandro Dal Lago, Rocco De Biasi and Nicolà Porro in Italy; Roman Horak in Austria; Ronit Lentin in Dublin; David Andrews in the USA; Hans Hognestad and Eduardo Archetti in Norway; José Sergio Leite Lopes, Rosilene Alvim, Guilerme Carvalhi do Ferreira, Marcos Nowosad, Fernando Vianna and César Gordon in Brazil; Pablo Alabarces, Maria Graciela Rodrigues and their colleagues at the University of Buenos Aires; Rafael Bayce and César Aguiar in Montevideo; John Hughson, John Nauright, Dennis Hemphill, Rob Hess, Bob Stewart, Bill Murray, Tony Hughes, Roy Hay and many others in Australia. The staff in the School of Social Science at the University of New England, Australia, were also great to work with during my year there as an exchange lecturer. I am very grateful to my football research groups in Aberdeen and Edinburgh, and to the fans that make up the 'Tartan Army', for their patience and humour during my studies.

In Aberdeen, I have to thank my immediate and extended family of parents, brother, grandparents, aunts and uncles and cousins. Among my oldest friends I'd like to thank Dave, Ronnie, Willie, Scott, Martin, Kenny and Steve and partners. Thanks too to Barrie and Mary O'Loan, Mike Gerrard and Terry Penny. Overseas, I have greatly enjoyed the friendship of Pino Sardo, Roberto

Merciadri and their friends in Genoa; Armando Rivarola and Maria José in Ascunción; Roberto Elissalde and family in Montevideo; and Andrew and Airlie Johnson, Peter Corrigan and Steven Thiele and family in Armidale, New South Wales.

Finally, in the course of writing this book, I have to thank Tony Giddens and his team at Polity for seeing the project through; and Donna and baby daughter Gabriella Rose for allowing me the countless hours to sit, read and write about football.

Glossary

AFA	Asociacion del Fútbol Argentino (Argentinian Football Association)
AFC	Asian Football Confederation
ASSH	Australian Society for Sports History
BBC	British Broadcasting Corporation
BSA	British Sociological Association
BSB	British Satellite Broadcasting
BSkyB	British Sky Broadcasting
CAF	Confédération Africaine de Football (African Football Confederation)
CCCS	Centre for Contemporary Cultural Studies (Birmingham)
CCTV	closed circuit television
CONCACAF	Confederación Norte-Centro-americana y del Caribe de Fútbol (North and Central American and Caribbean Football Confederation)
CONMEBOL	Confederación Sudamericana de Fútbol (South American Football Confederation)
CRASH	Creating Resistance to Society's Haemorrhoids
DFB	Deutscher Fussball-Bund (German Football Association)
EBU	European Broadcasting Union
EC	European Community
ENIC	English National Investment Company
EPO	erythropoietin
ESRC	Economic and Social Research Council (UK)
EU	European Union
EUI	European University Institute (Florence)
FA	Football Association (English)
FFACJA	Football Fans Against the Criminal Justice Act (UK)

FIFA	Fédération Internationale de Football Association
FSA	Football Supporters' Association
GAA	Gaelic Athletic Association
ISA	Independent Supporters' Association
ISL	International Sport and Leisure
ITV	Independent Television (UK)
KGB	Committee of State Security (Soviet Secret Police)
MBO	management by objectives
MLS	Major League Soccer (United States)
NASL	North American Soccer League
NASSS	North American Society for the Sociology of Sport
NBA	National Basketball Association
NCIS	National Criminal Intelligence Service
NFFSC	National Federation of Football Supporters' Clubs
PFA	Professional Footballers' Association (English)
PPV	pay per view
SFA	Scottish Football Association
Sky TV	Sky Television
SNCCFR	Sir Norman Chester Centre for Football Research (Leicester)
T y C	Torneos y Competencias (South American Television)
UEFA	Union des Associations Européennes de Football
WM	Football playing formation invented by Herbert Chapman at Arsenal in the 1920s

Foreword

The Passion of Peoples: the essential social appeal of football

Any discussion of world football must open with an acknowledgement of the game's global appeal. Though it may be increasingly passé to say as much, association football is undeniably the world's premier sport. No other form of popular culture engenders football's huge and participatory passion among its devotees. While this book seeks to explore the social, cultural and historical complexities of the game, the initial impression is one of curiosity that a single sporting form is able to entrance so many different kinds of people. Football's cross-cultural appeal extends from its established congregations in Europe and South America to the mass conversion of Australasia, Africa, Asia and even the United States. The game's cross-class profile in Latin nations is beginning to be duplicated in Northern Europe and the new football territories. Though football reflects the wider distribution of gender-related power in most societies, the game is also undergoing varying degrees of feminization among players, spectators, commentators and officials. Moreover, it is a sport that retains rather than relinquishes the loyalties of its followers throughout their lifecourse.

Certainly, football has some essential features which contribute to this popularity. Probably the most important is the relative simplicity of football's laws, equipment and body techniques. Only a few key rules must be observed if football is to be meaningfully played and watched. Outfield players cannot be allowed to handle the ball, hacking must also be prohibited, while opposing teams should attempt to beat one another by scoring more goals into a recognized goal. Even these rules can be amended to fit with training procedures or break up the routine of conventional play. Other rules – such as those relating to offside, fouling and penalties, team numbers, the duration of play or the precise parameters for playing and scoring – can all be agreed between the players before or during games. The relative plasticity of football's laws reflects the fact that its practitioners throughout the world will try to play in almost any circumstance: on standard pitches, certainly, but also in unmarked fields, public streets, gymnasia, beaches or even the family home.

Undoubtedly, the simple equipment requirements of football have been a major attraction for the lower social classes in most parts of the world. While football may be played in most informal, public settings, it requires no specialist attire or sophisticated technology, except the requisite-sized sphere with which to pass and dribble. Players need only learn to master some basic skills in trapping and manoeuvring the ball by foot to participate in games. The defensive skills of marking, tackling or goal-keeping may be encouraged initially among the technically less adept. Finally, football is increasingly peculiar in a sporting sense, in that it tends to encourage a heterogeneity of body shapes and sizes. Players of varying physical fitness, height, weight and age may find specific playing positions that are favourable to their body shape.

All these features follow from football's innate simplicity. On balance, however, all are outweighed and qualitatively transformed by the multiplicity of social influences within football. In other words, there is little essential to football that makes it so compelling for cultures throughout the world. Instead, my argument here is straightforward enough within the human sciences: specifically that the game's valued characteristics tells us something fundamental about the cultures in which it is performed. Nomadic football supporters are already well aware that, if they wish to encounter their host society and to understand the complexity of its social structure and moral values, then the nearest major sports event will conveniently condense and dramatize these elements before the visitor's gaze (see Cresswell and Evans 1997). Football in any setting provides us with a kind of cultural map, a metaphorical representation, which enhances our understanding of that society (see Bateson 1972). We should perhaps ensure that this metaphor does not forget how the map and its plotted subjects continue to interact in complex ways. Its cultural centrality in most societies means that football carries a heavy political and symbolic significance, to the extent that the game can contribute fundamentally to the social actions, practical philosophies and cultural identities of many, many people.

The leitmotif of this book demonstrates that football's diffusion across the world has enabled different cultures and nations to construct particular forms of identity through their interpretation and practice of the game. That diversity is increasingly undermined by the interplay of economic and cultural forces which are transforming the game's cartography into a global marketplace. Nevertheless, when we view the 'football world' in a historical sense, it does become possible to explore the long interrelations of football cultures. That cultural-historical perspective encourages me to periodize the key developments within football on a chapter-by-chapter basis. The book deals primarily with professional football, which is increasingly influential within the non-professional game, in terms of establishing key reference points for action, discourse, ethics and ambition among ordinary players. It is not intended to be a second doctoral thesis, but instead seeks to provide the first 'sociology of football' by exploring the game's major social properties and issues.

The Tactics of Analysis: locating the 'traditional', 'modern' and 'post-modern'

The text is not dominated by one philosophical tradition but instead draws upon a range of sociological perspectives and *maîtres à penser*. Each chapter discusses specific social and historical issues within football *per se*. I draw upon these philosophical perspectives according to their potential value and previous influence in explaining the issue under examination. I am also keen to discuss previous sociological research that is concerned with each specific issue. Inevitably, some topics (like football hooliganism) have received far more sociological investigation than others (such as football's playing styles).

Most chapters are structured around the historical trajectory of specific football issues. I argue that each of these issues has been through specific stages that may be categorized as 'traditional', 'modern' and 'post-modern'. My definition of these terms is conventionally sociological. When I discuss the 'traditional' I am talking about the 'pre-modern', where vestiges of the pre-industrial or the pre-capitalist era are still strongly influential. Generally, this involves the aristocracy or traditional middle class exercising their authority by convention, rather than by rational or democratic means. In international relations, Britain's imperial influence remains pervasive.

'Modernity' is associated with rapid urbanization and the demographic and political rise of the working class. A division is established between male (public, productive) spaces and female (private, reproductive) spaces. International events come to have an increased influence on everyday social life. Identity comes to be fixed along the axes of class, gender, age, locality and ethnicity. The rise of the mass media, improvements in the transport infrastructure, and the creation of a national education programme (as part of a welfare system) all serve to promote unitary senses of national identity. In industry, productivity and profitability are maximized through more complex divisions of labour. 'Fordism' involves workers being given specific tasks to repeat endlessly on the factory production line. 'Deskilling' becomes an occupational hazard for tradespeople and artisans. 'Taylorism' or 'scientific management' involves the use of time and motion studies to maximize the efficiency of individual workers. The factory system favours the production of identical commodities on a mass scale. In leisure and recreation, the class division between the bourgeoisie and working classes is reproduced through the differentiation of high ('legitimate') and low ('popular') culture. Modernity is also rooted in new kinds of rational social organization. Bureaucratic systems become ever more complex; social life becomes more regulated and predictable; public geography and architecture become more standardized. Temporally, 'early' and 'late' modernity can be distinguished according to different social levels of reflexivity and self-criticism. Yet throughout, the spectre that haunts modernity is its self-assurance, its faith in progress, its utopian conviction that problems and people can be 'put right'.

The contemporary age of post-modernity is signalled by the critical extension or actual rejection of modernity and its defining properties. Socially, post-modernity involves suburbanization; the rise of new white-collar forms of employment; and the splintering of the working classes. Social and cultural identities become increasingly fluid and 'neo-tribal' in their leisure orientations. Feminism challenges patriarchy, while a singular national identity is undermined by immigration and ethnic diversity. Globalization of people, technology and culture gives rise to a cultural hybridity and economic dependency of nations upon international markets. 'Post-Fordist' forms of industrial production involve workers being hired on short-term contracts; they must fit into all kinds of jobs on the factory floor; the products that they manufacture change constantly, in line with market demands; meanwhile, the new production system enables the flexible accumulation of capital for entrepreneurs. The division between high and low culture collapses. The power and status of professionals and bureaucracies are constantly challenged. Architectural styles favour pastiche and the 'retro' look. Overall, post-modernity is characterized by a philosophical scepticism towards science; an opposition towards 'meta-narratives' and 'grand theories' that purport to explain all history; and an instinctive distrust of modernity's faith in historical progress and human enlightenment.

I am not arguing that the 'traditional', 'modern' and 'post-modern' epochs can be easily combined to provide a study in football's uncomplicated, linear and irreversible (post-)modernization. None of these epochs is hermetically sealed from the others. For example, the 'globalization' of peoples through migration began long before the industrial revolution. In the 'modern' and 'post-modern' world, 'traditional' kinds of authority still have at least some residual influence (for example, the aristocrats who sit on the English Football Association [FA]). Moreover, historians and sociologists continue to argue about the degree to which each epoch is self-identifying. 'Traditions' are socially constructed by the powerful to protect their material and political interests, and to cement particular senses or 'myths' of national identity (Hobsbawm and Ranger 1983). The progressive and emancipating dimensions of 'modernity' ensure that it remains forever an incomplete project, paralysed increasingly by the self-critical and reflexive impulses that it promotes (see Habermas 1987a). Meanwhile, 'post-modernity' continues to be a highly contested term in its own right. Critical sociologists and philosophers argue that 'late modernity' describes the current historical age rather better than the more dramatic (but vacuous) appellation 'post-modernity' (see Jameson 1991;

Giddens 1990). Others point to the inner contradictions of the concept of 'post-modernity', notably its association with unscientific or irrational modes of thought, and its tendency to reject 'meta-narratives' through arguments that are 'meta-narratives' in their own right (see Lyotard 1984).

Nevertheless, I view these periodizations as 'ideal types' with an intrinsic heuristic and hermeneutic value. They are useful general concepts and categories for structuring our understanding of historical events and actions, though with the recognition that 'reality' will not always fit all that neatly into these categorizations. More powerfully, these historical categories help us to generate a 'documentary meaning' for specific events or developments within football, by relating them to the wider social and political context, or to the prevailing *weltanschauung* (world-view) of the time. Hence, for example, as I argue in chapter 7, the 'WM' playing system of Arsenal during the 1930s becomes meaningful within the wider context of the 'Fordist' mode of industrial production at that time. A 'hermeneutic circle' exists between using these grains of social life to understand the wider social context, and using the broader social context to explain one of its particular features (see Gadamer 1975). Football and other kinds of sporting practice are not 'dependent' on the wider society; they are instead influenced by and influential upon the broader social context. I should add here that this contextual approach is not neutral in terms of critique. I favour the socially engaged, critical wing of hermeneutics that 'exercises suspicion' towards the language, thoughts and actions of the powerful (Ricoeur 1970: 32–6).

The hermeneutic method has strong parallels here to the position of superstructural Marxism and critical theory. According to this viewpoint, sport and other particularistic forms of the 'popular culture superstructure' stand in a position of 'relative autonomy' to the remaining structures and superstructures of society. Pierre Bourdieu, that alchemist of divergent sociological traditions, explains the implications for sport very succinctly: 'The history of sport is relatively autonomous history which, even when marked by major events of economic and social history, has its own tempo, its own evolutionary laws, its crises, in short, its specific chronology' (Bourdieu, 1991a: 358).

My position throughout the book, therefore, is that the social aspects of football only become meaningful when located within their historical and cultural context. Football is neither dependent upon nor isolated from the influences of that wider milieu; instead, a relative autonomy exists in the relationship between the two.

The book is divided into eight chapters and ends with an afterword. The first two chapters discuss the history and general sociology of football. Chapter 1 examines the social emergence and global diffusion of association football. I also discuss at length the game's dichotomous meaning within social relations. Football gives rise to intense rivalries and oppositions, but also enables more positive forms of social 'belonging' to emerge, which point towards the game's religious dimensions. Chapter 2 expands on these points by looking at the shifting power relations within football throughout the twentieth century. The 'nation' becomes the most fundamental football unit, underpinned by class and localist social ties. As we enter the third millennium, however, we find that the new football nations (like the USA or Australia) no longer utilize the game to cement senses of national 'belonging'.

The remainder of the book is devoted to looking at the history and sociology of specific football issues. Chapter 3 examines supporter cultures in the UK, northern and southern Europe and Latin America. Football 'spaces', in particular football stadia, are discussed in chapter 4. I turn to look at the business dimension of football in chapter 5, and then examine the changing economic and cultural circumstances of football players in chapter 6. The historical aesthetics and playing styles of football are the subject of chapter 7; the final chapter looks at the contemporary cultural politics of football with regard to class, ethnicity and gender issues. I conclude the book through an afterword that synthesizes some of the key points of the earlier chapters, and outlines some issues for future sociological research.

1

The Essence of Football: the Historical and Social Bases of the Global Game

An Early Kick-Off: the prehistory of football

To explore football's social history we must begin by discussing the game's origins. Historical scholars have established that some of the earliest civilizations played folk variants of football. Some point to central America and the Amazon as football's cultural fountain, where ball games were played by the indigenous tribes as early as 1500 BC (Galeano 1995: 27). McIntosh (1987: 33) posits that the earliest forms of football were played in Antiquity, perhaps in the Roman game of *harpastum* or the *episcyros* of Greece. However, doubts remain about the proximity of these games to the sport we know today (Marples 1953: 4; Sweet 1987: 96).[1] More likely, China has the most compelling claim to the longest football history (see Walvin 1994: 11). Stone balls were manufactured to be kicked around in games in Shan Xi province during the Neolithic Age. Later, *cuju* was played during the Han Dynasty (206 BC–AD 220) with rules very similar to football.[2]

Other indigenous peoples played their own football games. Pilgrims arriving in North America in the early seventeenth century found the indigenous peoples playing *pasuckquakkohowog*, which might translate as 'they gather to play football' (Foulds and Harris 1979: 7–8). The indigenous peoples of Chile played *pilimatun* while those of Patagonia played *tchoekah*, long before the invasion of the Conquistadors (Oliver 1992: 2). The Romans had been responsible for introducing ball games to their conquered peoples, but such practices already had indigenous roots in northern parts as ancient religious ceremonies invoking fertility and worship of the elements. The Gauls of northern France, for example, performed ritual games in honour of the sun (Baker 1988: 43). Throughout the British Isles, folk football took numerous forms. The game of cad emerged at least a thousand years ago and was popular among all Celtic peoples, particularly in Ireland (Sugden and Bairner 1993: 71). In Wales, the game was known as *knappan* and, like Cornish hurling, could be played on horseback (Elias and Dunning 1986: 228). In the Orkney Islands, the *ba game* has been played between the 'Uppies' and 'Doonies' of Kirkwall since the eighteenth century, on Christmas and New Year's Day. More commonly, these football games were played in English and Scottish counties from the thirteenth century onwards as mass pastimes during breaks from work on holy days. Folk football was also played on the continent. French peasants have played the violent ball game of *soule* since medieval times (Bromberger 1995b: 276). Florentine *calcio* was played from the thirteenth to eighteenth century, becoming increasingly the preserve of the aristocracy and gentlemen of the Renaissance (Guttmann 1991: 57). The modern Italian game is still known by this archaic term (De Biasi and Lanfranchi 1997: 88).

Most of these folk games generated distrust or animosity among the ruling classes. In China, during the Ming Dynasty, the emperor Zhu Yuanzhang banned football in 1389; offending officers would have their foot cut off as punishment. The ban was repeated in 1625. Edward II banned football in England in 1314 to allow more time for archery practice (Strutt 1969: 94). James I of England later upheld this and further bans, empowering his officials to fine transgressors (Birley 1993: 42). During the sixteenth and early seventeenth century, the youth of Scottish towns like Aberdeen were regularly charged with profane conduct on the Sabbath, by drinking, dancing and playing football (Magoun 1938: 92). The declining influence of the monarchy did little to promote football. The puritanical Parliamentarians listed football as one of many proscribed sporting pastimes (Brailsford 1991: 36).

Historical interpretations of football's development, from these early games to its modern association form, have tended to follow the related perspectives of Max Weber and Norbert Elias. These emphasize the limited degree of 'modernization' to be found in folk football, in terms of rules and organization. Most games permitted handling and kicking of the ball (and other players). Opposing teams were rarely balanced in number or skill level, but were usually composed of rival groups of males from neighbouring towns and villages. There was little distinction between spectators and players, no playing parameters, and certainly no referee. Most commonly, the objective of the game was to wrestle the leather ball into the opponents' 'goal', the dimensions of which were highly variable (Signy 1969: 15).[3] Finally, there was no bureaucratic apparatus appointed to oversee the running of the games (see Weber 1978: 341ff).

Folk football might also be regarded as notably violent and 'uncivilized' compared to the modern game (see Elias and Dunning 1986). Daggers were commonly carried by players in the thirteenth and fourteenth century and liable to cause serious injury, as much by accident as design (Birley 1993: 32). Hacking, punching and general fighting were commonplace as old scores were settled by rival players; broken bones, serious injuries and deaths were not unexpected outcomes (Elias and Dunning 1970: 119–20). The play also lacked organization in terms of playing positions or team tactics.

The related Weberian perspective points further to the limited secularization of football (see Guttmann 1994: 2). By the sixteenth century folk football was most likely to be played on religious days, such as Carnival in Europe, or Shrovetide in England, when the carnivalesque would predominate as the symbols and figures of the ruling elite were ritually toyed with or inverted (Birley 1993: 60).[4] 'Boy bishops' were elected in some towns to preside over the people for the day. Games might be organized by the landed gentry or, in more urban areas, the masters of the guilds. Chaotic football matches between rival villages, towns or guilds, were important adjuncts to these periods of revelry, along with other rustic pleasures, such as cock-fighting and dog-tossing.

Durkheimian sociologists would argue here that folk football functioned to maintain social order and to integrate individuals at the local level. In the manner of many carnivals, these football matches promoted long-term social order by giving youth its head. Local apprentices practised the game to mark their elevation to the guild: through this male ritual, the *rites de passage* from adolescence to manhood were publicly consecrated. Generally, football fostered a strong sense of social solidarity. Matches were played parish versus parish, one part of a town against another, bachelors against married men, married women against unmarried women, school against school, or town against countryside (Magoun 1938: 136).

Public School Association: the early history of the contemporary game

The historical materialist perspective of Marx has the most immediate value when we turn to explain the specific transition of folk football to modern association football ('soccer'). The 'rationalization' and 'secularization' of the game (as discussed by Weberians and Eliasians), and its capacity for nurturing social order (Durkheim), were promoted in Britain by a privileged social class with its own material interests. Football may have been populist in character, but it was also keenly and regularly played by Oxbridge undergraduates from at least the sixteenth century (Walvin 1994: 24). By the early nineteenth century, England's public schools had degenerated into hotbeds of anarchy and incipient revolt with outbreaks of rioting regularly enlivening the curriculum (Dunning and Sheard 1979: 51–2; Mason 1980: 11). In 1828, Thomas Arnold became headmaster at Rugby and revolutionized the moral education of the nation's wealthy youth. Sport and physical culture became central to this mission. Games were introduced as character-building, teaching the virtues of leadership, loyalty and discipline, epitomizing the noble philosophy of *mens sana in corpore sano*. The new 'Christian gentlemen' would maintain the political and economic order at home and later underpin imperial expansion abroad (Hargreaves 1986: 39). The social standing of games was also improved in being 'elevated to the more serious and absorbing status of "sport" ' (Lowerson 1993: 65).

Football rules were codified and matches overseen by school house-masters. However, major inconsistencies soon emerged between the football codes of rival institutions. As Birley (1993: 257) reports, football 'was not so much a single game as an array of roughly similar tribal codes preferred by different public schools'. By the 1860s inter-collegiate fixtures had divided the young gentlemen into two general camps. Old Rugbeians and Etonians favoured a hacking and handling game, while Harrovians prohibited these actions. The latter's rules were adopted by the first football club, Sheffield FC, formed in 1854 by 'new money' classes, such as industrialists and merchants. Nine years later, Cambridge fell into line. The Harrovians took the initiative in printing rules as the Football Association was formed, leaving the Rugbeians to formulate their eponymous code with hacking and handling still permitted. Through the missionary-like zeal of C. W. Alcock, old Harrovian and FA Secretary for twenty-five years, the 'dribbling game' was introduced to all parts of Britain. In 1872, the FA Cup was first contested under the public school knockout system, and the first full international was played between England and Scotland in Glasgow (Walvin 1994: 48, 75). The laws of association football were formally codified in 1877, ironing out any remaining inconsistencies (Mason 1980: 15).

Technically, football's modernization seems to be highly Weberian. Certainly the folk game underwent rationalization; the new rules allowed for the establishment of sporting exchanges, initially between football playing schools, but then across regions and nations. As football developed its own autonomous field, so the FA became the organizing body to which all clubs and lower institutions were affiliated. The FA guaranteed the rules of the game among all members and exercised a disciplinary power that was guaranteed by the state (Bourdieu 1991a: 360). Nevertheless, the actual pace and direction of this process, and the conflicts that underpinned it, are more legitimately explained in Marxist terms, though not along simple 'capitalist versus proletariat' lines. As football expanded during the late nineteenth century, hegemonic battles took place along class and regional lines. The major conflict occurred within the middle classes, divided by region and over the question of professionalism (Mason 1980: 69–81; Lowerson 1993: 181–2). In the south, the FA's amateur ethos and general elitism predominated, symbolized by the Corinthian Football Club which refused to believe gentlemen would commit fouls and so declined penalties (Mason 1989a: 147). In northern England and the midlands, the professional middle classes, industrialists and petty bourgeoisie controlled the most successful clubs. Here, and in industrial Scotland, the power of capital prevailed. Olympian virtues were a poor reward for financial investments in trophy-hungry clubs (Wagg 1995b: 2; Tranter 1998: 46). Well-heeled directors were soon making undercover payments to the best players, especially the 'Scottish professors' lured south to educate the English in the fineries of the game. Another Scot, the draper William McGregor, became a director of Aston Villa and organized northern clubs into the Football League; the first championship was contested in 1888 with immediate success. A Scottish League followed two years later, although it was implacably opposed by the Queen's Park club, the Scottish equivalent of the Corinthians and still staunchly amateur to this day.

The FA failed to limit payment to 'reimbursed expenses' and so reluctantly recognized professional players in July 1885 (Birley 1995a: 32). More aristocratic southern teams were soon losing regularly to professional northern sides, although the Corinthians often defeated the northern FA Cup holders in challenge matches[5] while regular places (including the captaincy) were reserved for top amateurs in the England team. The 'gentlemen and players' dispute climaxed in the creation of the short-lived Amateur FA which operated in the south from 1907 to 1914 for the increasingly anachronistic, non-professional clubs. The new commercial order accounted not only for the best amateur teams, but also fledgeling professional outfits guilty of over-extending themselves. In Scotland, economic rationalization was severe: of the fourteen founder members of the League in 1890, six were out of business within a decade (Crampsey 1990: 7). The pace of change continued unabated as club after club converted from association status to limited liability company replete with shareholders and a board of directors (Birley 1995a: 42).

As the professional bourgeois model became established, so the number of consumers multiplied. Hutchinson (1982: 9–10) points out that, between 1820 and 1860, a huge vacuum had appeared in popular leisure. Old bucolic pastimes like bear-baiting, cock-fighting and village folk football had largely disappeared as the general populace moved into the towns for work. The new working classes came under the moralizing instruction of a civic bourgeoisie bent on eradicating all intemperance and uncivilized diversion. It was not until the 1860s, with the codification of association football and other old games, that the populace had a large sporting culture to immerse itself in once again.

Football's centrality to the new urban culture is highlighted by the changing size and class composition of late Victorian crowds. In England, average attendances rose from 4,600 in 1888 to 7,900 in 1895; they reached 13,200 ten years later and finished at 23,100 on the eve of the First World War (Vamplew 1988: 63).[6] Scottish gate receipts doubled between 1885 and 1914. Middle-class fans were squeezed from the terraces as football attracted the male working classes in droves (Lowerson 1993: 83), though these were 'skilled workers in the main, with relatively high wages and relative security of employment' (Mason 1980: 157). Football's mass appeal saw it sit neatly within a constellation of popular cultural practices that also included drinking and gambling. The game itself became an architectural extension of the urban industrial archipelago. 'Football stadia looked like factories around the little stretch of turf; the giant, civic crowds looked like the workforce going through the factory gates' (Inglis 1995: 53). Thousands stopped work on Saturday afternoons to watch the matches, risking summary dismissal; attendance money was set aside even during unemployment (Walvin 1994: 79).

The commercial embourgeoisement of football brought with it further aspects of early capitalist modernization. Match decisions were no longer settled through dialogue between two umpires provided by the opposing teams; instead, by 1891, one 'neutral' individual, the referee, was adjudicating solely during games (Agozino 1996: 171). But the vexed question of the new professionalism rumbled on. The amateur lobby regularly protested about professional instrumentality: ungentlemanly players intimidated referees; fouling and violent play were ever on the rise. These complaints were typically jaundiced by class antagonisms: 'toughness, it seemed, was acceptable as an expression of masculinity among middle-class men . . . but not as an expression of the will to win among working-class ones' (Wagg 1984: 10).

To maintain traditional class boundaries, football's authorities sought to limit the earning power of top professionals, just as the potential might of the labour movement was being colonized or resisted in industry and politics. English club directors complained that professionals were overpaid and undermining club finances. Yet the new market system was ill disposed to the imposition of a maximum wage. The biggest clubs favoured a free labour and contract market (in which they would ultimately profit). The £4 maximum wage, introduced by the FA in 1901, was constantly circumvented. Clubs provided under-the-counter payments or invented sinecure posts for players complete with generous salaries (Birley 1995a: 234; Mason 1980: 98–9).

Professionalism certainly reflected working-class football passion but other forms of stratification, including ethnicity and nationality, were also important. Scottish players were the most peripatetic professionals. Moreover, the real centres of footballing excellence were those areas strongly touched by Celtic migration and cultural influences. Liverpool had established itself as England's footballing bedrock by the turn of the century (Walvin 1975: 56). Soon after, the catholic Irish club of Glasgow Celtic rose to dominate the Scottish game, winning ten championships in thirteen years from 1905 to 1918 (Crampsey 1990: 49).

Trading Leisure: football's global diffusion

Northern working-class pre-eminence was reflected further in the export of football. Trade connections, rather than imperial links, were the most propitious outlets. Yet, this is not to say that football was ignored in the Empire's outposts. It became a staple of the curriculum of colonial schools and a common pastime for occupying troops. In India, football was regularly played between British troops and bootless local rivals, most commonly in Calcutta (Mason 1986: 76; 1992). Holt (1989: 216–17) suggests that the physical endeavour of football and its sister sport, rugby union, could not be accommodated by the more decorous, gentle body culture favoured by India's Hindus. It seems equally likely that the colonial elite simply preferred to teach the less energetic and more aristocratic sport of cricket to the natives.

In Australia, football lost caste with the gentry and never really recovered as local games like Aussie Rules were established (Daly 1988: 171; Hibbins 1992: 110–11). In Canada, Scottish immigrants introduced football almost upon its codification. A team of top Canadian players toured Britain in 1888, holding Glasgow Rangers to a 1–1 draw, and winning several other games against top sides (Jose and Rannie 1982). However, local climate and cultural pressures to invent a national sports tradition ensured ice hockey and US sports became much more established among new Canadians.

Football's spread in colonial Africa was heavily influenced by occupying soldiers and the white working settlers (Clayton 1987). European colonists in West Africa considered football unsuitable for the coastal townships, in some contrast to cricket which spread more rapidly (Jenkins 1992: 68). The game of *mwana-foot* (children's football) became the most popular pastime among the Congo's indigenous peoples during the 1920s, with many matches organized within the new urban communities. White Europeans sought to establish administrative control of football during the 1930s, but encountered resistance from many locals, reflecting the rising proto-nationalism of black Africans at this time (Martin 1991). By the early post-war period, British diffidence towards black colonial footballers had diminished. Touring teams were invited from Africa and the Caribbean and fêted upon arrival. The visitors were left under no illusion that they were to learn about not only the superiority of British football, but the rectitude of the political and economic systems favoured by their colonial masters (Vasili 1995: 55).

In Cameroon, French settlers already inured with the game played alongside an African expatriate elite brought in to help administer the country and make up the sporting numbers (Clignet and Stark 1974). Further south, while in some territories football could be a vehicle for the expression of proto-nationalism, its diffusion and the standard of play were severely inhibited by racialist political systems and obscene levels of material inequality. In South Africa, football was initially controlled by the African elite, but the colonial army helped spread the game among the urban working classes (Stuart 1995: 29). It became popular among black Africans in areas like Durban, and was controlled by a number of patrons or 'big men' from local to national level (Kuper 1965: 352; Jeffrey 1992). Later, black clubs would regularly cultivate wasteland to play on. However, apartheid laws that banned their ownership of property would be invoked, opening the way for non-blacks to take over these new football fields (Archer 1987: 236–7). At the height of apartheid, it was common to find up to one hundred black clubs competing to use a single football pitch (Kidd 1988:

660). Nevertheless, throughout Africa, football continued to be the favoured sport among Africans, principally because it was regarded as 'culture-neutral', lacking in Westernized values and practices (Mazrui, 1987: 219).

Football spread far more quickly and successfully on the European continent. Native Europeans returned from the UK with footballs and rule books, while British workers and school teachers or pupils organized fixtures on foreign soil. The first European clubs were established in Switzerland by English boys attending private schools (Baker 1988: 134). In Scandinavia, the game formed a counter-weight to Nordic gymnastics, first appearing in Denmark in 1879 (Eichberg 1992: 120). Scottish artisans took the game to Sweden in the late nineteenth century (Giulianotti 1993), while British connections brought football to Norwegians in the early 1880s (Goksøyr and Hognestad 1998). Cotton workers from Lancashire were said to be the first exponents in Holland during the mid-19th century (Wagg 1995a: 105), inspiring the first non-British FA to be formed in 1889 (Signy 1969: 36). English schools were central to football's popularization in Germany and Russia (Mason 1986: 69–70). Spanish football developed after it landed in the Basque country with British maritime and colliery workers playing the game during the 1890s (MacClancy 1996a: 182). In Italy, British sailors and those 'in trade' introduced the modern game to Genoa, Milan, Turin and Naples (Guttmann 1994: 54). In France during the *belle époque*, the first football teams were formed by Scottish and English exiles in Paris. The local bourgeoisie soon seized upon the game as a morally uplifting pastime, although it never quite lost its plebeian cachet, and so proved most popular in the extreme north and south of the country (Holt 1981: 62, 66, 76–7). Further east, English expatriates in Vienna secured football's future in Austria, Hungary and Bohemia (later Czechoslovakia) during the 1890s. It was soon included in the activities of most gymnastic clubs (Duke and Crolley 1996: 86).

In Latin America, trade connections proved the most fertile outlet for football colonization. Brazil's first encounter came through British sailors in 1864, but it was British-educated Charles Miller of São Paulo who became the game's most ardent proponent (Allison 1978: 218–19; Leite Lopes 1997: 55). Football also arrived on the Rio de la Plata as the 45,000 Britons who lived in Buenos Aires began to establish clubs, particularly via British schools (Archetti 1996: 203). British influence continued through the founding and naming of clubs by ex-pupils and railway workers, such as in the capital with clubs like River Plate, or the duopoly in Rosario of 'Newell's Old Boys' (founded by former pupils of an English teacher) and 'Rosario Central' (after the local train station) (Brisaboa 1996: 17–19). Spanish did not replace English as the undisputed language of the Argentinian football association until 1934. The first Uruguayan football-oriented club, Albion FC, was founded in June 1861 in Montevideo. Two decades later there were reports of football being played in physical education classes at the British high school (Krotee 1979: 145). British railway workers founded in 1891 what was to become the great Peñarol club. Their rivals, Nacional, were founded in 1899 by local students keen to uphold national Hispanic honour (Giulianotti 1999). The Scottish tea millionaire, Sir Thomas Lipton, donated the Lipton Cup in 1902, to be contested annually by Argentina and Uruguay (Forsyth 1990: 34). Similarly, in Chile, football was introduced by British sailors in the port of Valparaiso where the first team was formed in 1889. Six years later, the national FA was formed by nine clubs of mainly British origin (Oliver 1992: 639).

Evidently, British political and cultural influence was vital to football's international diffusion. Class differentials remained important. More imperial sports such as rugby and cricket prevailed in the dominions, whereas the new industrial game was more easily introduced through trading and educational networks. British cultural hegemony over football remained in these foreign fields. English was often the official language of local football associations, and English football terms (such as 'corner', 'referee', 'free-kick', 'penalty' and, latterly, 'hooligan') became standard among players and supporters. Moreover, the football publics in Europe and the Americas were particularly keen to watch touring British sides in action. Results against these tourists were the accepted yardstick for assessing the quality of local play. The hosts often copied and 'creolized' the playing style of touring teams.[7]

Meanwhile, many UK footballing coaches were embarked on endless peregrinations to proselytize on their game. The football nomads included Jimmy Hogan, William Garbutt, John Madden and John Hurley (Walvin 1994: 110–11; Buzzetti 1969: 7–8). Greater status may have been accorded to them abroad than at home, where the stricter class system held sway. British directors were typically dismissive of the soccer coach's importance and, until Herbert Chapman, tended to regard him as a medium for controlling players.

Overall, we may refer to this process of codification and diffusion as representing football's 'traditional' period. At home, football is still strongly influenced by the ideological assumptions of the established bourgeoisie who remain critical of professionalism. Abroad, British political and cultural hegemony over the international game remains unshakeable. I explore the subsequent modernization of football in detail in chapter 2. To conclude here, I wish to discuss the social and cultural underpinnings of football's diffusion at home and abroad. Specifically, I wish to examine how the *meaning* of this global game is manufactured to fit local conditions. In this way, the universal football code is employed to express particular forms of social and cultural identity.

The process of constructing a 'meaning' or an 'identity' for something is dependent upon two principles: *semantics* (establishing what something is in itself) and *syntax* (establishing what it is not) (Mills 1959: 42–3). In the remainder of this chapter, I explore these two principles of meaning construction, to demonstrate how they underpin the football identities of different societies. I begin by examining football 'syntax', in particular how the game is rooted in binary oppositions and rivalries in most societies. I then move on to the 'semantics' of football, examining how it helps to integrate people and reproduce the social order; particular attention is paid to the religious aspects of the game.

The Meaning of the Game (1): opposition and rivalry

In an early contribution to the sociology of sport, Heinilä (1966: 33) noted that the strongest senses of in- and out-group attitudes were created by team sports involving dual contests at the international level. Thus, at the Olympic Games, low levels of international rivalry tend to exist because many individual athletes from a multitude of nations compete in any one contest. Conversely, football matches involve two teams that represent specific geographical and cultural identities. These matches therefore give rise to the most potent dramatizations of binary opposition within sport.

The dyadic drama of football takes place at a number of levels: players, teams, clubs and countries. Each player is locked into a personal battle with his 'opposite number': the striker trying to evade the robust centre-half; the winger feinting and dribbling past the watchful full-back; the midfielders tussling for the ball against their mirror opposites; the play-makers manoeuvring and scheming against one another; and the goal-keepers, sharing a mutual respect and empathy found nowhere else in the game, but still cognizant that their personal success is still heavily dependent upon the other's frailties.

Equally, football clubs establish cultural identities through rivalry and opposition. Purest rivalries grow up between civic siblings. It was good economic sense during the game's infancy to establish two rival teams from the same locality, city or region (Hobsbawm 1969: 308). These 'derby games' promised comparatively large crowds due to the short distances travelled by local supporters. Culturally, derby matches sold themselves; rival fans lived, worked and socialized with each other, discussing, joking and theorizing endlessly on past and future encounters. Today, derby games like Rangers–Celtic, Everton–Liverpool, Roma–Lazio or Flamengo–Fluminense are said to be the definitive moments in the football season for opposing supporters, if not the most important dates in their emotional calendars.

The meanings of these football rivalries have tended to be underpinned by deeper historical and cultural divisions. Classically, the opposition is reinforced by localist chauvinisms that are mapped in spatial terms. Within the largest football metropolises, major football antagonisms exist within single zones. In London, Arsenal and Tottenham compete for supremacy in the north (Goodwin 1997). West Ham and Millwall vie for hegemony in the working-class east. In South America, clubs often represent *barrios*, and battle with indigenous opponents or their nearest neighbours. In Montevideo, one bitter *clásico* involves Rampla Juniors and Cerro, who each hail from the Cerro *barrio*. In the region of Buenos Aires, which dominates Argentinian football, duopolies have emerged within specific localities, such as Independiente and Racing Club in Avellaneda.

Two-club rivalries remain the norm in most cities, with spatial dimensions again serving to cement the oppositions. In Sheffield, United drew in greater support from the city's older localities until large housing projects were started nearby to Wednesday's Hillsborough ground (Armstrong 1998). The Roma–Lazio rivalry mirrors the cultural differences between the Eternal City and its surrounding rural region. In Genoa and Milan, the Genoa and Internazionale clubs were respectively associated with the civic centre (and claimed to represent it), while Sampdoria and Milan were more easily linked with satellite industrial areas. In Seville, the traditionalist side of Sevilla are counterpoised to Real Betis, who attract a strong left-wing and working-class empathy. In Hamburg, the working-class fans of Hamburg SV journey to the outskirts to watch their side, while their city neighbours St Pauli attract a bohemian crowd of 'happy fans' (such as anarcho-punks and leftist activists) to their compact, inner-city ground. In France, the new Stade de France in northern Paris has elicited the argument that a club should be created to fill it in opposition to Paris Saint-Germain who are housed in the exclusive west (Mignon 1996).

Within one-club cities, intense spatial rivalries may emerge as contests to represent provincial regions, such as the old north–east animosities between Newcastle and Sunderland, or the Battle of the Lakes between Brescia and Verona. In smaller nations, such rivalries may double as contests to represent the nation. The Benfica–Porto contest is a case in point in Portugal. The Feyenoord–Ajax clash becomes a struggle between Rotterdam and Amsterdam to represent Holland. It is also a symbolic conflict along ethno-class lines between the industrial, working-class superport and the commercial, Jewish, middle-class bohemia.

The deepest antagonisms between the classes, as expressed through football, have existed in South America and are permeated by severe ethnic cleavages. In Rio, the Fla–Flu rivalry was until recently underwritten by class and ethnic representation. Flamengo were the team of the *favelas*, confronted by the aristocratic Fluminense, who barely hid their contempt for black players and supporters. In Belo Horizonte, Cruzeiro's foundation by Italian immigrants has given way to their association with the local elite, and thus to be juxtaposed with their eternal rivals, Atletico Mineiro, the team of the lower classes. Peru's major club rivalry has traditionally confronted the white Universitario side and the proud, black Alianza Lima team (Stein et al. 1986). In Paraguay, the two strongest teams have class roots, with Cerro Porteño favoured by the workers and Olimpia housed in Asunción's most exclusive quarter. In Argentina, a similar class distinction exists in many great club rivalries: in La Plata, there is the 'rich' Estudiantes club versus the 'poor' team of Gimnasia y Esgrima; in Santa Fé the same binary conjoins the clubs of Unión and Colón; and in Rosario there is Newell's Old Boys against Rosario Central.[8] One may even add here the ethnic associations of Uruguay's top clubs: Peñarol (the team

adopted by Italian immigrants) versus Nacional (the Hispanic side founded by
the local *jeunesse d'ore*). Similarly, in the Middle East, most Israeli clubs grew
up from the youth teams of two rival political factions. The leftist Hapoel clubs
incorporate the internationalist hammer and sickle in their club badges, while
the more traditionalist, nationalist Maccabi clubs retain the Star of David in
their emblems. In Istanbul, Galatasaray are renowned as the historical team of
the gentry, while Besiktas are the proletariat's club, and Fenerbahce the side of
the middle classes. Athenian clubs also carry a class inflection, with AEK
Athens regarded as a leftist team (founded by refugees from Turkey),
Panathinaikos the former Generals' team now laden with money, and Olimpiakos
the truly working-class team from Piraeus. The 'sectarian' football teams in
Scotland and Northern Ireland also belong here, and are discussed later in this
chapter.

   Discourses of economic inequality are central to the structural syntax by
which the major football binaries acquire their social meaning. Popular clubs
like Schalke 04 in Germany or Fiorentina and Napoli in Italy are cognizant
that, whatever their fan base or financial infrastructure, they cannot match
their largest rivals, like Bayern Munich, Juventus and AC Milan (see Portelli
1993). In France, little clubs like Lens or Auxerre might nurture a provincial
distrust of the Parisian centre (and its representative, Paris Saint-Germain),
but they recognize that simple economics precludes consistent success. Even
in north London, the cultural history of the top two clubs might be partially
understood with reference to Arsenal's classically aristocratic, 'old money'
stewardship, in some contrast to the 'new money' and Jewish influences at
nearby Tottenham.

   In civic rivalries, the smaller club may counter this financial weakness by
claiming to represent the soul of the city (rather than a nationwide backing).
Torino have the sympathy of Turin while Juventus carry an industrial magnate's
backing and a global following. In Manchester, United possess similar support,
but City gain a disproportionate affection from its citizens. In Munich too, fans
of 1860 maintain that a greater civic support exists for their club, though Bayern's
attendances are bolstered massively by in-comers from Bavarian provinces and
beyond. Thus, while the major club transmogrifies into a modern organic institution, its smaller rival seeks to maintain the ideological upperhand, on their
community of fandom at the mechanistic, *gemeinschaften* level.

   The football dyad at club level may become an exterior site in which ethno-
nationalist tensions are symbolized and expressed. Catalonian and Basque
identities are synonymous with Barcelona and Athletic Bilbao respectively;
each displays a richer lustre in confrontations with Real Madrid (the team of
Castille and Franco) (see Shaw 1985; MacClancy 1996b). Against the backdrop of separatist politics, Italian fans from below the *mezzogiorno* line have
equipped themselves with the Confederate flag of the American south, to
express regional pride against northern hostility. Similarly, civic conflicts may
be read into matches involving Fiorentina (the heart of Italy's cultural renais-

sance), Roma (the politico-administrative centre), Juventus (industrial and football hegemony) and Milan (financial and populist power). In the UK, one might say that intense regional rivalries exist within both England and Scotland, between clubs from the north and south. In Israel, the emergence of the Arab team Hapoel Taibeh generated strong ethno-religious antagonisms between the Israeli police and rival fans and the Palestinian peoples (Carmeli and Bar 1998). The former Yugoslavia provides the most notable instance of club football's ethno-nationalism coming to the boil. The opening salvoes of the civil war occurred with the full-scale riot at a football match between the Croatian side Dinamo Zagreb and the Serbian team Red Star Belgrade in May 1990 (Lalic and Vrcan 1998).

Finally, football's highly competitive dimensions manifest themselves through nationalist antagonisms and international rivalries. In the UK, strong rivalries exist between the smaller Home Nations (notably Scotland) and England. The strongest continental grudge match features Germany and Holland. The Dutch recall not so much their war-time occupation as the moral injustices of the 1974 World Cup final, when a superior Holland side lost to the durable hosts in Munich. The French are similarly fired by their World Cup loss to Germany in 1982, and the assault on one of their players by the German goal-keeper during that game. Further east, Balkan politics ferment beneath the rivalries of Bulgaria and Romania, or Greece and Turkey. The latter animosity is dramatized in divided Cyprus where the Fédération Internationale de Football Association (FIFA) has sought to conciliate by ordering friendlies to be played between clubs from the south (overseen by Greece) and the north (annexed by Turkey in 1974) (*The Guardian*, 4 June 1997). One might look to other sites of post-war military conflict for natural football binaries. The former Yugoslavia again features here, in particular the new Yugoslavia–Croatia opposition. In the Middle East, Israel were granted admission to European qualifying fixtures for the World Cup, partly to save it playing neighbouring Arab nations. In central America, war began between Honduras and El Salvador in July 1969 following the return leg of a World Cup qualifying match between the two nations which El Salvador had won 3–0.[9] American geo-politics mean that the United States tend to be the prized target of football sides representing its satellite states. Further south, the oldest historical rivalry is the *rioplatense* derby of Argentina and Uruguay, which has often resulted in violence on and off the field (see Giulianotti 1999). The rising power of Brazil in the post-war period has also seen Argentina assume the mantle of the antithetical other.

It may be said, therefore, that football's dyadic relationships operate at all levels – player, team, club and nation – and that they are effectively rooted in the game's social ontology. The melange of norms in European, Latin American and West Asian societies all serve to promote competitiveness and sensitivity to the other, thus providing the vital hermeneutics for justifying football rivalries. In Europe and West Asia, we have the capitalistic and cultural mores of social individualism, competitive masculinity in industry and business, the legacy of war-like imperialism and its attendant cultivation of nationalism, often tinged with a religious conviction. From the Latin societies of the Mediterranean or the Americas, we may add the deeper chauvinisms of the family or village. But what if the wider society emphasizes other social values, such as harmony and collectivism? Does football's structural syntax still obtain in these circumstances?

In the old Second World, state socialism failed to inculcate new cultural mores among the citizens *de haut en bas*. In the Soviet Union itself, the most popular club has been Spartak Moscow, named by the rebel player Starostin after Spartacus, the leader of a Roman slave insurgency. Spartak stood in symbolic opposition to the four other Moscow teams who enjoyed the patronage of Soviet ministries.[10] In the East European satellites, football oppositions grew up against the state machine. Clubs patronized by the army or state police would often find themselves especially despised by opposing fans.[11]

While these football rivalries reflect the Second World's failure to 'harmonize' the public, it may be that East Asia will offer a less propitious setting for football oppositions. China, Japan, South Korea and their neighbours, with their economic and religious blends of spiritual Confucianism and state/market collectivism, promote the virtues of social solidarity and harmony. Mental equilibrium takes precedence over bodily exertion. Football cultures here are relatively young and, where they do not replay deeper military conflicts (such as South Korea and Japan), it is difficult to find evidence of fundamental opposition. Notably, the new football leagues here usually fail to feature two rival teams from the same city. In China at least, the football authorities have resisted such a move as contrary to the traditional culture in which social harmony and order are pivotal.[12]

The Meaning of the Game (2): the semantics of social solidarity

Discussion of football's binary oppositions helps to explain how social identities are constructed in most societies, save the new Eastern sports cultures. The syntax of such identity formation also raises questions about the semantic dimensions of football. These relate to the kinds of social solidarity that are established *within* football groupings, at club or national level.

In sociology, issues such as solidarity, social order and political continuity are central to writers working within the Durkheimian or neo-functionalist tradition. Their argument is that modern life tends to break up the community; industrialization, urbanization, rapid social and geographic mobility, and more complex divisions of labour, all erode the communitarianism and fixed social identities found in pre-industrial, traditional societies. Yet sport may repair much of this social damage by enhancing the cultural bonding and social integration of disparate individuals within modern societies.

Durkheim (1893) distinguished two models of society according to their social solidarity. In modern societies, the more complex, 'organic' solidarity prevails; in small and traditional communities, a relatively fixed and undifferentiated 'mechanical' solidarity exists. The formation of football clubs and the regular, voluntary association of supporters and players, help to counteract the feelings of atomization and alienation that corrupt individuals within large, impersonal cities. Participants in football are integrated into the larger social system as they meet and interact with those from other clubs. The clubs therefore help to promote deeper forms of shared identity or 'solidarity' at local, civic and national levels (Escobar 1969: 76).

It would appear that urban football clubs, with their complex division of labour, are clear illustrations of Durkheim's 'organic' solidarity. However, a more sophisticated use of Durkheim emphasizes the strong connections of many clubs to the more traditional, mechanistic model. Virtually all clubs are named emblematically after a particular 'place', and thus have the kind of affective tie to a specific locality that one finds in more traditional and localist societies. Players may also be strong supporters of the club, live near to the ground, and share a strong chauvinistic pride about the community. Such clubs are increasingly anachronistic within the modern football world of shifting fan loyalties, mobile professional players and ground relocation to suburban wastelands. Yet they husband an indefatigable localist identity that waves of football modernizers cannot fully submerge or drown. Even in the highly professional game, players are still adopted by the club's community; they play 'at home' and usually perform more effectively.[13]

Strong criticisms have been directed at the functionalists' emphasis on social integration, and this has a direct impact upon their interpretation of football's wider role. Functionalists are often criticized for their social conservatism and their conviction that power relationships are easily reproduced (Gouldner 1970). Where major change threatens, other factors are thought to intervene, functioning to preserve the political *status quo*. One such safety valve may be football. Its popularity seems to be perennially ripe for exploitation by the politically powerful as a safeguard against revolts from below. This functionalist argument echoes the viewpoints of 'left Leavisites' and some critical Marxists. The Roman satirist Juvenal first forwarded the thesis that political oligarchies could be sustained by supplying bread and circuses *(panem et circuses)* to the masses. Since then, it has often been suggested that a Machiavellian influence lies behind the popularization of sports.

The Latin nations of southern Europe and South America tend to receive this accusation most frequently. Umberto Eco (1986: 172) enquires of his native Italy: 'Is the armed struggle possible on World Cup Sunday? . . . Is it possible to have a revolution on a football Sunday?' Sebreli (1981) draws a critical connection between the football 'masses' and the emergence of social alienation, fascism and populism.[14] In Portugal in 1974, during the revolt to overthrow Salazar's regime, football match attendances were halved – suggesting that sports involvement and political agitation are two mutually exclusive practices (Hammond 1993: 76). Most stridently, an early paper by Lever (1972) considered Brazilian football to be the *de facto* opium of the people. Rachum (1978: 199) concurred, arguing that football 'ultimately tended to alleviate possible social and political tensions'.

Mason (1995a: 129) accuses Lever of making a 'tempting but fundamentally mistaken' analysis of Brazilian football's social relationship to politics. 'The game could never eliminate the conflicts caused by vast inequalities of wealth. On some occasions, football clubs have been vanguard organizations for promoting the democratization of Brazil.'[15] Others share Mason's optimism; football 'may be one of the sources of an authentic Brazilian nationalism, at once popular and liberating, and more immediately potent than polemical campaigns of the Left against multinational companies' (Evanson 1982: 408).

Three further criticisms of this functionalist, 'false consciousness' thesis may be added. First, empirically, there is ample historical evidence to show that football may enable the masses to protest against the ruling elite. For example, Scottish football fans at international fixtures voiced their opposition to the deeply unpopular Conservative governments that had been elected primarily by English voters. In South Africa, at the height of apartheid, football provided one of the few legal avenues through which Africans could organize to debate and contest their marginal status (Nauright 1998). When Romania qualified for the 1990 World Cup finals by beating Denmark in Bucharest, the fans went on extended celebrations that rapidly developed into anti-government protests and rioting. Ceausescu failed to suppress these sentiments at a public rally, and was overthrown soon after. In South America, football was one of the first forums of dissent for Paraguayans during the reign of Stroessner (see Archetti 1992). In north Africa, the football stadium is a 'privileged arena' for the dissemination and expression of political dissent or revolt, particularly among the young (Fates 1990: 69).

Secondly, the 'bread and circuses' thesis is rooted in an intellectualist disdain for sports, barely concealing an underlying disdain for the 'masses'.[16] The Frankfurt School are notable examples, as they forward a dismissive critique of post-war 'mass culture', for stupefying its consumerist populace through the trifle of playing and watching games (Adorno 1991: 74–8; see Baudrillard 1983: 12–13).[17]

Thirdly, it is increasingly difficult in complex societies to identify how competing interests and many different social elements interact and function to benefit the whole. Clearly, football 'seeks to serve many functions and many masters' (Taylor 1988: 539); these include amateur players, spectators, individual clubs, sponsors, new soccer markets, different governments and social systems. It is impossible to sketch, in functionalist terms, how these interests interact to preserve some imagined social order.

Football and Religion: the rituals of conflict and consensus

The functionalist position produces a richer vein of thought when analysing the cultural belief-systems that sustain social order and solidarity. According to Durkheim (1965), religion is highly pervasive in small, traditional societies and 'functions' to bind the members together. Religious ceremonies may seem to involve the simple worship of sacred totems, but for Durkheim they served to establish the influence of the collective (its *conscience collectif*) over individuals. As modernization took hold and societies moved from mechanical to organic solidarity, the social significance of religion declined, thereby contributing to greater individualism and senses of anomie.

A historical and symbolic relationship is identified between religion and sports, especially football. The modern game is said to have replaced religion as the institution that binds people together, while giving rise to states of emotional ecstasy previously associated with religious ceremony. Yet football and religion need not be mutually exclusive cultural phenomena. The two interact in complex ways.

Superficially, religion still holds a key influence on many of football's most important social actors. Deep personal faith carries European football people, like England ex-manager Glenn Hoddle and Fiorentina striker Gabriel Batistuta. In the West, the post-secular turn to alternative religions is reflected most famously by Italian internationalist and Buddhist, Roberto Baggio, 'the divine ponytail'. Meanwhile, following Durkheim, we find that religious devotion is strongest in less modern, more 'mechanistic' societies, where Catholicism or Islam is most prevalent. In Brazil, a special association of football players with strong religious beliefs has been founded. The players of Catholic Ireland visited the Pope during the 1990 World Cup finals. George Weah is a committed Muslim, as are many top North African players.

Inevitably, football dramatizes the religious conflicts and inequalities that exist in the world. The football calendar itself is drawn up with Western rather than Eastern sacred moments in mind. There are no World Cup qualifiers played on Christmas Day. Yet, as the Egyptian team found to their cost in 1996, the African Nations' Cup finals can easily fall in the middle of Ramadan, when devout Muslims cannot eat or drink during daylight hours, thus severely handicapping their playing performances.[18] More seriously, some of football's fundamental oppositions are rooted in senses of religious antagonism or conflict, within both the developing and developed world. Such cases serve to highlight Taylor's (1988) point on global complexity within football and the difficulty of identifying precise 'functions' for the sport.

The religious tensions between Hindu, Muslim and Christian groups in the Asian sub-continent can precipitate sporadic outbursts of violence at matches. The religious politics of the Middle East are also fraught with potential dangers. A violent encounter between Libya and Egypt in 1978 effectively dramatized the conflict within the Arab states over the Israeli question (Baker 1987: 288–9). In the war-torn states of Western Africa, where tribal conflicts are reinforced by religious tensions, football clubs may come to represent distinctive denominations (see Richards 1997). In the West, residual religious divisions can continue in football. The Flemish and Walloon populations of Belgium are split by their respective allegiances to Catholicism or Protestantism and secularism, as animated culturally through their football identification (Duke and Crolley 1996). The oldest religious-based divide within football involves the major football clubs of Scotland and Northern Ireland. To examine the complex interplay of religion and football within a modern society, it is worth discussing this case in some depth.

In Scotland, the football–religion division centres on the 'Old Firm' of Glasgow Rangers and Glasgow Celtic. Historically, Rangers have maintained a staunch Protestant and anti-Catholic tradition that includes a ban on signing Catholic players. The club's cultural history is closely tied to the Unionist majority of Northern Ireland, whose livelihood was strongly associated with the shipyard industries of Belfast and Glasgow. Celtic were founded in Glasgow's east end in the late nineteenth century as a benevolent club for poor Irish Catholic immigrants. It soon became a symbol of sporting and cultural success for the disadvantaged minority. Celtic never adopted an employment policy based on religious denomination, but remain proud of their Irish connections. They continue to attract many supporters among Irish Catholics and regularly play friendly fixtures in the Republic of Ireland (Finn 1991a, 1991b). The rivalry and violence between supporters of the two clubs extend back to their 'Brake Clubs' of the late Victorian era. Infamous 'razor gangs' sprung up during the inter-war years. Violence continued throughout the post-war era with Rangers fans becoming particularly notorious during the 1970s and 1980s.

The 'sectarianism' of the Old Firm and their fans has attracted diverging explanations from social and historical researchers. The pioneering work of Bill Murray (1984) has contributed much to our understanding. Murray treads a careful path in seeking to apportion blame equally between the two clubs, but may underplay the deep structural inequalities that Irish Catholics experienced in Scotland. A 'modernization' thesis has been advanced by Walker (1990) and some notably less credible writers, arguing that major financial investments have encouraged Glasgow Rangers to outgrow their anti-Catholicism since the mid-1980s. The signing of the known Catholic and former Celtic player, Mo Johnston, is forwarded as evidence of reformation. Other signs of modernization seemed to be the signature of famous English internationals such as Terry Butcher and Graeme Roberts, and the takeover of the club by the Edinburgh businessman David Murray. Yet, it appears all of these anomalous cases were assimilated by Rangers' Unionist club culture (Finn and Giulianotti 1998). Moreover, Rangers' main officials have all lent open support to the Conservative Party and its Unionist principles during general elections and the Scottish referendum on devolution. 'Catholic' players signed from overseas were regarded by many loyal Rangers fans as not in breach of the famous ban on Irish Catholic players. Meanwhile, the new players were advised not to bless themselves when taking the field for fear of antagonizing their supporters (Finn 1997).

To date, Finn (1991a, 1991b, 1994a, 1994b, 1997) has presented the most convincing explanations for the Old Firm rivalry. His research indicates that Rangers had acquired custodians of strong Unionist beliefs and anti-Catholic prejudices before Celtic had even been formed (Finn 1991a: 90). Meanwhile, the deep-seated distrust of Irish Catholics within Scottish society has led to a historical disinclination to allow Celtic to celebrate their 'dual nationality' (as a Scottish and Irish club) (Finn 1991b). Myths about the Old Firm rivalry are rooted in an over-simplified understanding of religious 'sectarianism' to the extent that it would be better to drop the term altogether (Finn 1997).

The religious differences of Rangers and Celtic find their historic referent in the troubled history of Ireland, where football has again dramatized the deep-seated, ethno-religious conflict, principally in the north. During the struggle for home rule, violence flared between Unionist and Nationalist clubs, with the latter's Belfast Celtic worst affected.[19] Violence continues to bedevil matches between clubs from opposite sides of the religious divide (Bairner and Shirlow 1997). Security problems forced the Nationalist-supported club of Derry City to withdraw from the North's Irish League in 1971; in 1985 it joined the South's League of Ireland, winning the league championship four years later. Derry City always presents itself as a neutral institution that even hired a coach from the loyalist Linfield club. However, it cannot escape the political context, not least its location in a nationalist area and its dislike by isolationist Protestants for competing in the Republic (Sugden and Bairner 1993: 85–6).

Clearly then, football and religion are interrelated in complex ways. Even in the most 'modern' of societies or football clubs, religious intolerance and prejudice may still contribute greatly to senses of internal solidarity that are nurtured among players, fans and directors. Sociologists and historians have looked particularly at the kinds of religious conflict that may emerge within football, such as in Scotland and Northern Ireland. Alternatively, anthropologists have shown a greater interest in researching the complex and diverse belief systems and religious rituals that come alive within football. Perhaps the most enchanting yet fundamental aspect of this religious belief within football comes from Greenland. There, the native Inuit people believe that the spectacular movement of stars, known in the West as *aurora borealis* ('northern lights'), displays a football match between the spirits of the dead.[20]

In Africa, it is not uncommon to find witchcraft being practised by team officials and supporters. Some football teams from the former Zaire believed that pre-match magical rites, rather than their own 'professionalism', could secure results (Reefe 1987: 63). In Tanzania, teams practise *juju* (witchcraft) through their *mganga* (medicine-man), who prepares a *kafara* (offering) for the pre-match ritual sacrifice (Leseth 1997). A similar use of sorcery for football purposes has been found among Zulus (Scotch 1951), Cameroonians (Clignet and Stark 1974: 416–17) and Nigerians (Igbinovia 1985: 142–3). The rituals include wearing charms on fingers or toes, urinating on the field, smearing players' faces with the blood of sacrificed animals, or burying the latter beneath the pitch.

Western observers may ridicule such 'savagery' while conveniently forgetting that all players and supporters practise their personalized forms of witchcraft as pre-match 'superstitions'. Professional footballers are renowned for such fatalistic practices as eating a particular pre-match lunch, being last onto the field, not wearing their shirt until they reach the field, sporting lucky socks, talking to or avoiding specific team-mates, and shooting into (or purposefully missing) an empty net in the pre-match warm-up. Supporters are little different, ritually availing themselves of their charmed attire, digesting their 'lucky' football nourishment and securing their favourite seat.

The football match itself involves a number of religious rites. Rio's Maracanã stadium provides the most profound setting for worship. The atmosphere intensifies as the attendance rises before kick-off. The colours of the *torcidas* ('supporters') designate their tribal identity as distinguished from their distant opponents banked high in the other world opposite. Their incantations of totemic support sweep through the covered ends, in extended two-syllable mantras: 'Va-sco, Va-sco', or 'Fla-m'ngo, Fla-m'ngo'. Fervour is added by the rival fans jumping in unison to their hymns. Beyond the Maracanã, nature prepares the stage for play; Rio's mountainous topography juts above the huge stadium roof, piercing the sharp blue sky. Firecrackers and flares greet the entry of the teams; another act of communion is symbolized as the rival sides opt to 'defend' the goal behind which their respective fans are situated. The game kicks off while the Maracanã sits in semi-eclipse, its grandeur split between day and night, sun and shadow. The play itself is a paean to grace and divine favour, swinging rhythmically between slowness and speed, perambulation and pace, to the accompanying beat of the supporters' drums. Touches of genius by the athletic demi-gods are hailed as acts of revelation by the practising footballing mortals massed high upon the terraces. Goals are moments of ecstatic delivery from the anxiety of attendance. The game's second half soon sees the ground cleansed of the last vestiges of daylight; floodlights illuminate the focal event upon the green centre, its drama slowly closing. The final whistle draws the ceremony to an end; acclaim and disdain pursue the winners and losers as they disappear back into the Maracanã's temple, pursued by scribes and photographers seeking graven images. The congregation melts away into Rio's balmy night: the victors in tumult and noise; the vanquished quietly and with shirts worn inside out, to exculpate their fate. There is nothing in Europe to match this quasi-religious experience, although we may observe that many matches in southern nations are played on the Sabbath as a climax (or alternative) to Mass.

Death and the Game: cultural differences at pla

If football is an analogue of religion, if each enables its devotee~~ ..~ ..~.~..~p
what is sacred about themselves, then moments of the greatest existential
importance will be marked by special ceremonies within both institutions.
Death, and its cultural commemoration, is probably the most significant existential moment; it is 'the great extrinsic factor of human existence' (Giddens
1991: 162).[21] The rituals before and during modern deaths may be increasingly
private, yet the ceremonies that mark bereavement remain essentially public in
character, especially for heroes and celebrities. Football deaths have particularly rich, associative sequels; cultural beliefs about the nature of being, social
life, heroism and adulation, are distilled and openly displayed in rituals of
mourning. Their religiosity is undeniable and universal, but the content remains very particularistic.

Within the space of three months in 1993, I witnessed the contrasting public
ceremonies surrounding the lives of two late football club chairmen, Paolo
Mantovani (owner of the Italian club, Sampdoria of Genoa) and Dick Donald
(owner of the Scottish club, Aberdeen). Each dramatized the social essence of
their local football and popular cultures: one was public, vibrant and celebratory; the other, private, sombre and understated. The Genoese ceremony began
with a funeral service, well attended by fans and dignitaries alike, with the
coffin serenaded on its final journey by a New Orleans jazz band. A day later, a
stadium full of fans chanted and waved flags for over two hours at Sampdoria's
home defeat to Roma. Conversely, the Aberdeen ritual involved a private
service at the local kirk with only a handful of onlookers outside in the rain. At
the club's next home game, the pre-match minute's silence was observed with
customary (if distracted) solemnity, before a bizarre electrical fault shrouded
the ground in darkness.

Donald's funeral is one illustration of the immense discomfort with which
Protestant northern Europe handles public death (see Ariès 1983; Elias 1985).
It is often intolerant of the strong culture of public association that one finds in
southern Europe and Celtic nations. Invariably, the Catholicism of these nations, and the use of mourning rituals to celebrate life, are viewed with deep
suspicion. The 1989 Hillsborough disaster brought this opposition into stark
relief. Afterwards, football supporters journeyed to grounds throughout the
country (but especially Hillsborough and Liverpool's home at Anfield), to lay
personal emblems of memory for the dead, such as scarves, flags, flowers and
wreaths. Ian Taylor (1991a: 4) described these grounds as 'shrines' and the
mourning as 'a mass popular rite largely without parallel in Britain this
century'. But Liverpool was also a city in mourning for its economic decay and
cultural marginality. It had been heavily influenced by Irish immigration, Catholicism and the culture of Celtic expressiveness. The city was devastated by
post-industrial 'restructuring' throughout the 1980s. Hence, after Hillsborough,

a counter-discourse emerged outside Liverpool, that dismissed Liverpudlians as laden in sentimentality and self-pity (Walter 1991: 607–8; Scraton et al. 1995: 274–5). The English culture of reserve had been deeply unsettled by Liverpool's Celtic rituals of commemoration, of the dead and of itself.

Football and death: Protestant and Catholic, Anglo-Saxon and Celtic (or Latin), white and black, north and south, rich and poor. The constellation of these historical and cultural identities encapsulates the complexity of football identity *per se*. Culturally, each football society may play according to the rules of association football, but the meaning of the game within each setting is heavily dependent upon local conditions. Syntactical kinds of identity are particularly important in football. The game dramatizes senses of rivalry and opposition like no other sport. However, football and its associative rituals can also enable societies to celebrate themselves as part of a latter-day religious ceremony. While the 'secular' potentialities of Protestantism seem to prevail in Anglo-Saxon societies, a more symbolic and celebratory faith emerges in Celtic and Latin societies. Discomfort and disharmony ensue when the two cultures collide, particularly in their divergent understandings of that 'great extrinsic', death.

Football's early history reflects the material and ideological power of northern European societies like the UK relative to more peripheral cultures in southern Europe, Africa or South America. The game of football may be an extraordinary outlet for local senses of pride and rivalry at the interpersonal or cultural levels. Yet these intrinsic properties of the game would count for nothing against the social history of football. There would be no 'global game' without the sporting imperialism of British workers, teachers and soldiers during the late nineteenth century. In the next chapter, I turn to examine football's social history during the twentieth century, with particular reference to relations between the old and new worlds.

2

The Twentieth-century Sport: Football, Class and Nation

Football is one of the great cultural institutions, like education and the mass media, which shapes and cements national identities throughout the world. Football's international diffusion during the late nineteenth and early twentieth century occurred when most nations in Europe and Latin America were negotiating their borders and formulating their cultural identities. Major towns and cities were under construction, to be filled by new citizens drawn from the countryside or abroad. The characteristic processes of modernization (industrialization, urbanization and widespread migration) unravelled the old social and cultural ties of rural communities. Modern nations required to find fresh ways of unifying disparate peoples as an 'imagined community' (Anderson 1983).

A shared language, educational system and mass media of information became vital cultural tools for disseminating senses of modern nationhood (Gellner 1983). Each nation produced an 'official history', celebrating heroic figures who had fought to defend 'the people' from hostile forces. More potently, popular culture provided these resources with aesthetic and ideological components. Sports events, especially football matches, have become the most important contributors. Football teams from different parts of the country may represent rival localities, but within the unifying framework of a national league system. At internationals, the team embodies the modern nation, often literally wrapping itself in the national flag, and beginning matches with a communal singing of the 'national anthem'. The technological power of the mass media ensures that every corner of the nation can share the action (and thus participate) by watching on television or listening on radio (Gruneau et al. 1988: 273).[1]

The modern nexus of football and nation is underpinned by the increasing complexity of social and cultural life. Cultural complexity refers to the quantity of information ('knowledge') which actors use in dealing with the world. Social complexity refers to the social interaction of these actors, the breadth of their social positions, the relationships that they form (Archetti 1997b: 128). Using these axes of change, we may identify how football has become more complex. Socially, greater levels of interaction occur between players, fans, officials and other actors (such as television reporters, politicians and business sponsors) within any one nation. Moreover, as football has become more global, so the number of social actors and their frequency of interaction has multiplied. Old boundaries between the local, the regional, the national and the global are routinely penetrated or collapsed. The rising cultural complexity or 'hybridity' of football further reflects this globalization. Time–space differences are increasingly compressed (see Harvey 1989). Technology permits football information to be global rather than national in character. The mobility of players, reporters, officials, supporters, and more importantly football images, collectively ensures that individuals now bring an immense diversity of information to playing or watching the sport. Appadurai (1990) employs the term 'flow' to describe the global circulation of cultural products, people and services. The global 'flow' operates across a number of 'scapes', such as the mediascape or financescape. We might add the 'soccerscape' to these, to refer to the geo-cultural circulation of football's constituent parts: players and coaches, fans and officials, goods and services, or information and artefacts.[2]

In this chapter, I examine how the complex social and cultural relations within the 'soccerscape' have moved from predominantly 'modern' and 'national' ones to 'post-modern' and 'global' ones. I begin by discussing the general historical developments that lie behind the switch of political and cultural control over football, from Britain (and the old world) to FIFA (and the new world). I then adopt a case study approach to explain some of the soccerscape's common or differing features within specific football nations. From the 'old' football world, I look at England, Scotland and Germany; from the 'new' football world, I look at Argentina and Uruguay. All are 'modern' football nations, the game having played a key part in the formulation of their dominant idioms of national identity. I conclude the discussion by examining three nations (USA, Ireland and Australia) which privileged other sports during their 'modern' nation-building. Latterly, as each has reconstructed its national identity within a global environment, football has featured prominently as a 'post-modern' sporting facilitator.

Football's Modernization: the British game goes to FIFA

In a global political sense, the soccerscape's modernization is marked by two phases: first, the gradual transfer of hegemony from the British Isles to Europe; then, the late modern ascendancy of the new world within FIFA.[3] This recounts a story of football's global diffusion politically and culturally, and cruelly exposes Britain's failure to adjust strategically and ideologically to a declining international status.

After spreading the game globally, the British did little to preserve their lead in political and administrative terms. Seven European nations stepped in to fill the vacuum in 1904, founding the Fédération Internationale de Football Association (FIFA), replete with a significantly Francophone title.[4] In its infancy, the Home Nations maintained a policy of distance to FIFA, disturbed by the prospect of discussing their sport on an equal footing with foreigners. Problematically, unlike Britain's opponents at cricket or rugby, these footballing rivals were not incorporated within the British Empire but free to pursue their own cultural development. Moreover, they were either Britain's opponents in the pre-war scramble for colonies, or her 'trading partners' when business was still viewed as vulgar by British football's aristocratic custodians (Wagg 1984: 14).

The new football powers still deferred to Britain's symbolic hold over football, continuously soliciting British expertise to run the game, and appointing the FA treasurer D.B. Woolfall as FIFA President in 1906 (Perkin 1992: 212). FIFA further agreed to British demands that the Home Nations be admitted as separate members with autonomous voting rights. However, FIFA–British relations were regularly conflictual. The Home Nations joined up between 1905 and 1911, but resigned in unison in 1920 when FIFA favoured the membership applications of Germany, Austria and Hungary. Readmission in 1924 was cancelled *en bloc* four years later after disagreements over the expenses for 'amateur' players (Duke and Crolley 1996: 13). During the inter-war period, the Home Nations viewed FIFA's growth with a mixture of suspicion and jocularity. They declined to enter the first three World Cup finals (1930, 1934, 1938), retraining their sights on the extraordinary mass spectacles of domestic football as attendances increased phenomenally.[5] British self-preoccupation meant the respective football associations spent more time discussing Irish Home Rule than international matters (Walvin 1994: 130).

Evidence of Britain's international decline could not always be dismissed. Routine victories over teams from the dominions failed to mask the emerging continental threat. England's first overseas loss came in Madrid in 1929, a narrow 4–3 defeat by Spain. The brilliant Austrian side of the early 1930s, the bourgeois 'wonder team' of the 'Viennese Football School', thrashed Scotland 5–0 and only lost 4–3 to England (see Horak 1992, 1995).[6] At around the same time, Scotland lost 2–0 to Italy in Rome. Comfortingly, England entered the war after beating Germany home and away in 1935 and 1938; a poor FIFA select was seen off, while the 1934 'Battle of Highbury' against the world champions of Italy finished 3–2 to the home side (Birley 1995b: 302).

After the war, the UK's isolationist mentality slowly relented. The Home Nations rejoined FIFA in 1946 / 7 and England sent a team to the 1950 World Cup finals in Brazil. Scotland declined a qualifying place because it had failed to win the Home Championship that year – again indicating where the British priorities resided (Forsyth 1990: 180). International defeats, however, soon had a seismic impact on British notions of superiority. In 1945, the brilliant

Moscow Dinamo side (in reality, the Soviet national team) visited the UK, astonished huge crowds with their skills, and returned home undefeated in four matches (Edelman 1993: 87–91).[7] In 1950 England lost to the Scottish-influenced style of the USA in Brazil; Scotland became the first British national side to lose at home (1–0 to Austria). Most momentously, the 'Magical Magyars' of Hungary arrived in November 1953 and handed out a football lesson to the English, winning 6–3 at Wembley and then 7–1 in Budapest a year later. The first game acquired a mythological status in English football's genealogy. It shook English football traditions to the foundations and forced a rethink on Britain's world status, just as the Empire's colonies were showing their thirst for independence. Scotland fared rather better against the same Hungarians, losing by two goals in two matches home and away. Uruguay inflicted double blows on British self-respect at the 1954 World Cup finals in Switzerland, annihilating Scotland 7–0 then beating England 4–2. While the four Home Nations qualified for the finals four years later, only Wales and Northern Ireland made it through to the later stages, both losing in the quarter-finals. By that stage, Britain's claim to footballing excellence had been visibly deflated. Television pictures were beaming images back from Sweden of the Brazilians' brilliance. The *jogo bonito* ('beautiful play') of their illustrious front five – Didì, Garrincha, Vavà, Pelé and Zagalo – was unmatched in Europe, let alone the UK.

The process behind this modern footballing decline is perceptively identified in Willy Meisl's neglected classic, *Soccer Revolution*, published in 1955. Meisl was particularly critical of the English football hierarchy for failing to innovate or take foreign teams seriously. Although English sides scraped victories over continental sides between the early 1930s and 1950s, few admitted that they were regularly outplayed by technically superior foreigners. The English FA had ignored a 1936 report by Stanley Rous, calling for measures to safeguard England's international position. Fourteen years later, English journalists and football officials departed *en masse* after the England team were eliminated from the World Cup in Brazil, believing that nothing of interest could emerge from the later rounds. The Scottish response to overseas skills was even more atavistic; the crack Hungarian side of 1954 was tackled with undisguised violence. Regular humiliations of British sides became inevitable once modern continental sides had shaken off the pre-match nerves of playing football's traditionalist 'custodians'. At club level, the exceptional Manchester United side that perished in the Munich air disaster of 1958 might have withstood the great south European sides, like Real Madrid, Benfica, Internazionale and AC Milan. However, the epic 1960 European Cup final between Real Madrid and Eintracht Frankfurt, played in Glasgow before 135,000 fans and a nationwide television audience, left no doubt about British stagnation.

As power on the park was transferred from Britain to the modern footballing hotbeds of Europe and Latin America, administrative control was also being modernized. A rationalized pyramid of authorities controlled the increasing global complexity of the new soccerscape. FIFA remained football's universal power and invested its member associations with authority at national level. To ease administration and organization of competitions, FIFA also sanctioned the formation of continental football confederations as middle tiers of control between the national and the global.[8] These confederations empowered smaller football nations, such as those in Africa and Asia, with voting rights at a global level. The Confederación Sudamericana de Fútbol (CONMEBOL) had already been founded in 1916 to organize South American tournaments and represent 'new world' interests overseas. In 1954, the Union des Associations Européennes de Football (UEFA) was formed to administer European football. Although UEFA reflected the broader range of post-war European alliances that were the genus of today's EC, it was intended to contain the rising influence of the new world (Sugden and Tomlinson 1997: 3–4). Meanwhile, the Asian Football Confederation (AFC) was formed out of a meeting of nations competing at the Second Asian Games in Manila. The Confédération Africaine de Football (CAF) was founded three years later, just as Ghana heralded the drive for African self-government by gaining independence from the UK. North and Central America fell into line with the foundation of the Confederación Norte-Centro-americana y del Caribe de Fútbol (CONCACAF) in 1961.[9] The Oceania Football Confederation was founded in 1966; its belated formation reflected the low national importance of football in the Antipodes.

Notably, within this modern organization of the global game, the key political and administrative unit was established as the nation-state. With the privileged exception of the UK (and its four Home Nation associations), membership of FIFA remains dependent upon national recognition by the UN. In the West, separatist politics within nations must be set aside. In Spain, the rival 'nationalities' of Castille, Catalonia and the Basque region (not to mention the separate cultural identity in Andalusia and Galicia) are fiercely expressed at club level, but papered over to allow these disparate players to represent Spain (or, exceptionally, France). Civil wars in the old Second and Third Worlds have destabilized the FIFA status of affected nations. During the Yugoslavian civil war, UEFA refused the 'Yugoslavia' team the right to compete in the 1992 European Championship finals. Latterly, clubs from the new state of Bosnia–Hercegovina were barred from European competitions because they did not compete in a single national football championship, but were instead divided into Serb, Croat and Muslim leagues.

Initially, the new football pyramid of power did not produce major political changes. FIFA's Presidents continued to be drawn from France and England; the World Cup finals alternated between South America and Europe. However, the final reign of the Old World came with Sir Stanley Rous, whose naive internationalism precipitated his personal demise. Rous failed to appreciate the political ramifications of the new global soccerscape. The new member states from Africa and Asia held equal voting rights at FIFA's congressional meetings and were understandably keen to advance their collective interests (Sugden and Tomlinson 1997, 1998). Rous did not read this mood, nor was he shaken from his simplistic belief that football and politics should be kept apart, thereby alienating large numbers of delegates from the developing world. Rous's 'neutralist' stance resulted in the mishandling of sensitive political issues relating to China's football and world status, Pinochet's brutal regime in Chile, and the apartheid system of South Africa. In 1974 the Brazilian delegate João Havelange was elected President after travelling the world in search of support. He set about maximizing FIFA's commercial activities in exchange for increasing the new members' influence, notably through representation at the World Cup finals. Havelange was succeeded by Sepp Blatter in 1998 and his late modern legacy of commodification and political expediency has had real consequences for the UK. FIFA's International Board, where the UK has its final vestige of privileged influence, has come under regular pressure to revolutionize the laws of football, to make it more appealing to new consumers (rather than established football followers).[10]

Overall, throughout football's modernization, gradual shifts in power take place. During early modernization, administrative influence shifts from the UK to the European continent, to be followed predictably by a transfer of hegemony on the park. Late modernization sees the new world gain political ascendancy. Neither process revolutionizes the political framework of world football, in which the nation-state represents the fundamental unit. Nevertheless, as I shall argue, football's continued modernization potentially undermines the centrality of the nation-state; in Giddens's (1990: 139) apt metaphor, the juggernaut of modernity may crash through these barriers, out of the control of its initial drivers. To explore this possibility, I introduce the notion of football's 'post-modernization' and look at the 'post-national' cases of Ireland, Australia and the United States. To arrive at that point, however, I wish to provide a bridging discussion which looks at the historical cases of some established football nations. I therefore look at the old enemies of England, Scotland and Germany in Europe, and the oldest Latin American rivalry between Argentina and Uruguay. Each of these nations has been through 'traditional' and 'modern' football phases; they have since entered a 'post-modern' period, in which new, predominant senses of national identity require to be reconstructed within the global milieu.

Studies in Football and National Identity: the old enemies of England, Scotland, Germany; Argentina and Uruguay

England has been perhaps the most complex venue for football's contribution to the construction (and deconstruction) of national identity. English football's 'traditional' period involved a huge working-class popular culture centred on football, class conflicts over amateurism, and an isolationist policy abroad. As we have seen, the English had codified and practised the people's game for longer than anyone else, and so presumed to remain its masters. During the inter-war years of early modernity, English football's decline was masked by deference from overseas and narrow international victories. The modern, early post-war period saw English international football (much like British influence overseas) enter serious decline, with the contrived exception of the 1966 World Cup finals. The English game remained steadfast in its traditions while the economy and national culture stagnated in the nostalgia of former greatness. In its late modernity, English football's hooligans battled each other and their European counterparts with a ferocity matched by Margaret Thatcher in her pursuit of enemies at home, in Europe and in the engineered Falklands war (see Critcher 1994: 86–7). Though English club teams relied heavily on the other Home Nations and colonies to dominate Europe, the national side's failings could not be disguised. In the post-modern period of surface reinvention, the English game has been graced by service-sector monies and outdated European influences. English football grounds do remain the Labour Party at prayer. But, the cloth-capped male congregation of early modernity has been exchanged for new middle-class, Blairite couples and families. Meanwhile, the English national game trades on its heritage: bids for major international tournaments are delivered with the jingle that football should 'come home'.

The dominant strains of Scottish national identity are traditionally bound up with football and a structural dependency upon England. Football's traditional period was rooted in a strong, masculine, working-class culture; ethnic and religious divisions rooted in the Irish Question; and a relatively friendly rivalry with England. Scotland's football contests with England were viewed as beneficial to the Union, which also favoured the functional 'separateness' of Scottish state apparatuses (Paterson 1994). Scotland's wider modernization, and its football economy, relied heavily upon English influences. Scotland's late modernity during the 1970s saw a deep intensification of football rivalry with the English, the discovery of oil, and nationalist fulminations of politicians and *kulturkritiks* against the '90 minute patriots' (Nairn 1981; McIlvanney 1991; Jarvie and Walker 1994). The post-modern milieu has seen Scottish football and the wider society refocusing upon new European and global horizons, aided by the establishment of the Scottish Parliament before the millennium. Yet there remains a residual reliance upon England as a vital reference point for defining senses of Scottishness, in football and elsewhere (Finn and Giulianotti 1998).[11] Scots continue to support every opponent of England, even Germany, as a reflex technique for identity construction.

In contradistinction to the UK, German football traditions lacked any 'folk' prehistory; the association game was predominantly 'lower middle-class', at least until the 1930s (Lanfranchi 1994). Many clubs were dominated by the aspirant new white-collar workers, such as clerks, sales assistants and engineers; their organization was modelled on exclusive student fraternities and the respectable *bürgerliche* societies (Eisenberg 1989). During German football's mid-century period of early modernity, this hegemony was increasingly challenged by working-class clubs from the Ruhr. Schalke 04, the 'Pole and Prole club' from Gelsenkirchen, won seven league titles between 1934 and 1958 (Gehrmann 1994). Latterly, the modern West German game was dominated by the pan-national enterprise of Bayern Munich, while the national sides, under the influence of Beckenbauer, displayed an even greater capacity to succeed (Kuhn 1996). Nevertheless, in the post-modern milieu of a united Germany, support for the national side reflects opposing senses of national identification. On one hand, there are the *neckermanner* ('football tourists') who back the national side so long as it wins. These fans mirror the *Verfassungsnationalismus* ('Constitutional Nationalism') that prevails in Germany, based on what Parsons might call 'system integration', which survives so long as the constitution functions effectively. Conversely, the 'hard core' fans have a more affective association with the national team. They reflect a form of German identity rooted in 'social or moral integration', and which is maintained whether the team (or economy) wins, loses or draws (Giulianotti 1996c; Kreckel 1997).

A similar genealogical structure underlies the relationship of football to forms of national identity and history in South America. In Argentina, football became a key cultural medium for forging the first senses of traditional and popular national identity. The game went professional in 1931, as the early modern Argentina established itself as a leading football nation. Football quickly stood alongside other mythical national symbols, such as the *gaucho*, tango and *asado* (meat) (Archetti 1994). The Argentinian game became an important populist tool during the first period of Peronist rule (1946–55). However, by the modern era of the late 1950s and 1960s, Argentina's marginal economic and political status was replicated by the failures of the national team (Alabarces and Rodrigues 1999). The nation was traumatized by the disastrous 6–1 loss to Czechoslovakia at the 1958 World Cup finals (Levinsky 1995, quoted in Arbena 1998). During the late modern 1970s, the military junta struggled to reunify football and politics by hosting the World Cup finals; political alienation and military terror often collided violently in the national stadia (Archetti and Romero 1994). Subsequently, Argentina's crisis became dramatized in the 1980s through two opposing models of football style (Archetti 1996). On one hand, the 'traditionalism' of Menotti celebrated the Latin virtues of style, honesty and spectacle (Mason 1995a: 128). On the other hand, the modern pragmatism of Bilardo employed European techniques of discipline, work and organization (Di Giano 1995). Today, Argentinian football and society have entered a post-modern period. Political neo-conservatism and *laissez-faire* fiscal policies have encouraged the growing influence of television stations over an indebted domestic game (Alabarces 1998).

In Uruguay, football became a highly potent vehicle for the formation of national identity. As in Argentina, Uruguayan football was initially controlled by the British elite and local professionals. At the same time, huge waves of European immigrants were arriving and settling in Montevideo. The new Uruguayans had few cultural symbols to unite them as a 'nation', but football soon filled that vacuum. Uruguay's early modernization coincided with the rise of the national team, which first won Olympic gold medals in 1924 and 1928, then the inaugural World Cup Finals in 1930 (Giulianotti 1999). By 1932, the Uruguayan domestic game had gone professional. The process of modern nation formation reached its apogee in 1950 with the epic Maracanazo, when Uruguay beat Brazil 2–1 to win the World Cup (Reisch 1991: 83). The valiant performance of the captain, Varela, embodied a determined and definitive sense of modern 'Uruguayan' character. It also crowned Uruguay's political ascendancy to being the most democratic and orderly nation in Latin America. Uruguay's small population, vulnerable economy and peripheral global status were gradually replicated on the more modern football field. The brutal military junta (1972–1985) failed to arrest the decline; increasingly aggressive football tactics proved equally ineffectual. In the post-modern, post-military democracy, Uruguayan football and society stand in a paradoxical relationship. The nation is one of the most stable in Latin America, yet the national mood is deeply pessimistic. The explanation may lie in the parlous state of contemporary Uruguayan football, and the struggle of the national team to qualify for major tournaments. Accordingly, it cannot repay the deep emotional and nationalist investments of Uruguayans in the national game.

Continuities and Differences: traditional, modern and post-modern football nations

These case studies indicate that each nation possesses some unique features in its football history and identity. The early constitution and administration of football belongs to England, as does the reputation of leading hooligan nation. Argentina's mixture of football and political populism is unparalleled. Scottish football has been peculiarly obsessed about its relations with a neighbour. Lower-middle-class hegemony over football, and the impacts of national reunification, are solely German. Many nations may claim to be 'football crazy', but none matches the Uruguayans' national dependence on the game.

Nevertheless, these national football histories do harbour important commonalities. During football's 'traditional' period in these nations, in the late nineteenth and early twentieth centuries, the game privileged amateurism. Football was usually controlled by the aristocratic or middle-class urban elites, who sought to inculcate particular notions of national identity through the game, assimilating new immigrant groups. Lower-class interest in football multiplied, leading to their domination among fans and players.

Football's 'early modernity' is signified through the professionalization of players and the rise of working-class teams. International competition became more established; particular national styles became more pronounced through regular inter-continental matches. British hegemony on and off the park was seriously pressurized. The game's later modernity began after the Second

World War; its features became increasingly marked during the 1970s and 1980s. International club competitions were established; the expanding 'financescape' of football guaranteed the rise of the richest clubs; international player transfers multiplied. The old dominant nations, such as England, Argentina and Uruguay, experienced a decline in world terms on and off the pitch.

Latterly, football has entered the period of 'post-modernity'. Deindustrialization has fractured the nexus of the working classes with inner-city clubs. Television dominates the finances and administration of football leagues and their member clubs. The largest nations benefit, importing players from throughout the world, while smaller nations become dependent on overseas transfers. The global circulation of labour and ideas begins to undermine footballing 'traditions', increasing the hybridity of playing styles.

This is not to say that the 'traditions' of nationality within particular football cultures are destabilized by 'post-modernity' alone. Inequalities have always existed between nations, during football's 'traditional' and 'modern' phases, thereby undermining the capacity of weaker nations to formulate national identities through the game. In the post-modern epoch, football's role in reproducing national identification in Argentina and Uruguay is threatened by the sale of players to Europe. However, this structural inequality, and its threat to 'nation-building', has long existed. Uruguay and Argentina were heavily reliant on the British for learning the game; hybridity is central to their 'national' football traditions. During the game's early modernity, their football successes were wounded by Italian sharp practices. Top South American players became *oriundi* in being granted 'dual nationality' so they could play for Italy. The Argentinians Orsi, Monti and Gualita played for the 1934 World Cup winners; the Uruguayan Andreolo played at centre-half for the 1938 champions. During the 1950s, the Italians recruited the Argentinian 'trio of death' (Maschio, Angelillo and Sivori) and the brilliant Uruguayans Schiaffino and Ghiggia. The 'late modern' dependency of Argentina and Uruguay upon the Old World continued; each borrowed tactically from Spain and Italy, as players and managers sought their fortune abroad. Yet, in the post-modern era, the sale of top and mediocre players has never been more institutionalized. South American agents employ numerous European contacts to transfer the players at increasingly young ages.

Class and Nation: tensions and paradoxes

In classic modernist fashion, the nation has been the principal administrative unit within football throughout the twentieth century. Concomitantly, *nationalism* within the game encapsulates the strength of national identification of specific peoples, so that particular kinds of identity are celebrated while 'others' are categorically excluded. Yet national identities are never static nor mononuclear. There may be a multiplicity of national identities within any one nation, which are distinguishable along specific structural or ideological lines, such as those relating to religion, or class, or ethnicity, or identification with a specific sovereign. In multi-cultural societies, the heterogeneity of nationalist voices is particularly striking. For example, when France won the 1998 World Cup on home soil, the victory was hailed by all shades of political and ethnic opinion; people of North African extraction unfurled the traditional tricolour alongside the Algerian national flag.

The cultivation of nationalism, and the stoking of nationalist antagonisms, have tended to be at their height during football's early modernity. In Western Europe, we may refer to the 1920s and 1930s, when football internationals were inevitably influenced by rising nationalist sentiments and militarization. In Latin America, Peron paved the way for generals throughout the southern cone to seek to exploit the nationalist potential of football. Nevertheless, a major debate remains among scholars and the people themselves regarding how instrumental or efficacious the military leaders actually were in delivering populist football policies (Arbena 1990; Scher 1996; Giulianotti 1999). Today, football nationalism of a corporatist state variety is fuelled by the battle to host major international tournaments: for example, England and Germany clashing for the 2006 World Cup finals; Japan and South Korea's earlier struggle for the 2002 tournament. Meanwhile, rival fan groups vie for national prestige by capturing the global imagination. The violence of some hooliganism at international fixtures might partially be explained by reference to their nationalistic ethos and rhetorics, though we must examine other factors (such as youth cultural identity or the bodily aesthetics of violence: see chapter 3). Equally, the non-violent fans actuate their nationalism when they battle to become officially recognized as the world's best supporters.

While football's nationalism emerges episodically at international fixtures and tournaments, it is local and civic concerns that underpin the game at grassroots level. The everyday loyalties of fans and players tend to be bestowed upon individual clubs rather than nations. At club level, we find important symbolic reflections of the industrial, urban, early modern period in which football emerged as a national sport, in both the old and new worlds. Except for those from the largest conurbations, most team names proudly announce their ties to an urban locality. Most clubs had been founded during football's 'traditional' or 'early modern' period, when a geographical home was favoured; the clubs were created for local social and cultural purposes, rather than as modern 'franchises' for maximizing sports revenues. In the UK, especially, the second names that the clubs choose underline this civic, associative dimension: teams represent the 'City', or bring together its citizens ('United'). Modern geographical mobility (from a recognized home) may be emphasized ('Wanderers', 'Rovers' or 'Rangers'). These modernist appellations are in some contrast to the 'post-modern' nomenclature found in American sports, in which teams are named totemically after natural forces or creatures, for example, Chicago Bears, Atlanta Ravens, Toronto Maple Leafs (Laughlin 1993: 97). In Latin

America, this modernist connection is often reflected, with teams like Peñarol or Rosario Central named after local railway works.

In the UK, intense nationalism at the outbreak of war in 1914 did not prevent class-based differences surfacing. The press, politicians and middle-class public contrasted the gallant bravery of young soldiers with footballers, who were failing to 'do their bit' by staying at home and playing games (Crampsey 1990: 57). Stronger criticisms centred on football's debilitating impact on the war effort, as thousands of potential recruits were alleged to have put their spectating before conscription (Birley 1995b: 70–2). In reality, attendances did decline, but northern working-class football enthusiasts still showed a strong passion for the game, particularly when celebrating the winning of trophies.

In terms of practising and spectating, clear class-related differences exist in the early football histories of the UK and the rest of Western Europe. Before and after the First World War, Scandinavia, Germany, Italy and France saw an explosion in the involvement of socialist and communist movements, in organizing mass sports participation, with football a key component. UK labour movements failed to challenge middle- and upper-class hegemony over working-class recreation. A more passive relationship to sport inevitably followed; pervasive commercial interests encouraged drinking, gambling and spectating (John Hargreaves 1992: 134). Edwardian football clubs were meanwhile dominated by bourgeois ethics. Club officials felt duty bound to save working-class youth from moral dissolution and physical licence by expending its energies in this healthy, manly pastime (Redhead 1995: 43).[12] By the early 1960s, a number of policy reports had enshrined this ideology.[13] Yet, thirty years later, the actual value of football clubs as *de facto* 'crime prevention units' was highly questionable (Robins 1992).[14]

Football's traditional and modern forms have therefore cut across three key kinds of social identification: nation, class and locality. While those of nation and class can often be irreconcilable, the 'intense physical and temporal compression and fierce partisanship' of matches often mean that local ties usually predominate over national ones (Marqusee 1995: 54). Football clubs from strong working-class areas are integral to the local 'structure of feeling'. The earliest social scientists to write on football culture in the UK emphasized the deep connections between the club and its working-class community.[15] The football ground becomes a vital space for male association, along with the local pub and factory or industrial plant. The affinities of club and supporters can sometimes be expressed politically during collective struggles. In recent years, Borussia Dortmund offered free seats to striking steelworkers, while Liverpool players displayed slogans supporting the sacked Merseyside dockers in their long-running industrial dispute.

In the epoch of post-modernity, three contemporary pressures undermine this class-centred 'structure of feeling'. First, within club football, there is a growing polarization between two kinds of support. On one hand, the 'local publics' type of support is analogous to the old working-class fandom; the intense partisanship and loyalty of fans are channelled through the local team (see Leifer 1995: 85). In contradistinction, clubs like Manchester United, Liverpool, AC Milan and Bayern Munich adhere to the 'national publics' model. Their supporters follow utilitarian principles: 'Winning teams amass followings, and losing teams are inevitably abandoned' (1995: 86; see Alt 1983). Football's economics ensure these latter sides increasingly dominate competition and media coverage of the sport.

Secondly, globalization brings with it a disembedding of local social and political ties between club and community. The international movement of players also entails the greater circulation of political grievances and cosmopolitan perspectives. Today, the political involvement of football players is much more likely to touch upon international than local issues. For example, Swiss, Norwegian and Sampdoria players demonstrated against French nuclear tests in the South Pacific. Sampdoria players also made pre-match protests in the Italian league over the Yugoslavian civil war.

Thirdly, in class terms, the 'lower-class' sport has become increasingly the property of middle-class popular culture. I discuss this transformation more fully in chapter 8, with regard to the growing fashionability of football attendance in Northern Europe. We may add that this process is also manifested in Latin America in the class composition of fans and players. 'Crack' internationalists such as Redondo of Argentina and Francescoli of Uruguay hail from stable middle-class backgrounds. Francescoli in particular represents a new Latin American role model, in possessing the cultural capital and psychological equilibrium to settle and play successfully in France, Argentina and Italy during a long and nomadic career. Meanwhile, the living conditions of the urban underclasses have declined during the last quarter of the twentieth century. Unemployment, illiteracy, poor housing, malnutrition and chronic illnesses simply vitiate the pursuit of personal fitness and sharpened dexterity, the prerequisites for any sports career. Hence, the more successful players of lower-class origin hail increasingly from farming areas that provide young men with more nutritious, meat-based diets and regular exercise.

In contrast, southern European nations have always had a relatively classless football culture. The differences are highlighted in the meanings that emerge from football-related ceremonies. For example, the World Cup finals of 1994 in the United States saw the superstar 'Three Tenors' (Pavarotti, Domingo, Carreras) performing together as part of the festivities (Hannigan 1995: 195), just as Pavarotti's rendition of Puccini's 'Nessun Dorma' had become the anthem to the 1990 finals in Italy. In northern Europe, this marriage of opera and football marked middle-class entry to the game, via a post-modern collapse of high and low culture. Conversely, in southern Europe, from whence these great singers had emerged, the concerts merely confirmed the classless fabric of football culture and popular opera.

Football and the Post-modernization of Nation-States:
the USA, Ireland, Australia

While football, national identity and modernity appear to be deeply interrelated, they are neither evolutionary nor universal processes. As I noted in chapter 1, many societies have undergone modernization and nation-building processes without any meaningful contribution from football. In such cases, other sports cultures have been employed to cement distinct senses of national identity (Taylor 1988: 538). In the United States and Ireland, and to a lesser extent Australia, the old colonial sports legacy was transmogrified to invent new national sports traditions, including further variations on football. Yet, in each case, association football's new cultural and social importance has emerged in the post-modern era, after the modern process of nation-building has been completed.

In the United States, soccer has never belonged on the roster of American pastimes, such as American football (gridiron), baseball and basketball. Soccer had been practised keenly by European immigrants in eastern cities since the 1900s (Bazzano 1994: 113), while the Church helped in its promotion (Reiss 1991: 106). The professional game enjoyed a short east coast boom in the 1920s and early American teams did produce some astonishing results.[16] Yet the game continued to be associated with ethnic groups reluctant to assimilate or 'Americanize' (Mormino 1982; Pooley 1976; Walter et al. 1991).

During the late 1960s and 1970s, American soccer leaders adopted a glitzy modern strategy to market the game. Teams were organized into the large North American Soccer League (NASL), games were staged in huge state-of-the-art stadia, aged overseas stars were recruited to play (Sugden 1994: 242–5; Miller and Russell 1971: 36–7). Though successful for a while in attracting ethnic audiences (most notably in New York), the venture foundered largely on the nation-building question: the reliance on foreign players effectively alienated Americans. By the early 1990s, large numbers of foreign players in college soccer teams reflected poor grassroots interest (Bale 1991a: 55–7).

In 1994, the USA successfully hosted the World Cup finals, symbolizing a watershed both in the game's American fortunes and in the nation's sense of identity. Major League Soccer (MLS) was launched soon after, employing the modest, post-modern business philosophy of 'downsizing', with only twelve team 'franchises', limits on the purchase of foreign stars, team salary caps of $1.19 million, rules demanding more intimate stadia for matches, and a long-term planning strategy that accepted first year losses of $19 million. The long-term goal of MLS is to tap into the huge market of organized American soccer players, reckoned at between 12.2 and 16 million (Giulianotti 1996a: 326). Most are white, middle-class suburban children. For many, the game is a cultural enclave from violent playing ethics or Afro-American domination (Andrews et al. 1997; Wagner 1990: 401). To establish a modest but lucrative niche in US sports, MLS hopes to tap this market and appeal to those hyphenated Americans from Europe, Central America and the Far East with an established football interest.[17] Instead of being a modern mechanism for uniting the nation through sport, soccer's survival depends upon exploiting post-modern class and ethnic divisions.

In Ireland, the post-modernization of national identity has been a key facilitator of football's new appeal. Historically, football in Ireland was regarded as the 'garrison game', a British sport at odds with the 'traditional' Gaelic Games of hurling and Gaelic football that had been institutionalized and popularized during the late nineteenth century. The latter were controlled by the Gaelic Athletic Association (GAA) which threatened to expel members who played the colonial sport. Ireland's partition in 1921 granted full independence to 26 of its 32 counties, the northern 6 remaining under British jurisdiction. The GAA continued to organize the Gaelic Games on an All-Ireland basis, thereby reflecting the new Republic's commitment to reunification. The GAA monopolized sport's contribution to Irish modernization. It symbolized a break from the colonial past, professed to be the national sports body, and presented its games as insolubly 'Irish'. However, Ireland never really established itself as a 'modern' nation. The countryside remained the more populous, cultural 'soul' of Ireland; secularization was very limited; mass immigration stunted demographic and industrial growth; partition meant that Ireland deemed itself territorially incomplete (O'Toole 1994). Tellingly, Gaelic games dominated rural areas, while the cities of Dublin and Cork indulged also in football.

Recently, Irish football has flourished, particularly in internationals. Qualification was secured, first, for the 1988 European Championships, and then for the 1990 and 1994 World Cup finals. A pragmatic selection policy saw top players born overseas drafted in to play for Ireland through their Irish ancestry. This approach also reflects the 'post-modern' condition of Ireland, in recognizing the diaspora's consequences, whereby 'Irishness' cannot be conveniently restricted to a single island (Giulianotti 1996a and 1996b). Selecting non-white players like Babb, McGrath and Phelan, compelled the indigenous Irish to confront the racist elements within their culture. Moreover, the Irish team, authorities and fans seek collectively to distance themselves from the sports nationalism of the GAA by adopting an agnostic approach towards the politics of Ireland (Holmes 1994; Hunt 1989: 19). As Fintan O'Toole remarked, 'the team has allowed people in the Republic to celebrate their identity without being encumbered by the dark complications of the North' (*Irish Times*, 29 June 1994).

As in the United States and Ireland, soccer in Australia was traditionally marginalized. The formation of Australian national identity throughout the nineteenth century was dominated by relations with Britain and sport was a key medium of this cultural hegemony. The resulting passion for sport never saw soccer supplant the popularity of Australian Rules or Rugby League (Vamplew 1994a: 208). After the Second World War, indigenous soccer became the preserve of the new, south European immigrants; the Anglo-Saxon majority maintained a soccer interest through televised British matches (McKay et al. 1993: 16). Confirming the marginality of Australia's ethnic communities, soccer was disparagingly referred to as '*wogball*' (Vamplew 1994b: 3). Relations between ethnic soccer clubs tended to reflect the frictions and enmities of Balkan politics. Incidents of fan disorder were grossly exaggerated by the Australian media (Hughson 1992: 14–15; Mosely 1994). In response, the Australian Soccer Federation sought to 'Aussify' the clubs by demanding that they change their ethnic names – hence, for example, Sydney Croatia became Sydney United. This crude 'harmonization' represented a denial of Australia's post-modern multi-cultural make-up and failed to Anglicize the clubs or the indigenous football culture (Hughson 1997a). The top clubs and the Australian national team all continued to be dominated by these ethnic groupings. Meanwhile, the part-integrationist, part-multicultural schizophrenia at the clubs has jeopardized their future in Australia. New ethnic minorities (particularly from the Far East) are not drawn to clubs that retain an ethnic symbolism. Yet many second or third generation European immigrants have been well integrated into Australian cultural and industrial life, and so have little desire, time or energy to work for the clubs to keep them alive (Hay 1998).

Football in the United States, Australia and Ireland demonstrates that senses of national identification are not neatly packaged within political borders. Identification with an 'imagined community' of fellow nationals can stretch into many other geo-political territories (as in the case of Ireland). Internally, one 'nation' may house many conflicting senses of national identity (as in Australia and the United States). A policy of tolerant 'multiculturalism' may seem to be a sensible and liberal response to these problems. However, 'multiculturalism' assumes that antagonisms between minority groups can be papered over, which is not always the case (as demonstrated in Australia). It forgets that competing senses of ethnic or national identity will continue between different strata *within* the same 'national' community (see Hughson 1997b).

The global pressures upon national unity affect all football societies. The national integrity of football leagues is undermined by small and indebted clubs who wish to 'relocate' to another nation, while still competing in the same domestic competitions.[18] It is more seriously jeopardized by business ventures to establish elite continental leagues such as that regularly proposed in Europe. In the final four chapters, I look at how globalization and the deconstruction of national borders have impact upon football's business side, the position of players, the mass media, playing techniques and aesthetics, and some of the contemporary political questions within the game. In the next two chapters, I look at fan cultures and how their spatial environment for watching the game has been modernized.

3

Spectator Cultures: Passion at Play in Europe and Latin America

Since the late 1960s, UK football sociology has been strongly associated with the study of football supporters, and more particularly football hooligans. Concomitantly, there has been an enormous political, social and media concern with UK football hooliganism, providing academics with a large public audience for research and (during the 1980s) a jealously guarded source of funding. Public concern with fan violence peaked in Scotland in 1980 when Rangers and Celtic fans fought a pitched battle after the national cup final; in England the apogee arrived in 1985 with the pitch invasion by Millwall hooligans at Luton, and the deaths of football fans in Birmingham and, most tragically of all, at Heysel in Brussels.

The violent persona of English fans has been slowly refashioned since the late 1980s, encouraging UK sociologists to examine other aspects of football fandom. A more international and interdisciplinary field has emerged to examine violent fan groups and other, non-violent forms of spectatorship.[1] These comparative studies highlight the cultural differences that exist between supporters, at the local, regional, national and continental levels. Nevertheless, the UK remains a dominant influence within this international field in terms of financing and disseminating this body of research.

This chapter is devoted to a discussion of international football supporters, and the kinds of sociological analysis that they have attracted. I begin with a substantive critical assessment of the three major social explanations that were advanced to explain English football hooliganism, from the late 1960s to the late 1980s. These are the Marxist perspective of Ian Taylor and others, the social psychological position of Peter Marsh and his Oxford colleagues, and the figurational explanation forwarded by Eric Dunning and his Leicester contemporaries. Some of these scholars might prefer to close the debate on fan violence and move on to examine different football-related issues, such as those discussed throughout this book. However, football hooliganism is still

present in the UK and overseas and remains a relevant subject of enquiry. It
would be unwise to grant these perspectives, with their various strengths and
numerous limitations, the 'final word' on fan violence.

Subsequently, I turn to discuss alternative studies of football hooliganism
undertaken by myself and other fieldworkers in the UK. I examine key issues
relating to research methods, the changing social and cultural elements of
hooliganism in Scotland and England, and the psychosocial 'pleasures' that are
enjoyed by hooligan fans. I contrast these findings with research into the
militant fan sub-cultures of southern Europe (the *ultràs*) and South America
(particularly the *barras bravas* of Argentina). The chapter closes with an
analysis of two new, 'post-hooligan', European fan groups: the carnival fans
who follow national teams like Scotland, Ireland and Holland; and the political
fan movements, such as football fanzines and independent supporter associations, which have become prominent in the UK since the late 1980s. The
overall discussion draws heavily on personal fieldwork undertaken over the
past decade into supporter groups in the UK, Ireland, continental Europe and
South America.

English Sociologists and Football Hooliganism:
Ian Taylor and the Marxist perspective

The British sociological analysis of football hooliganism began with Ian Taylor
(1969, 1970, 1971). Drawing upon a Marxist and 'new criminological' perspective, Taylor argued that football hooliganism must be explained according
to wider economic and social changes. He viewed football as traditionally a
male working-class sport, in which the clubs were tied inextricably to their
surrounding communities. Working-class fans felt the club was a 'participatory democracy', where their views had some purchase within the boardroom
or on the park. According to Taylor, club directors had sought to undermine
this deeply affective (but ultimately unprofitable) tie by promoting the game
among a wealthier, more respectable, middle-class audience. Clubs shifted
their emphasis from satisfying existing 'supporters' to attracting modern 'spectators' or leisure 'customers'. Symptoms of this purported 'bourgeoisification'
included football's 'spectacularization' (such as pre-match displays, more comfortable ground facilities), its 'professionalization' (for example, highly paid
players bought by transfer), and its 'internationalization' (for example, more
competition with European teams).

The commercialization of 'their' sport alienated working-class fans, particularly the young, 'sub-cultural rumps' which began to assemble regularly at
matches. Their initiation of modern English football hooliganism came in
1961, through a televised pitch invasion at a match between Tottenham and
Sunderland. Increasing violence between opposing soccer gangs, vandalism,
and the provocation of police and rival fans were further symptoms of the

Taylor - 1969, 70, 71 - 1990's
Methodological no facts

rump's alienation. Taylor interpreted these outbursts of disorder as inarticulate acts of 'resistance' to football's commodification which could not be quelled by more aggressive policing.

Later, Taylor adopted an increasingly critical perspective on football hooligans. He argued that the marginalization of football hooligans would also encourage fascistic political movements to target them, and thus result in even deeper social problems within working-class and immigrant communities (Taylor 1982a and 1982b). He abandoned his political teleology on fan violence and developed a less empathetic, 'left-realist' approach. Turning to Phil Cohen's (1972) studies of urban change during the late 1960s, Taylor argued that two hooligan identities predominated. Upper-working class or 'yuppie' youths had benefited materially from Thatcher's self-interested, *laissez-faire* economic and social policies; conversely, 'lumpen', lower working-class youths, were unskilled, under-educated and effective 'fodder' for far-right xenophobia and racism. Both social groups were increasingly threatening towards working-class citizens and immigrant communities (Taylor 1991a). He later opined that the 'terrace culture' of the 1980s held few romantic attractions, being 'one of rampant racism, crudely sexist banter, and of aggravation conducted by groups of young white males of little education and even less wit' (Taylor 1991a: 14–15). In the early 1990s, Taylor (1991b) reconstructed his position once again, claiming in a short newspaper article that the entire culture of football fandom was changing (Taylor 1991b). In the post-Italia '90 atmosphere of English football, he argued, fans were better behaved, and keen to copy the displays of the Italian *ultràs*. Hooliganism was '*passé*'; the game had become 'fun'. To illustrate his point, Taylor referred to a recent match between Nottingham Forest and West Ham at which Hammers fans were photographed in fancy dress.

Taylor's work has some analytical strongpoints. He forwards an attractive, trenchant critique of football's commodification, though it would be economically reductive to attribute football hooliganism solely to this process. His early work challenged some public stereotypes about hooligans. Cohen and Robins (1978) and Horak (1991: 535) (in Austria) confirmed that young fans labelled as 'hooligans' were far more committed to the club than those they counter-labelled as the 'rich assholes in the stands'. Likewise, Clarke (1978) argued that from the 1960s, young fans were no longer under the social influence of their parental group, but did attend instead as part of large peer groups with their own sub-cultural values.

Over the course of twenty years, however, Taylor appears to have completed an explanatory somersault on football hooliganism. He had began with the idea that hooligans were popular 'resistance fighters', but then abandoned this in the 1980s, to define them as serious social menaces. In the 1990s, he concluded that hooliganism was 'out-dated'. This U-turn was mirrored in his analysis of football commerce. Ground facilities were derided as bourgeois affectations in the 1970s; after Hillsborough, they became part of the spectator's human rights

U Turn on who Hool's were - challenged stereotypes.

(Taylor 1991a). It might be claimed that Taylor's changing arguments on hooliganism reflected developments within the phenomenon itself. However, the major weakness in Taylor's work is its lack of empirical grounding. He readily accepted in the early 1970s that his writings were 'speculative' and not based on real fieldwork. He spent most of the 1980s in Canada.

Hence, it is hard to believe his initial argument that working-class fans viewed clubs as 'participatory democracies'. Football has been a serious business since at least the 1890s; directors have almost always protected their investments rather than pursue the fans' interests by over-spending on players or ground facilities. Taylor's subsequent point on fascist agitation among young fans was in line with media reports from the mid-1970s onwards, but the actual recruitment of hooligans to these political movements is a question that 'speculation' cannot answer. His later use of Phil Cohen's (1972) studies to identify two hooligan identities was imaginative, but more than a decade overdue. Finally, though hooliganism did decline in the late 1980s, it certainly did not disappear. Ironically, at Taylor's illustrative Nottingham Forest–West Ham match, there were over 140 arrests. Moreover, few English fan groups really borrowed from the Italian *ultràs*. In fact, the latter's terrace displays and social energy had originated through meticulous copying of the English terrace culture of the 1970s. We might conclude that Taylor's analytical depth in explaining fan violence was greatly undermined by a genuine lack of empirical content.

English Explanations Continued: Peter Marsh and early fieldwork

The dearth of ethnographic research into English football hooliganism was partially repaired by the social psychologist Peter Marsh and his Oxford associates in the late 1970s (see Marsh, et al. 1978; Marsh 1978a, 1978b). To investigate 'hooliganism' at Oxford United, the researchers employed the techniques of 'participant observation' and qualitative interviewing with young fans. They found that the 'aggro' (social aggravation) of rival fan groups was subject to specific 'rules of disorder' (Marsh 1978b: 24). Social exchanges between rival fans were typically limited to exaggerated threats, ritualized insults, and the denial of the opponent's masculinity (Marsh, Rosser, Harré 1978: 131–3; see Archetti 1992). Fans might intimidate one another with chants such as 'You're gonna get your fucking head kicked in', but 'Happily, the threats are rarely translated into action' (Marsh 1978a: 64). Deviant hooligans who were genuinely interested in harming opponents, for example by carrying weapons like knives or ammonia, would be considered 'out of order' by their peers, and labelled as 'nutters' to reflect their 'outrageous' character (Marsh et al. 1978: 70).

Order was maintained internally through a pyramid hierarchy of members (Marsh 1978a). At its apex were the Graduates, an older grouping of young

Handwritten margin notes: Marsh et al / social psychologist / mid-late 70's / only / Ethno / at Oxford Utd

males, who had accumulated respect and status, and thus no longer required to indulge on a regular basis. The 'aggro' was instead taken care of by the younger Rowdies; beneath them were the Little Kids or Novices, learning the ropes of football gang interaction, and probably initiating the 'aggro' which Rowdies would then seek to convert into a symbolic victory for the group. On the fringes of this highly structured organization were the self-explanatory Chant Leaders and the Nutters. Collectively, the hooligan group retained a strong sense of territoriality. During the 1970s, young fans would congregate in rival 'ends' (behind the goals), chanting and singing. Their match-day objective was to drive their rivals from their end, and so 'take' it, thus claiming a symbolic victory (see Armstrong and Giulianotti 1995).

The researchers accepted that real violence did sometimes happen, but they argued that such incidents were largely precipitated by the excessively sensitive response of powerful social groups to the 'problem' of 'football hooliganism' *per se*. The media, police, magistrates, school teachers and politicians were criticized for dehumanizing young fans by referring to them as 'animals' and 'savages', and thereby 'amplifying' the seriousness of their 'aggro' (Marsh et al. 1978: 134). When this happens, 'order is threatened': the 'hooligan' comes to take on at least part of the violent identity that is ascribed to him, and expects his peers on either side to do likewise. A 'positive feedback cycle' begins, as the distance between hooligans and authorities becomes ever more polarized and difficult to bridge. The solution is to show more tolerance to the young fans; 'perhaps in the end we will have to live with a bit of aggro' (Marsh 1978a: 80).

Marsh and his colleagues certainly enhance, through fieldwork, our qualitative understanding of fan violence. The major problem concerns their explanation of what causes 'aggro'. Marsh argued that 'aggro' is precipitated by human aggression, which is deemed to be innate rather than socially learned, and therefore common to all men, women, societies and civilizations. Aggression is defined as a helpful, indeed functional aspect of human nature; it is part of our survival instincts. If tolerated and given suitable social outlets (such as through sports or small-scale battles), aggression can benefit any society by enhancing social integration. Conversely, societies that ostracize aggression find their future is 'a frightening one'; by way of illustration, Marsh (1978a: 93) referred to real injuries suffered within football hooliganism, as well as to the violent and unpredictable streets of New York and Detroit.

This 'ethogenic' portrayal of aggression is ahistorical and asocial, and goes against the basic 'socialization' approach favoured by all social scientists for explaining social behaviour. The researchers also underplayed the complex social and hermeneutic aspects of 'aggro' among the young fans themselves. The explanations that young fans offer for their activities are seen as mere verbal symptoms of an innate aggression. Furthermore, behind any rivalry between two sets of supporters, there are complex social, historical and cultural factors at work, which the Oxford researchers would again generally discount. For example, even in a small nation like Scotland, the antagonisms between Glasgow Rangers and Celtic fans are very different to those involving Aberdeen fans and those who follow the Glasgow clubs.

Researchers into football hooliganism have also been suspicious of the fact that Marsh and his colleagues were supported by some 'pop academics' of the time, notably the psychologist Dr Anthony Clare,[2] and the anthropologist Desmond Morris (1981). More seriously, it is disappointing that the group of fans which they studied, followers of Oxford United, were not exactly the most notorious hooligan formation in the UK. Additionally, the vintage of their research (mid-1970s) suggests it may have become rather dated.

English Explanations Continued: the 'Leicester School'

Since the early 1980s, the leading contributors to the UK debate on football hooliganism have been the group of sociologists based at the University of Leicester, namely Eric Dunning, Patrick Murphy, John Williams, Joe Maguire and Ivan Waddington. This group received substantial funding from the old Social Science Research Council and the Football Trust at a time when political and public concern with fan violence was at its zenith. The term 'Leicester School' has been coined by others, to reflect the group's admitted hegemony in football sociology (Dunning, Murphy and Waddington 1991: 460); and to highlight the group's unity over their theoretical perspective, research methods and conclusions (Clarke 1992; Giulianotti 1989a). The group explains football hooliganism, indeed all sports related issues, according to the 'figurational' or 'process sociological' perspective created by Norbert Elias, a former colleague at the University of Leicester (see Elias 1978a, 1997). Critics have argued that the Leicester research was conceived and designed simply to confirm (rather than test) Elias's standpoint (e.g. Taylor 1987; Armstrong and Harris 1991; Lewis 1996). Indeed, the chief researcher working within the group, John Williams, found Elias's influence too oppressive, resulting in his acrimonious departure from the Leicester School in the late 1980s (Williams 1991).[3] To explain the Leicester perspective on football hooliganism, it is therefore essential to examine the sociology of Norbert Elias.

Elias's sociological viewpoint is rooted in his notion of social 'figurations'. People are linked into networks of social interdependency; power relations are fluid and in a permanent state of flux (Elias 1978a). More substantively, according to Elias (1978b, 1982), a 'civilizing process' has been underway in Western societies (particularly England and France) since the middle ages. This process is influenced by a complex of long-term, interrelated developments, which include economic growth, an expanded division of labour, state monopoly of taxation and violence, and social democratization (see Dunning 1993: 47). The civilizing process has involved an increasing everyday concern to monitor, control and shield the body and its functions from public scrutiny

Leicester Sch. - Methodological early 80's →
copied N. Elias.

(e.g. table manners, private toilets). Related to these processes is our growing intolerance towards public acts of aggression or violence. Elias notes that the civilizing process originates in court societies, reflecting the watchfulness of an elite figuration that was undergoing scissors-like pressure from the growing powers of the state above it and the citizenry below. Though the powers of the court society became increasingly ceremonial, its civilized manners have percolated through the social structure, into the bourgeoisie *(ad nauseum* with the Victorians), and down among the upper-working classes by the early post-war period, rendering both of these classes increasingly 'respectable'. Such a wide-ranging historical account inevitably encounters anomalies, such as warfare or violent revolution, in which the civilizing process seems to be ill-fitting. To rebut this counter-evidence, Elias introduces the notion of 'decivilizing spurts' which temporarily reverse the civilizing process (see Dunning 1989: 44). Since the civilizing process remains incomplete, it has yet to significantly influence the lower or 'rough' working classes and other groups at the base of the social pyramid.

The civilizing process is used by the Leicester School to explain football hooliganism in two main respects. First, the researchers examine how our broader social attitudes towards violence at football matches have developed over time; second, they attribute fan violence *per se* to social groups largely unaffected by the civilizing process. In their major work, *The Roots of Football Hooliganism*, the Leicester researchers draw upon press reports, official documents and some arrest figures to argue that football matches in the UK have always been venues for violence. Until the First World War, this violence tended to be 'relatively high' and 'affective'. It was 'generated mainly by more directly match-related causes such as perceived bias on the part of referees, perceived "foul" and "unfair" play by visiting players, or simply ... by the dynamics of the interaction between opposing fans' (Dunning et al. 1988: 90). The researchers argue that violence declined during the inter-war period and after the Second World War. Football crowds became more 'respectable' in class composition; working-class people benefited from economic growth and more inclusive social policies. Modern football hooliganism dates from the early 1960s, during which Britain entered a 'decivilizing spurt', as socio-economic weaknesses emerged and inequalities hardened. Violence at football matches emerged *de novo*. This time, rival gangs of young supporters attacked each other more deliberately, consistently and 'instrumentally'. 'Respectable' fans started to abandon the game to these 'rough' lower working classes. The 'moral panic' surrounding this hooliganism served both to reflect the wider society's more civilized abhorrence of public violence, and inadvertently to attract more 'roughs' to football in the hope of engaging in fighting. Drawing upon the work of Suttles (1968, 1972) on Chicago's black slums, the Leicester researchers contend that an equivalent is to be found in the UK, in the housing estates filled with the unincorporated, lower working classes, which represent the zones of socialization for the nation's football hooligans. They add, nevertheless, that there are also 'rough' middle- and upper-class fans who fight at matches (Dunning, Murphy and Waddington 1991: 474). To bolster their arguments on modern football hooliganism, the Leicester researchers draw upon the fieldwork of John Williams with England fans and young men in a Leicester housing scheme (Williams, Dunning, Murphy 1984; Murphy, Williams, Dunning 1990: 129–66); a 1985 television documentary on West Ham United's hooligan formation, the Inter-City Firm; and arrest figures at football matches uncovered by previous researchers (Harrington 1968; Trivizas 1980).

The Leicester researchers have attracted strong criticism from fellow academics on most key points. Analytically, Elias's figurational sociology has been criticized for failing to provide a genuine theory, rather than a medley of 'untestable' and 'descriptive' generalizations (see Rojek 1985; Horne and Jary 1987). It is, for example, impossible to test the 'civilizing process' if one falls back on 'decivilizing spurts' to 'refute' counter-evidence. The same may be said for the researchers' expedient discovery of 'rough' middle- and upper-class hooligans. Historians and anthropologists have argued that Elias's civilizing process is historically inaccurate, evolutionist and ethnocentric, and that it implies that earlier or non-industrial societies are underdeveloped, savage and barbaric (Robinson 1987; Leach 1986; see Mennell 1989: 230). Elias's lack of empathy and fit when crossing cultures is reflected in the Leicester School's work on football. Researchers from Scotland, Italy and Argentina have highlighted the separate social histories of football in these nations. Concomitantly, the violence of these fans cannot be simply pinned on the lower working classes and their peculiarly 'rough' socialization (Giulianotti 1989b, 1993, 1994c; Dal Lago and De Biasi 1994; Archetti and Romero 1994). For example, many of the modern Scottish hooligans, the 'casuals', come from fairly stable upper working-class and middle-class areas, especially in cities like Aberdeen and Edinburgh (Giulianotti 1996c). Moreover, Glasgow Rangers fans were the most notorious in Scotland during the 1960s and 1970s; they tended to be Protestant and employed in skilled manual work, as opposed to the poorer, Catholic fans who have tended to follow Celtic (Finn 1991a and 1991b). In Italy, Roversi (1992: 11) reports that the *ultràs* groups 'are usually formed by youths who share common and unifying cultural models instead of a common and disadvantaged material condition', as attributed to the lower-working classes by the Leicester researchers.

English researchers have pinpointed major methodological weaknesses in the figurationists' work. The Leicester group were unwilling to engage with hooligans; most fieldwork was carried out with 'official' England fans and young lads in a deprived housing estate (Hobbs and Robins 1991: 560). It would have been far more pleasing methodologically to have seen their study begin within a genuine football hooligan formation (as, for example, undertaken by Armstrong [1993, 1994, 1998]). The use of the West Ham television documentary, to bolster the key argument that hooligans are essentially lower-working class, is also rather disingenuous. West Ham are, after all, the most famous working-class club in England, being based in London's East End (Korr 1986). A better test of their argument would be to investigate the class background of other hooligan groups, such as that following the west London club, Chelsea. Even research undertaken in the working-class city of Sheffield found that the lower working classes were *not* significantly involved in fan violence (Armstrong 1998; see Melnick 1986: 12–13)

Finally, as if to confirm the earlier criticisms, one might say that the figurationists' use of Elias is rather weak ethnographically. They make no meaningful attempt to employ Elias's figurational approach at the everyday level. The Leicester researchers fail completely to examine the complexity of figurational dynamics *within* a football hooligan group, such as the interdependency of individual hooligans or the fluidity of power relations within the group generally. Clearly, the emphasis has been on deploying the 'civilizing process' to explain football violence historically. Yet, even here, its application has been strongly questioned. Lewis (1996: 335) describes the Leicester thesis as 'historically inept, lurching from one absurd generalization to the next when discussing pre-1914 England in an attempt to sustain the viability of the "civilizing process".' The complaint here is that, again, the evidence has been manufactured to fit Elias's theory.

These published criticisms mask what is often a deeper, more bitter professional relationship between the figurationists and their opponents, especially those in England. Part of this reflects the tendency of Dunning and his colleagues to dismiss the work of other researchers, and to over-react (even by academic standards) to any criticism of their work. During one exchange in the *Sociological Review*, the Leicester group were again criticized by an eminent anthropologist and her young researcher for undertaking weak fieldwork (Armstrong and Harris 1991). The Leicester defence rather overstepped the mark by rhetorically 'suspecting' that their critics were football hooligans themselves (Dunning et al. 1991: 467–8).[4] Elsewhere, the figurationists have been strongly condemned for their tendency to misrepresent the arguments of their opponents when seeking to respond to criticism (see Hargreaves 1994: 13–16). It is perhaps here that the figurationists have had the least positive impact on UK football sociology. Certainly, the often rancorous and highly unproductive atmosphere of UK debates has no real equivalent in sports studies on the continent, the United States or Australia.

Fieldwork with Hooligans: some methodological problems

As I have sought to emphasize, one of the basic problems faced by these early researchers is methodological: the lack of worthwhile data on which to found a realistic explanation of football hooliganism. Only the Oxford researchers managed to get inside a hooligan group for any length of time, but that was in the late 1970s and with a less than notorious formation.

There are some good practical reasons for this methodological weakness. Conducting ethnographic research with football fans, especially the young fan sub-cultures, is not a simple exercise. Formal interviewing is problematic, as the research subjects may not attend at the agreed time or place (Dal Lago and De Biasi 1992). They may, quite understandably, feel that the researcher should repay them for their time and information. The Mediterranean *ultràs* interviewed by Bromberger (1993, 1995b) hoped that his professional position would secure influence inside the clubs, and gain them access to the star players. The hooligans of Aberdeen and Hibernian regularly suggested that my comparative research could be 'mutually beneficial' in helping the two sides to organize a major fight (Giulianotti 1995b). I did manage to avoid playing that role nor did I become a direct participant in any actual violence.

In the UK at least, research with hooligan groups has become an increasingly difficult exercise. During the 1970s, Marsh (1978a 1978b; Marsh, et al. 1978) and his colleagues interviewed juvenile hooligans with few reported problems. Similarly, Cohen and Robins (1978) suffered little more discomfort than social embarrassment at asking daft questions. But throughout the 1980s, the political, media and juridical onslaught on fan violence served to transmute the hooligans' reception of would-be interviewers and researchers, from the old cocktail of youthful boasting and mockery of outsiders, into an ingrained distrust of these potential 'grasses'. Hence, the social skills of the intending researcher must be far more acutely honed. Entrée to the hooligan group involves a social process of constant negotiation and renegotiation (Armstrong 1993; see Hughson 1996). The researcher must win the trust of key individuals while maintaining the stated boundaries of participation within the studied formation (Giulianotti 1995b). Comparative analysis is particularly hazardous when conducted on both sides of a major hooligan rivalry, as I found when researching hooligans following Aberdeen and Hibernian (1995b). Work of this kind now needs to be undertaken by those of the same generation as the hooligan group (Redhead 1995: 91). Lofland once observed that academics become increasingly 'chair-bound' as fieldwork gives way to teaching and writing; the ageing process means they lose touch with the activities and thinking of young people.

Fieldwork research is not made any easier when previous sociological 'explanations' of hooliganism are taken into account. Many hooligans are well acquainted with established sociological thinking on their activities, having done the odd social studies course at college, or encountered these academic views through newspapers or television. The hooligans' contempt for 'expert' celebrities is not based on an unreconstructed anti-liberalism or anti-intellectualism, as is conveniently argued. It is reserved instead for outsiders who so obviously identify and distort spurious features within the phenomenon to fit with a 'pet theory'.[5] Some academics attract particular scorn for developing media profiles and research careers out of their initial flirtation with the subject. Hence, few hooligans are particularly excited to meet a budding researcher. There is a palpable expectation that he will trot out another diagnosis of social pathology about 'uncivilized socialization' or 'nationalist xenophobia' or 'troubled masculinity', just like his predecessors. Yet for anyone who really meets with the hooligan groups themselves, what is most striking is the ordinariness of it all. A first glance at their clothes, girlfriends, parents, homes, cars, jobs, wider environment and leisure interests, testifies comprehensively to the mundane, even banal lifestyles of those who are well incorporated into mainstream UK society (though perhaps not the polite endogeny of academic conferences and dinner parties). Immediately, and embarrassingly, the new researcher realizes just how far off the mark the received wisdom in sociology actually has been.

Football Hooligans: tradition, modernity, post-modernity

Drawing on a mixture of long-term fieldwork and historical analysis by other researchers, we may say that football hooliganism in the UK has changed immensely over the years. All historical research indicates that association football in England and Scotland has always involved some degree of crowd violence, to the extent that it has become a 'tradition' of the game. Greater archival research is required to explain adequately the social background and cultural practices of the earliest violent fans during Victorian times (Tranter 1995). Nevertheless, football hooliganism in its contemporary sense refers not to 'traditional' outbreaks of disorder, but instead to the social genesis of distinctive fan sub-cultures and their engagement in regular and collective violence, primarily with rival peers. In Scotland, this begins at least as early as the 1920s and 1930s through the various 'razor gangs' that followed Glasgow Rangers and Celtic (Murray 1984: 144–5), although the consistent disorder associated with these sides' unofficial supporters' clubs ('Brake Clubs') suggests the record may go back to the turn of the century. English and other Scottish cities were not affected greatly by this 'early modernity' of hooliganism until the late 1950s and early 1960s, when young fans came to attend more regularly in large groups (Robins 1984; Clarke 1978). At that time, 'youth' emerged as a distinct social category with its own cultural styles and practices, while the violent sub-cultural aspects of Scotland's west coast were experimented with in other UK cities.

During the 1960s and 1970s, while some incidents of disorder occurred outside the ground, the most significant violence took place inside. Young fans sought to earn prestige for their hooligan formation by 'taking' the 'end' or 'kop' which 'belonged' to their rivals. Pitch invasions also occurred, particularly when the favoured side was losing. The police and football authorities introduced perimeter fencing, 'caging' fans into ends, and segregating home and visiting supporters into different ground sections (Hall 1978; Armstrong and Giulianotti 1995, 1998b). These crude, modernist measures inadvertently served to intensify football hooliganism. Violence became gradually displaced away from the ground, enhancing the hooligan groups' distinct senses of identity and their formal differentiation from the general body of supporters.

In the early 1980s, football hooliganism entered its period of 'high modernity' through the massive emergence of the 'soccer casual' style at most UK grounds. The old, visually aggressive styles of 'militant' fandom (for example, skinhead haircut, Doctor Marten boots, multiple scarves) gave way to the 'casual' style of expensive sportswear (such as Lacoste sweatshirts, Fila tracksuits) and designer menswear (for example, Burberry jackets, Armani sweaters, Rockport shoes) which dispensed with all club colours.

In Scotland, the soccer casuals were a radical departure from the sectarian-based rivalry of established hooliganism, and a collective repudiation of the Scottish Office claim that indigenous hooliganism had been eradicated by a post-1980 ban on alcohol consumption among fans. In England, the casuals were rather less revolutionary in impact, but served to extend existing club and regional rivalries within the hooligan sub-cultures. Informal networking took place among UK hooligans. The nationalistic dimension of fan identity intensified at matches overseas. England fans acquired a more extensive hooligan reputation, though its centrality to these supporters was greatly exaggerated. Meanwhile, Scotland fans adopted an 'anti-hooligan' persona to differentiate themselves from the English before their foreign hosts. For a while, the style revolution helped UK casuals to avoid police monitoring. But, by the late 1980s, police forces had began to initiate new anti-hooligan measures, such as greater plain-clothes policing, covert operations within hooligan groups, and closed circuit television (CCTV) inside grounds, while the government and magistrates were imposing tougher custodial sentences on violent fans (Armstrong and Hobbs 1994; Giulianotti 1994b). By the early 1990s, it had become obvious that the hooligan formations had fallen significantly in number, perhaps by 50 to 80 per cent, so that in Scotland, for major clashes, the top 'mobs' were down from four or five hundred to one hundred or less. Police measures against hooliganism have continued through 'hooligan hotlines' for the public, the creation of hooligan files and centralized databases by the National Criminal Intelligence Service, and the detention (without charge) of fans under the Criminal Justice and Public Order Act 1994.

The 'post-modern' epoch of football hooliganism is signalled most obviously by changes in its political and media treatment. In England, it has been 'deamplified' so that it no longer undermines bids by the English FA to host major international tournaments (especially the World Cup). In Scotland, it has been 'rediscovered' in the wake of an increasingly competitive circulation battle among the tabloids. But, in Scotland at least, the 'post-modernity' of football hooliganism is also highlighted by the casuals' recent preoccupation with the national question. Some groups of casuals have suppressed their club differences to form a national 'mob', which even operates outside of Scottish internationals. Other Scottish casuals remain opposed to this alliance, although it is notable that all have increased their interest in following the national team, in the light of fewer opportunities for violence at club fixtures (Giulianotti 1998a).

Fieldwork research in Scotland and England calls into question some earlier and dominant assumptions about football hooligans.[6] Contrary to the terminology employed by police and media to describe them, the contemporary casual groups are not organized along the lines of military bureaucracy, into 'generals', 'lieutenants', 'armourers', 'foot-soldiers', etc. Instead, each formation does carry 'top boys', whose status is secured in classically masculine terms by their regular involvement and 'gameness' in confrontations; they tend to form the 'front line', and represent the most prized targets for opposing casuals. Involvement in the hooligan groups also takes place on a very voluntary basis, which encourages us to describe these formations as a loose network of small groups of friends. These friendships may owe their origin to long-term involvement within the casual group. They may also reflect shared friendships that began and continue outwith the football scene, such as in work, in school or further education, in the family, or in a particular leisure space (for example, pub or night club). Accordingly, the hooligan group is a strong illustration of the open-ended urban 'neo-tribes' that Maffesoli (1996) identifies within contemporary Western societies.

The main objective of hooligans is to enhance the status of their formation in confrontations with rivals. Each side seeks to 'do' the other, by 'standing' and attacking the opposition, 'decking' them, forcing them to back off, or chasing them. Various degrees of prestige and respect are retained by hooligans who have stood and fought 'gamely' while still coming off the worst, but those who have turned and ran from a confrontation are considered to have been humiliated. Finally, there is no prestige (but plenty of ridicule and disdain) to be gained from attacking 'illegitimate' targets, such as ordinary supporters. However, there are occasions when this 'code' is suspended, such as when the rivalry of the two clubs is very intense, or when the so-called ordinary fans start 'acting wide' or 'taking the piss' in front of hooligans.

Pace the Leicester arguments, football hooligans rarely hail from the poorest locales in cities. Fieldwork with UK hooligans suggests that they are far more *incorporated* within mainstream society rather than structurally excluded from it. The hooligan's 'habitus' demands that the individual possesses economic and cultural capital. Money is important for socializing in pubs, clubs, football grounds and so on; for travelling to matches in the UK or abroad; for purchasing menswear or other commodities. Consumption of goods also requires a sub-cultural *savoir-faire*; hooligans exercise a distinctive 'taste' in buying and consuming particular menswear or other leisure products. Finally, for wider social groups in cities which are involved in consuming popular culture, hooligans have tended to be a compellingly attractive sub-culture, in being 'where the action is'. In football grounds, they have influenced ordinary fans of the same generation, with regard to where they sit (not in the ends), what they wear (more fashionable menswear and fewer colours), and how they view the match (with greater irony and detachment). Outside football, city centre spots initially frequented by hooligans have often been highly successful, 'in' places (Giulianotti 1993).

In Scotland, though their numbers have declined, the hooligan formations tend to experience a relatively slow turnover of lads. The vast majority have been part of the group since the mid-1980s or before. Hence, whereas in the mid- to late 1980s the average age of each group would be in the late teens or early twenties, today the majority of hooligans are in their late twenties or early thirties. This maturity has enabled them to formulate an informal information 'network' stretching across the UK and Europe. Individual hooligans come to recognize their rivals from years of fighting; they meet by chance in court, in police vans, in cells; in clubs and pubs; at other football matches; at work or on holiday. The internet provides further potential for the expansion of this network. Information is exchanged about recent events and the relative merits of particular sides. The network helps to foster alliances or 'friendships' between two hooligan formations, such as those that exist between individual Scottish and English teams. It offers the opportunity for 'pre-planning' or 'organizing' confrontations without police interference. Mobile telephones allow hooligans to keep in touch with their rivals on match-day, so they can discuss when and where the chance for confrontation is most likely to appear. Although they have occurred in the UK, organized battles remain a surprisingly rare feature of hooligan violence in the light of this grapevine and new technology.

Continental hooliganism is rather farther down this road than the UK. In March 1997, a clash between Feyenoord and Ajax fans on wasteland beside a motorway, saw one of the Ajax hooligans beaten to death *(Four-Four-Two*, September 1997). Mass arrests led to the conviction and imprisonment of 46 hooligans, in sentences ranging from 6 months to 5 years. In Germany and the Low Countries, individual hooligans value their connections with UK formations from the 'home of hooliganism'. This cultural deference to the UK is reflected in the European hooligans' belated and wholehearted adoption of the casual style, with a few local or national variations.[7] In Germany, 'friendships' between hooligan groups often reflect those that exist between the wider supporter groups, and these are more routinely encountered and systematically reproduced than one finds in the UK. The information network was also more formally established through the German hooligan magazine *Fantreff.*

Football Violence: the buzz of 'steaming in'

Sociologists have tended to underestimate the psycho-social pleasures of football violence. Hooligans routinely refer to the overpowering emotional 'buzz' that they experience when 'steaming in' against opponents (Giulianotti 1996d; Allan 1989: 132ff; Ward 1989: 5). Finn (1994c) and Pilz (1996: 53) both explain the first-hand account of hooligan sensations according to the concept of 'flow', advanced by Csikszentmihalyi (1975). Another applicable term here is 'edgework' (Lyng 1990) while 'liminality' is employed by Armstrong and Young (1997: 180–1). Use of these concepts suggests that hooliganism falls into a wider category of voluntary risk-taking leisure pursuits, such as scuba-diving, hang-gliding, and bungee-jumping. In these 'high-risk' sports, the pleasure of facing danger is socially acquired. Participants learn from one another how to enjoy the intense emotional states of the hooligan experience. Moreover, risk-taking pursuits 'involve not only activity-specific skills but also a general ability to maintain control of a situation that verges on total chaos . . . the ultimate goal of those who pursue edgework is to survive the experience' (Lyng 1990: 871, 875). The hooligan's aim is to walk in and out of an apparent maelstrom with mind and body intact. Concepts like 'flow' and 'edgework' further suggest that social class differences become secondary within hooliganism; risk-taking sports are, for example, renowned for their large middle-class constituency.

If we move the 'edgework' or 'flow' sensations of fan violence into a more cultural explanatory framework, we begin to uncloak its aesthetic and phenomenological components. In its modern sense, the 'aesthetic' refers to the perception and meaning of beauty, primarily within high culture. But in its post-modern or relativistic sense, its meaning expands to allow for the 'aestheticization' of everyday life (Rojek 1995: 165). Consequently, the aesthetic is no longer decided by 'epistemology', or by rational debate and reflection upon an object's artistic integrity. Instead, it is located in the 'ontological'; in the physical or emotional reaction to a specific cultural form or social situation (Boyne 1991: 281). Thus, and no matter how disturbing the thought to the reader, football violence may be said to contain its own aesthetic form. The innate and intense momentary beauty of hooliganism is revealed only to those who stride somatically into the very eye of the storm, the hooligans themselves.

Police measures against hooliganism may have reduced the frequency of these 'peak moments', but they remain highly desirable to large numbers of prospective participants (see McInman and Grove 1991: 348). To cater for the pent-up demand, a post-modern market has opened in the reproduction or simulation of football hooliganism, in print and in film. Hooligans (both old and new, real and imagined) may visualize the violence of themselves and others.[8] Autobiographies by hooligans or edited collections describing fan violence in vivid detail sell in their thousands (see Allan 1989; Ward 1989; Brimson and Brimson 1995, 1996, 1997, 1998; Francis 1997). Television documentaries on hooligan groups have a particular appeal where they contain 'live' incidents, which may be played, replayed and analytically dissected in full pornographic detail.[9] Fictional films on 'football hooligan' gangs, such as the British offerings *The Firm* or *ID*, tend to be regarded with some disdain by the hooligan cognoscenti. These impure replicas of genuine violence appear over-simulated and unbelievable, in the same way that 'soft-core' sex suddenly becomes staged and false when set against hard-core pornography and its immersion in the action.

Ultràs: South European fan sub-cultures and football violence

While in the UK and latterly northern Europe the 'casual' hooligan style (and network) holds sway, militant football fandom in southern Europe has explored a rather different trajectory (Giulianotti 1994d). Here, the *ultràs* model of participatory fandom holds sway. The *ultràs* name originated among Genoa's Sampdoria fans in 1971, and subsequently spread throughout Italy to southern France, Spain, Portugal and the former Yugoslavia. The *ultràs* represented a younger, more organized and militant form of fandom than had been previously known in Italy. While the northern European hooligans abandoned club colours and displays during the 1980s, the *ultràs* took audio-visual passion to new heights. *Ultràs* gather inside each *curva* (end) of Italian stadia, hours before kick-off, and cover their territory in banners which proclaim their identity and their fidelity to the club. Some *ultrà* leaders employ microphones and small amplifiers to lead the chants. When the team takes the pitch or scores, the *ultràs* will hail the moment with an intensified chant or a fiesta of fireworks. Smoke flares bellow out the team's colours; firecrackers and sparklers blind the senses. The *pièce de résistance* of the display may include the pre-match unfurling of an enormous flag covering one or two tiers of the *curva*.

Italian social scientists and journalists often badly misinterpret the *ultràs*. One study dismissed them as 'not really interested in the football matches', but there 'merely for a chance to give vent to their emotions' (Zani and Kirchler 1991: 19). Not only are *ultràs* among the most committed fans, their social practices are rich in hermeneutic terms, expressing very complex senses of social identity (Dal Lago 1990: 49ff). The names of *ultrà* groups tend to reflect three identifying elements: the club that they support; the political turmoil and paramilitarization of Italian society during the 1970s and 1980s; and their interests in global youth culture (Dal Lago 1990: 99; Roversi 1994). For example, at Roma, there is the Commando Ultrà Curva Sud, designating the south *curva* of the capital's Stadio Olimpico where the Roma fans congregate. At Milan, there is the Brigate Rossonere, signifying the red and black colours of the club; similarly at Verona, there is the Brigate Gialloblù, indicating their colours of yellow and blue. Aspects of youth culture are reflected by the Drughi at Juventus, named after the gang from the novel *A Clockwork Orange*; the Teddy Boys at Udinese; the Skins at Inter; or even the Freak Brothers who follow Ternana. Although these titles tend to hold centre stage within the *curva*, the other *bandieri* of the *ultràs* reflect their heterogeneous interests and composition. Different youth cultural styles, such as the British ones of skinheads, mods and punks, are often prominent in the same *curva*. Signifiers of social diversity also feature, such as references to 'girl' members or rastafarian and black power flags (see Dal Lago and De Biasi 1994: 79–80). While the casual-like *paninaro* style became sporadically popular during the mid-1980s, most *ultràs* retained a strong commitment to the 'display' side of fandom, including the ready donning of club colours.

Within the cultural politics of Italian football, the *ultràs* possess a distinctive organic relationship to both their club of support and its official supporters' association. All Italian clubs help to organize their official supporter groups. The biggest have several hundred fan clubs throughout Italy and abroad. Supporters' associations may have the ear of the club's owner and directors, occasionally influencing policy. More significantly, they provide its commercial wing with outlets for selling tickets, organizing match-day travel and marketing merchandise.

In contrast, the *ultràs* groups are organized as more informal, autonomous and populist forums for the more visible expression of support. They arrange their own transport to fixtures away from home; they elect their own leaders, develop their own symbols and merchandise, and have their own club premises. In exceptional cases such as with the Genoa *ultràs* group, the Fossa di Griffoni, the commercial interests of the leaders may override the affective concerns of the members (with regard to supporting the team). The *ultràs* do not originate with a formal relationship to the club, although one may evolve. The club may contribute to the costs of manufacturing large flags (although at fixtures it may still admonish fans for covering advertising boards with their banners). It may meet with *ultràs* leaders and help to sell their merchandise. In some exceptional cases, such as with the late Paolo Mantovani (owner of Sampdoria), the club's paternalism may see the leading *ultràs* employed by the club. Such a strategy shows some foresight in regard to football violence. The peers of disorderly fans may help to defuse situations through mediation, by acting in the role of club representative (see Lewis 1982b: 202). Not only are the *ultràs* behind the match-day pyrotechnics, they also tend to be the most vocal in expressing criticism of their club.

Externally, each Italian *ultrà* group is located within a network of social ties between it and *ultràs* following other clubs. This network is far more formal and collectively orientated than the informal 'friendship' networks that exist at the individual level between most ordinary UK club supporters or hooligans. Usually, an *ultrà* group will be friendly towards one lineage of other *ultràs*, and hostile towards an alternative lineage. For example, in the early 1990s, Sampdoria's group (known as the Ultràs Tito Cucchiaroni, after a former favourite player) were located in a lineage of friendship with *ultràs* following Verona, Inter, Atalanta, Cremonese and Fiorentina (see Roversi 1992: 56–8). Latterly, some friendships with *ultràs* following Parma and Cagliari emerged. Sampdoria *ultràs* were also hostile to those following Genoa, Torino, Bologna, Milan, Pisa and Lazio. In cities where there are two clubs (such as Genoa), these oppositions are often rooted in the hostility between local rivals:

Sampdoria's *ultràs* cannot display empathy towards the friends of Genoa. Nevertheless, the haphazard evolution of the amities and enmities within *ultrà* politics ensures that these lineages are not purely symmetrical.[10] More significantly, in exercises of proto-democracy, *ultràs* who follow sides that dominate Italian football (Juventus during the 1970s and early 1980s, Milan during the late 1980s and early 1990s) tend to be ostracized by other *ultrà* movements. This can result in civic rivalries like Sampdoria and Genoa being suppressed when Milan's *ultràs* are in town.

It would be palpably wrong to conceive of the *ultràs* as southern Europe's equivalent to the north's football hooligans. The cultural and historical specificities of Italy and its Mediterranean neighbours mean that such a simple comparison is ethnocentric with an Anglo-Saxon bias (Giulianotti et al. 1994: 4). Moreover, unlike their northern European 'peers', football hooliganism is not the *raison d'être* of the Italian *ultràs*, although violence involving them, the police and rival fans is a consistent part of their match-day repertoire. Prodigious reputations are held by some *ultràs* groups, such as the 'barbarians' of Atalanta (from Bergamo). Others, such as those following Parma or Juventus, are not noted for violent behaviour, to the extent that they are derided as 'rabbits'. Often, the violence between *ultràs* groups will actuate the geo-cultural animosities that fracture Italy's sense of national identity. Medieval hostilities across the *mezzogiorno*, between Italy's north and south, continue in matches like Atalanta and Napoli. Moreover, the heterogeneity of Italy's party politics has stoked *ultrà* rivalries as their clubs and home towns have become associated with particular leanings. The extreme right is considered to be particularly strong among fans of Verona (where separatism has strong support) and Lazio (the favoured club of Mussolini). Conversely, Bologna's communist tradition used to flavour the symbolism and animosities of the club's *ultràs*; Atalanta *ultràs* initially tended towards the left, but have since inclined towards the separatist Lega Nord. Italian researchers have produced opposing interpretations of the extent to which the *ultràs* have been influenced by right-wing political extremism. Some argue that *ultrà* organizations resist any prescriptive political leanings, and have been largely ignored by the youth groups of the radical left or right (De Biasi 1996: 123). Others point to the generalized rise in racism among Italian fans as conjunctural to the new and direct links that have been established between neo-fascist movements and right-wing *ultrà* groups in Verona, Rome and even Bologna (Podaliri and Balestri 1998: 97–9).

Latin Violence: the culture of hooliganism in Southern Europe and South America

Since the late 1980s, the violence involving Italian *ultràs* has attracted regular political and media attention. The policing of *ultràs* centred on segregation and the enforcement of order on the ground, while sentences against offenders were unaffected by media hyperbole. Clubs sought to calm the atmosphere by winning the consent of fans, rather than coercing them into passivity. Italy's long memories of totalitarian government and greater respect for informal public association seemed to exclude the surveillance and intelligence-gathering practices routinely used by UK police against football supporters (Armstrong and Giulianotti 1998b). Much of the disorder tended to take place inside the grounds (against the police) in response to on-the-field events, or immediately outside as the rival groups of *ultràs* converged on one another.

Nevertheless, several incidents of serious violence seemed to signify a watershed in the social response to the more militant *ultràs*. The murder of the Genoa fan, Vicente Spagnolo, by a Milan *ultrà* in January 1995, followed the Brescia–Roma match two months earlier, at which visiting fans had seriously wounded two high-ranking police officers. In the same season, violent clashes took place outside the ground at the Sampdoria–Genoa derby match, critically injuring one police officer. These and other incidents precipitated a qualitatively different response from the Italian state, including the widening of intelligence-gathering strategies and 'dawn raids' on suspects. Yet, the disorder continued, particularly when Fiorentina took the 1996 Italian Cup against Atalanta in Bergamo, sparking widespread rioting that hospitalized scores of fans and police.

In Spain and Italy, some *ultràs* factions have been accused of extortion against their clubs and the media. During the early 1990s, the Real Madrid fan group, the Ultrà Sur, had reportedly attempted to extort money from the club's players and officials, to pay for banners and match-day travel expenses. Latterly, nine Roma *ultràs* were charged with a number of conspiracy offences, after a long-running police investigation that included heavy surveillance measures such as telephone tapping used more commonly against terrorists and the Mafia. The accused were said to have demanded monies from camera crews filming on the terraces, and blackmailed Roma into selling cut-price tickets by threatening riotous behaviour at matches.

On the surface, these offences certainly seem synonymous with extortion. Yet, they also smack of the rather desperate attempt by some dedicated and powerless fans to bolster their organization and its attendant expenses. More powerful participants in football culture (such as players, journalists and sociologists) are well versed in claiming fees from television companies in return for their time and thoughts. In Roma, there seems to be a supporter group trying to do the same, in exchange for the rights to film their carnival in the stands.

In southern Europe and Latin America, we find that fan violence which is external to the match is often precipitated by the supported club. Followers of Torino and Fiorentina have rioted after their relegation or the sale of star players to richer clubs. Other fan groups have attacked players at training or at their homes for persistently poor performances. Real Madrid, Benfica, Napoli,

Torino, Roma and Genoa fans are just some of the *ultràs* groups who have violently confronted their club's players and officials when results or management policy were displeasing. In Brazil, following a dismal run of form, coachloads of Corinthians fans attacked and pelted the players' team bus with missiles, while returning from a match in Santos. Such assaults may be dismissed psychologically as expressive of irrational, collective frustration, but usually the supporters explain their motivations in more cultural and social terms. The professional team, which is usually well paid and multinational in composition, is typically accused of lacking important personal and communitarian virtues, such as integrity, pride in performance, and respect for the local public.

The strongest connections between fan organization, football club politics and criminal activities (including hooliganism) are found in Argentina. Within their various groups of *hinchadas* (fans), all of the top Argentinian clubs have their militant fans, known as the *barras bravas*, whose numbers can run into several thousand. These fan groups resemble south European *ultràs*, with their voluble chanting and pyrotechnic displays at matches. Some Argentinian journalists describe the *barras bravas* simply as 'hooligans', other sports writers and sociologists more accurately regard the two as discrete social entities. The *barras bravas* have long been the militant wing of South American football culture.[11] Certainly, not all associates of the *barras bravas* are involved in football violence, while the fan formations themselves are active in other, non-hooligan practices.

What distinguishes the *barras bravas* from southern Europe's *ultràs* is the structure of Argentinian football. Argentinian football clubs are organized as private member associations, whereby the office-holders are elected by fan members. As the *barras bravas* tend to be the only distinct fan groupings within each club (and certainly their most vociferous), candidates for office often seek their support. Conventionally, the candidate's populism involves giving match tickets and even money to the main figures within the club's *barras bravas* (Duke and Crolley 1996). At two former clubs of Diego Maradona, evidence suggests that the political influence of the *barras bravas*' leaders had been rather more nefarious during the mid-1990s. At Boca Juniors, a *barras bravas* group known as La 12 was brought to trial; nine were convicted of serious crimes, including the new offence of 'illicit association'. Their leader El Abuelo (the Grandfather) was sentenced to thirteen years' imprisonment for an extortion racket aimed at top club officials (*Olé* 11 April 1997). Five others were each given twenty-year sentences for homicide, while a sixth was handed a fifteen-year term (*Super Hincha*, September 1997). At Argentina Juniors, a relatively poor club that had slipped into decline, the *barras bravas* effectively took over. The leaders set up home in the club's facilities, stole gate-money, and assaulted an official who had threatened to inform on them. Sometimes Argentinian football club officials are also active in mainstream politics, through party membership or contesting local elections as individual candidates. In this way, their association with *barras bravas* leaders may provide them with an intimidating political weapon. Again, a former President of Boca Juniors benefited from the support of the *barras bravas* when they broke up the meetings of political rivals.

To most European observers, the political influence and violence of the *barras bravas* is far removed from the 'carnival' image of neighbouring Brazilian fans. However, that reputation masks a more complex and specious history within Brazilian fan culture. Brazil's carnival football fans emerged during the early 1940s, first among the followers of Rio's most popular club, Flamengo. Fans known as the Charanga Rubro Negra[12] gathered inside the Maracanã and other stadia, dressed in team colours and playing uplifting music in support of their team. These supporters tended to be socially settled, being aged in their thirties and forties and married with children, and were lauded by the media and football authorities for their celebratory support and sporting atmosphere. They were eventually displaced by a younger, more partisan and aggressive fan culture. The transformation first occurred in 1974 with the appearance of the Gaviões da Fiel at Corinthians, the most popular club in São Paulo, partially as a response to their failure to win the state championship in twenty years. However, the new fan association also provided one of the few opportunities for organized public gatherings during military rule, hence the spread of its framework to all major clubs in Brazil. The equivalent group at Flamengo is known as the Raça. Socially, the Gaviões da Fiel has remained the most influential, with over 12,000 members and its own samba school, which took top prize in the 1996 São Paulo carnival. But these clubs also became heavily linked with hooliganism (including several deaths) during the 1980s and early 1990s. They were formally 'banned' from São Paulo stadia: no banners or flags depicting the fan clubs were allowed to be displayed. Hence, it seems that the carnival reputation of Brazilian fans says less about the essential nature of Brazilian fandom and more about the age and wealth of Charanga fans relative to the younger fan movements. Nevertheless, many European national fans work with the carnival model of Charanga fans in the battle to become the 'Brazil of Europe'.

Northern European Carnival: Scottish, Irish, Danish fans and others

The 'carnival' form of football spectating has emerged in northern Europe since the early 1980s. These fans have become renowned for following their national sides, especially at tournaments abroad, in an extremely gregarious, good-humoured, colourful and raucous manner. They are noted for intense singing in support of their team, and open friendliness rather than hostility towards rival fans and local hosts. Carnival fans are also renowned for their colourful, often extravagant dress, such as wearing their 'national costume', heavily equipping themselves with their national colours and flags, and wearing face paint. Some carnival fans travel in tow with their own musicians, such as the Dutch jazz band or the individual Scottish pipers. The most renowned examples of carnival fans include the 'Tartan Army' which follows Scotland (Giulianotti 1991, 1994a, 1995a), the *roligans* following Denmark (Peitersen 1991; Eichberg 1992), the *drillos* following Norway (Giulianotti 1996a), or the *oranji* following Holland (van den Brug 1994). Irish football fans have also become well known for their 'carnival' persona (Giulianotti 1996a and 1996b; O'Kelly and Blair 1992).[13] These fan groups see themselves as sharing key interpersonal and cultural characteristics, though the appellation of 'carnival' fans is primarily a sociological one and rarely used by the supporters to describe themselves.

These supporter groups are usually presented as paradigmatically opposed to the other north European fan model, the hooligan. While the practices of hooligans and carnival fans may seem to be antithetical, they do share some underlying commonalities. Both are strongly committed to support for their team; both engage in high levels of alcohol consumption, though with seemingly divergent results. Additional similarities exist in terms of their wider social stratification. For example, the Scottish Tartan Army tend to fall into the same kinds of employment and age categories as hooligan groups have in the past. Both have included significant numbers from the upper working-classes, and a large majority which falls into the young male age bracket (Giulianotti 1994a). Women tend to be more numerically prominent among the Scottish Tartan Army than among hooligan groups, but still constitute a small minority (less than 15 per cent). They have little 'feminizing' impact upon the men's behaviour, since this routinely involves drinking, swearing, mock aggression or adopting traditionally masculine practices towards other females (Finn and Giulianotti 1998). Finally, research indicates that hooligan fans can also be carnival supporters. For example, some 'carnival' fans following Scotland or Germany are also dedicated hooligans at club level.

It has been suspected that, because of their capacity for advancing football's image, 'carnival' fans are a construction of the media and football authorities. Certainly, in Denmark, the *roligans* have their own association, and in Scotland the police and football authorities have encouraged the Tartan Army in 'self-policing' and to join the Scottish Football Association's (SFA) Travel Club. FIFA and UEFA present 'fair play' awards to supporter groups that encapsulate the 'sporting spirit of football'. Scottish, Danish and Irish fans have won this award in recent years, to the obvious delight of supporters and authorities alike.

However, the 'manipulation' thesis seriously underplays the fans' motivation to reproduce their reputation, and the complexity of the social and historical background to the creation of the carnival culture. Some of the hard-core 'Tartan Army' look back to a match in Israel in 1981 for the 'origins' of their carnival identity. At that match the local press and populace had provided glowing reports about the Scots' behaviour, who then resolved to establish their popularity elsewhere. An important aspect of the Scots' new carnival identity was their cultural nationalism, specifically their desire to differentiate themselves from the English. During the 1980s, as the English became notorious for hooligan behaviour, the Scots adopted a simple binary opposition when presenting themselves abroad: they were 'Scottish fans not English hooligans'. For Norway, Denmark and Ireland fans, the structural factors which facilitate the carnival culture will be equally specious to that society.[14]

Moreover, there are times when social order breaks down within the carnival. Fans may become disorderly or overly intoxicated, leading to their arrest; old club rivalries among carnival fans may resurface rather than be suppressed; intense national animosities may see these carnival fans engage in violence with opposing fans (for example, Holland v. Germany, Scotland v. England). In such circumstances, the authorities and the fans may be working with rather different understandings of the carnivalesque. Both may agree with the basic principle that it can 'bring together in amity people from different classes and ethnic and religious groupings' (Cohen 1993: 129). For the authorities, the carnivalesque may be perceived within a functional light as 'authorized transgression'. It may be licensed to take place only in 'certain places, certain streets, or framed by the television screen' (Eco 1984: 6). The authorities may designate specific areas, away from local businesses, for the carnival to develop; they may encourage the carnival bands to play in particular ways before and during games. Conversely, the fans may actuate the traditional properties of the carnivalesque by mocking or inverting power hierarchies and celebrating all manner of excesses (see Ivanov 1984). Leading figures within the national football association may be strongly abused; property may be damaged as the carnival gets out of hand. As Bakhtin noted, the laughter within carnival always carries with it the possibility of violence (Hoy 1994). Resisting the organizational intentions of the authorities is not simply a statement in 'cultural politics' or done to establish popular control. It is also about maintaining the aesthetic pleasures of participating in the carnivalesque. This is because the bodily *jouissance* of carnival is deeply associated with the possibility of social breakdown. The psychosocial buzz of the carnival is therefore not entirely divorced from the liminality of hooligan confrontations. Both may symbolize forms of supporter resistance to the 'monitoring order' within football, the authorities themselves (Fiske 1993).

Football's New Social Movements: fan power, militancy and the 'fanzines'

Since the mid-1980s, football in the UK and elsewhere has given rise to more explicit cultures of resistance among supporters. The most important representatives of this new culture are the 'fanzines' and the independent support-

ers' associations (ISAs) (see Jary et al. 1991). Football fanzines are fan magazines that are produced at club and national level by supporters. They offer a
direct alternative to the 'Pravda school of journalism', such as club magazines
and match-day programmes, which eschew criticism of football's powerful
figures (Perryman 1997). Fanzines seek to provide a far more representative
picture of supporter views than one finds in the mainstream media, routinely
expressing discontent about the club, its custodians and players (Giulianotti
1997a; Rowe 1995: 160–5). A proto-fanzine called *Foul!* emerged in the early
1970s, but was unable to fend off libel threats (Redhead 1991a: 41–5). It was
not until the explosive cultural influence of the punk 'do-it-yourself' phenomenon in the late 1970s that the fanzine became a sub-cultural form. After
Heysel, fanzines emerged to demonstrate to hostile politicians that most supporters were not hooligans. New technology also helped, as the first fanzines
were printed off early PCs and photocopied *en masse* for sale outside grounds.

Many fanzine writers and editors had been socialized into football while the
game was undergoing a populist political assault. In England particularly, the
Thatcherite crusade against football hooliganism seemed to have a deeper
agenda: deconstructing the cultural playground of the working classes, just as
monetarism had flattened their industries (see Taylor 1987). Football supporter
organizations were as ill-equipped to repel this assault as had been the unions
in heavy industry. The National Federation of Football Supporters' Clubs
(NFFSC) had little influence within the football industry. Its aged leadership
offered few criticisms of football's establishment and an unenlightened analysis of fan violence (Taylor 1992: 170). It was increasingly out of kilter with the
culture of criticism, irony and parody then emerging among young football
fans. The latter adopted situationist tactics to express their political views,
through the chanting or spray-painting of slogans that decried players or officials. The situationist format of the football fanzines was to provide a crucial
outlet for this participatory and spontaneous culture of resistance.

Football supporters have also developed more organized forums to protect
their interests. After Hillsborough, the Football Supporters' Association emerged
as a far more effective voice for supporters than the old NFFSC, although its
membership remains low. At club level, ISAs such as those at West Ham,
Manchester United and Tottenham, have organized protests against the more
blatant, commercial practices of their club's directors, such as the selling of top
players or the inflation of admission prices. An ISA at Charlton was instrumental in returning the club to its home, the Valley; others at heavily indebted clubs
like Brighton and Doncaster have generated financial and symbolic backing
from other supporters and business figures to help their survival.

These supporter actions must be located within the broader epochal shift
from modern formal politics to post-modern cultural politics. Since the late
1960s, there has been a rise in the popularity of new, single-issue social movements at the expense of old political parties (see Melucci 1988). Young people
in the UK are more likely to join up with the anti-hunting movement, environ-

mentalist protests, marches in favour of sexual equality or football campaigns organized by ISAs. Movements like these submerge class differences. They focus on single issues that usually relate to lifestyle and leisure interests. Their participatory culture opposes the rigid hierarchical structures found in political parties. The egalitarianism and situationism of movements like football fanzines and ISAs are far more attractive to young and critical supporters than the conservatism and inertia of official supporters' clubs.

Many clubs have sought to defuse the political relevance of these supporter groups by setting up their own 'community projects' with 'community officers'. In a few cases, such as at Millwall, the project has been designed to enhance relations between the club and its surrounding community. More commonly, these projects are public relations exercises for the club's commercial wing, with a lot of emphasis placed on building up new 'consumer markets' and local talent-spotting for top young players.

Noticeably, the UK fanzine culture and the wider social movements of fans are not duplicated abroad. 'Fan projects' have been set up by the local authorities in northern European nations like Germany, Denmark and Sweden, to wean young fans away from hooligan activities without dissembling their subcultural activities *per se* (Pilz 1996). These projects also provide a forum and meeting-place for young club supporters to discuss their views, with some literature resulting from this function. In southern Europe and South America, by contrast, the autonomous structures of the *ultràs* and the *barras bravas* would resist such a pedagogical institution. In southern Europe, the multitude of specialist football media (such as *Supertifo* and *Super Hincha*) helps to fill the critical aporia that the fanzines have identified in the UK. Moreover, the *ultràs* provide an older form of alternative, non-official football organization for southern European supporters.

Global Diffusion and Cultural Diversity: fan sub-cultures and research towards the millennium

Football's fan sub-cultures therefore display significant geographical and cultural differences between one another. Historically, each nation shows itself to have certain unique features in the development of militant forms of fandom. Hence, the genealogy of football hooliganism in England and Scotland is different, just as we find that Holland, Germany, Belgium, Sweden and other north European nations have their own histories of violent rivalry and symbolic opposition between fans.

Nevertheless, within an increasingly global cultural framework, it is possible to identify some continuities. In northern Europe, the most participatory fans may be generally dichotomized as 'hooligan' and 'carnival'. In the UK, the soccer casuals represent the most recent incarnation of the hooligan style, while 'carnival' fans most obviously hail from the Celtic and Nordic societies when following their national teams. Latterly in the UK, a further category of supporter sub-culture has emerged, in the shape of politicized social movements, such as football fanzines and ISAs. This Weberian process of heightened differentiation between supporter categories does not obtain in Latin football societies. In southern Europe, the *ultràs* display particular elements of the 'hooligan' and 'carnival' style, although it is important to emphasize the culturally and historically specific dynamics and properties of these supporters. Fans in South America, such as the Gaviões da Fiel or the Raça in Brazil, and the *barras bravas* in Argentina, extend this fusion of spectacular pyrotechnics and violence. The membership structure of South American clubs enhances the political role of these militant fan groups, notably in Argentina.

Meanwhile, there are increasing signs of international exchange. The *ultràs* borrowed and 'creolized' the British terrace culture of the 1970s, taking it in new directions that were locally meaningful. UK fan sub-cultures of the late 1990s have started to experiment with aspects of the south European model, through the use of Latin chant patterns and musical bands. There is clear evidence that football hooliganism has undergone similar processes of globalization. North European hooligan groups tend to provide local or national variations on the casual model, while Italian and Spanish fans have experimented with this style. The southern European fan models (particularly Spanish ones) are also involved in sizeable social and cultural exchanges with South American fans, notably the *barras bravas* in Argentina. In the other direction, one relatively new English fan magazine, which is full of information on hooliganism, is entitled *ULTRA*. More generally, the globalization of football literature and fan paraphernalia (such as scarves, T-shirts, badges, magazines and so on), means that individual fans can easily 'buy into' the supporter cultures of other societies.

Academically, the worldwide body of research into fan sub-cultures is somewhat uneven. Western European nations are well represented; elsewhere there are large gaps in the sociological field. More research is certainly needed in South America to tease out the particular genealogy of supporter sub-cultures in each region or nation. Knowledge of the social and cultural properties of supporter groups in eastern Europe is also relatively weak, though the former Yugoslavia has attracted attention (Lalic 1993; Vrcan 1992). Ideally, future research in these areas will be more 'reality congruent' than was the case in the UK until the 1990s.

In the UK, at least, it is possible to periodize the social and cultural forms of these fan sub-cultures by introducing the temporal categories of the traditional, the modern and the post-modern. As I have noted, there are important national differences between the English and Scottish experience. In England, the attempt to construct a normalized, pacified, 'post-hooligan' identity for the supporters sits rather uneasily with the continuing activities of real football hooligans, and with those supporters who are part of supporter social movements. A key issue for many of these fan groups has been the post-Hillsborough redevelopment of football grounds. While ground safety and general facilities have been upgraded, these improvements may be at the expense of higher seating prices, the corporate takeover of the best stand areas, and the loss of atmosphere at matches (Brown 1998: 50–67). It is to the issues of ground redevelopment, and the general spatial organization of football, that I now turn.

4

Football Grounds: Emotional Attachments and Social Control

Stadia Development: the historical and cultural dimensions

In pre-regulation days, football's limited enclosure of play mirrored the game's weak codification. Folk football was played in village centres and fields where natural obstacles (such as walls and ditches) determined the spatial parameters of play, perhaps with village churches serving as rudimentary goal areas (Bale 1989a: 146; 1993a: 123). Today, the haphazard and imprecise boundaries of play are found in the improvised football of children in yards, parks and streets. Jackets are placed to form goal-posts; the imagined height of the bar is resolved through dialogue; a fence encloses play. However, the ontogeny of young players, it seems, does not duplicate the phylogeny of early football. The use of standard football rules, and relatively fair and equal competition between teams, show that children's games are more modern than folk in their practice.

At the elite level, football spaces have undergone periodic change in every nation. Britain constructed the earliest and grandest football grounds. Of the 92 English league clubs in 1993, 70 were playing at grounds built before the First World War; 34 had been playing 'at home' since the nineteenth century (Duke 1994: 130). Scottish grounds were no less venerable: 28 of the 38 league clubs in 1990 were first ensconced in their ground before 1910 (Inglis 1987: 10). These 'traditional' grounds tended to be built near transport terminals, notably railway stations, allowing supporters to arrive and disperse with ease (Inglis 1987: 12). Building grounds near to major industrial employers encouraged the growth of a large home support (Fishwick 1989: 54). The design of traditional grounds was strikingly classical. UK clubs regularly engaged the architect Archibald Leitch to build three open terraces offset by a two-tiered grandstand running the length of the pitch. The earliest grounds were often elliptical in shape; banked terracing swept round in a baroque variation upon the majestic

Roman amphitheatres. Later, as finance and inner-city space caused constraints, the grounds became rectangular, following the pitch parameters and placing spectators in closer proximity to play.

Class was at the core of the traditional ground's social ethnology. The directors and middle-class audience annexed the more expensive seats in the grandstand; the large, working-class audience stood on the terraces. In northern England, many rectangular grounds possessed elevated terracing behind the goal. The erection of these high, banked ends enabled their working-class custodians to commemorate a senseless tragedy that had befallen their comrades in battle. In January 1900 British soldiers were ordered to mount an uncovered and suicidal assault on the Spion Kop, held by the Boers during that eponymous war. Hundreds of the resulting dead and wounded came from the football heartland of Lancashire. Their memory lived on through the naming of these ends as 'kops' (Bowden 1995: 116).

In Europe and South America, other structural factors influenced the location and architectural ambience of new stadia. In northern Europe, especially Scandinavia, all-purpose sports parks were part of major city-building projects and owned by the local authorities. In the Low Countries, Germany and France, municipal stadia tend to be all-purpose, part of wider sports complexes, and located in the wealthier suburbs (for example, Düsseldorf, Monaco, Vienna). Privately owned grounds or those in smaller cities tend to be more football oriented, rectangular shaped and initially piecemeal when constructed (such as Eindhoven, St Etienne, Brussels). In southern Europe, great stadiums were typically erected during periods of political dictatorship, when public spaces were established to generate nationalist feelings. Mussolini constructed the Stadio Olimpico for the 1934 World Cup finals; Franco built the Bernabéu from 1944 to 1947; Salazar erected the Estádio da Luz in Lisbon in 1954 (Lanfranchi 1995: 127–8). Some provincial municipalities (notably in Italy) erected modest versions of the Olympic-style stadium; others (as in Spain) acknowledged football's sporting centrality by assisting clubs to build rectangular theatres.

Stadia owned by municipalities and leased to football clubs have relatively few opportunities for commodifying spaces. The magnificent stadia completed for Italia '90 lacked the executive boxes that are now mandatory in modern UK grounds. Italian grounds omit the restaurants, corporate hospitality suites, conference chambers, hotel facilities and retail outlets that may also adjoin the standard football theatre. Instead, many Latin grounds are located well away from industrial areas; internally, they house training centres and gymnasia as well as swimming pools, tennis courts or athletics tracks around the pitch. In Iberia and Latin America, these facilities are designed for easy use by the club 'members' *(socios)* as part of their subscription fees.

Within this global setting, the balance of power has shifted in terms of major football ground capacities (Bowden 1995: 139–40). In the 1900s, Glasgow housed the three largest stadia, the 'tribal theatres' of Hampden Park, Ibrox and Celtic Park. Today, the developing world possesses all but one of the twenty most capacious grounds. The great stadia of Latin America were built on the principle of mass. Brazil's Maracanã is the greatest jewel in the crown though its compatriot structures bear comparison: the Morumbi in São Paulo, holding 150,000; the stadia at Belo Horizonte, Pôrto Alegre, Salvador and Maceio, which hold over 100,000; and those of Curitiba (180,000), Belém (120,000) and Fortaleza (120,000) (see Rachum 1978: 198). Safety restrictions have significantly reduced these capacities, but the spectating principles of informality and mass still prevail.

Global differences in the spectator's environment contrast with the few important amendments made to the accommodation afforded team officials. The track-side 'dugout' was first introduced in Aberdeen in the 1930s, built with a shelter and excavated below ground level to allow the coach a 'worm's eye view' (Webster 1990: 22–3). After Everton took the concept south, the dugout gradually became a ubiquitous feature at all British then overseas grounds. The advantage afforded by proximity to the play was offset by diffi-cult sightlines within a less than panoramic view. Many grounds retain a variation on the 'dugout' through a sheltered 'bench' at ground level. Some managers have retreated to the centre stand, dispensing tactical instructions by walkie-talkie to their trackside assistants, although most prefer to stay close to the field of play. During his tenure at Barcelona, Johan Cruyff introduced a potentially revolutionary measure by having television monitors installed in his dugout for studying the game's progress from a number of angles (Radnedge 1997: xv). The innovation seemed to challenge the professional assumption that management is more intuitive than logical and so has hardly been copied elsewhere.

By the late 1980s, an important cultural hiatus had opened up between the UK and other European nations in terms of stadia development. Germany, Spain, France and Italy upgraded their largest grounds to host major interna-tional tournaments. Architectural modernism tended to emphasize the formu-laic and undermine ground individuality. Functional exigencies came to dominate architectural thinking: spectator safety, comfort and control; access to parking spaces, toilets and food kiosks; viewing sightlines. Meanwhile, the old UK grounds were proving increasingly incapable of meeting the most basic human needs. Yet just as at the start of the century, other football nations had looked to the UK for geometric aesthetics in play and ground architecture, so towards the new millennium, the English would effectively compel the world to rethink stadium design through the triple tragedies of Bradford, Heysel and Hillsborough. I will look at these and other stadium disasters later in this chapter. However, at this stage it is important to outline some of the key findings by researchers studying football grounds. In particular, I shall look at the social meaning of the ground, and the relationship of crowd composition to stadium geography.

Football Space and the Emotions: topophilia and topophobia

John Bale is the researcher and critic who has done most to legitimize the study of sporting spaces within the academic realm, through his superb series of monographs, edited collections and articles.[1] Bale's work blends the disciplines of social geography and contemporary cultural theory and draws upon worldwide fieldwork. His most significant contribution stems from his use of Tuan (1974) to explain the affective dimensions of sports grounds (see Bale 1991b, 1994). Tuan uses the term 'topophilia' to describe the deep affection of people towards particular social spaces, or 'places'. In contradistinction, people may also have feelings of fear or anxiety towards other places: Tuan (1979) applies the term 'topophobia' to describe such a sentiment. In both cases, a psychosocial relationship to these spaces has emerged, as they acquire an embedded meaning for the people that encounter them.

Tuan's notions have a strong resonance within football culture. For most players who enjoy the game, entry into the football space is a familiar, topophilic experience, no matter where they are playing. The player may be stimulated by the unfamiliarity of the setting, and its mixture of grass and sand, sky and cloud, football stands and terraces or open landscape. Yet, this disorientation is soon counterpoised by the familiar signposts of football; the pitch markings, the goal-posts opposite one another and the ball in the centre circle, evoke images and sounds of previous games, memorably enjoyed or best forgotten.

For players and spectators, an important stimulant is the 'atmosphere' of the game, especially at professional level: the more intense the 'atmosphere', the more pleasurable the game. Baudrillard (1996: 43) states that 'atmosphere is always both warmth and distance'; the interplay of the natural and the cultural and the confrontation of opposites. Football supporters express intense warmth and affection towards their team, but a categorical and physical distance still separates them. Rival teams may express warmth and mutual respect before or after games, but a basic competitive opposition remains during play. Strong rivalry between the two sets of fans typically exceeds their amity. The spatial organization of the ground, in permitting or undermining these relationships, plays an important part in constructing 'atmosphere'. Fixtures lacking this tension of warmth and distance, perhaps where there are no 'away' fans in attendance, where home fans turn up in low numbers, or where the players do not have a competitive edge, are said to lack this atmosphere. The topophilic sensations of participation are markedly reduced. Conversely, when the balance tilts the other way, the match is said to possess an excess of atmosphere, becoming 'poisonous' or 'evil'.

In professional football, topophilic or topophobic sensations are more readily associated with supporter–ground relationships. Supporters harbour topophilic feelings towards their grounds, including those lacking aesthetic or functional refinement. As Hopcraft (1988: 141) explained of the late 1960s,

'Football grounds are not often attractive places in the ornamental sense. Their beauty is the special, environmental kind, appreciable only to people who relate the setting to their emotional attachment'. The ground *qua* place evokes memories and excites anticipation. Its idiosyncratic features are particularly cherished: the sloping pitch, the nearby gasworks, the colour of the brickwork, the architectural folly of one stand. Each signifies the ground's special status relative to other stadia. Accordingly, football grounds are held to possess their own socio-geographical character, emblematic of the fans' community. Nevertheless, football supporters of the modern age belong to an 'imaginary community' of those that follow the same club. They may never encounter these fellow fans, nor even attend the club's home fixtures, yet the sense of communitarianism continues undiminished. So it is with distant supporters and their relationships to the ground. Topophilic sensations will strike when a mere sign of the ground is encountered. These imagined, symbolic aspects may be so strong that an actual visit to the ground proves disappointing; its ordinary 'realness' comes to fix the attention (Eichberg 1995: 323–4).

Equally, topophobic sensations will strike spectators as they anticipate visiting grounds where the home team is commonly successful, or where the fans have notorious reputations. Topophobic relationships may exist between the ground and its neighbours (Bale 1989a: 129–37). On match-days, the social geography of the entire locality is transformed. Streets become congested with cars, football fans urinate in gardens, sporadic fights break out, vandalism occurs, and rowdy behaviour appears (Bale 1980, 1990; Penny 1992; Walvin 1986: 120). These 'negative externalities' may serve to shape an antagonistic relationship between club and the local community, promoting a topophobia towards the ground on match day (see Humphreys et al. 1983; Mason and Moncrieff 1993; Mason and Roberts 1991).[2]

In England, the club that produces the most extreme ambivalence among local residents and opposing fans is Millwall FC. Based in the working-class heart of south-east London, Millwall's supporters have acquired a violent reputation that far outstrips the club's Second Division status. Their long history of ground closures, fines and reprimands for spectator misconduct goes back to the early 1960s. For many opposing fans, particularly rival hooligans, a visit to 'the Den' generated extreme trepidation, and a deep sense of 'topophobia'. Among local residents, litter and crowd congestion were regular problems on match-day. Yet, profound sentiments of pride and love of place underpinned the Millwall fans' support for the club; the ground was a key touchstone to their football aesthetic, their local 'structure of feeling' (Robson 1996). It would be easy to deride the occasional, 'parochial' outbreaks of disorder involving these fans (Williams 1995: 235). Violence was only one manifestation of the deeply protective and jealous reverence that they felt towards their 'home':

> Millwall was like our home. You wouldn't let someone walk in through your front door without interrogating them, would you. You'd want to know what

they were doing there. The Den is the same. Football's a man's thing, and fighting was a matter of pride, pride about your place, your ground. Our ground is a pony little ground, but we love it. Brick for brick, slate for slate, I'd die for it.

(Fan, quoted by Lightbown 1992: 14)

To nurture neighbourly relations, Millwall opened a community development scheme in 1986, offering a range of non-commercial contacts with local people. In the early 1990s, however, economic pressures largely dictated that Millwall should build a new ground near the original Den. The move was deeply unpopular with many Millwall fans; some invaded the pitch and threw mud at directors at the final game in the old ground. After a long residence in one place, moving home can be a traumatic experience.

While UK cultural geographers have carried out the best studies of the local cultural meanings of the ground, continental researchers have produced strong ethnologies of football crowds inside the stadium. Dal Lago (1990: 88) presents a rich social portrait of Milan's San Siro stadium, before its redevelopment for the 1990 World Cup finals. He identifies different kinds of supporter primarily according to their ground location. Hence, the *amatori* (passionate fans) sit at the foot of the stands, near to their idols on the park; the *militanti* (militant fans) stand on the *curve* (ground ends), opposite one another, chanting for their team. However, the cultural peculiarities of Italian fans are best brought out by Dal Lago's identification of the *loggionisti* (theatre-type fans), who sit in cheaper seats above the expensive main stand. Dal Lago compares these fans to the ordinary lovers of Italian opera and theatre, who cannot afford the best seats but still want to be near the optimum vantage-point.

The French anthropologist Christian Bromberger undertook similar qualitative research at grounds in France and Italy. Bromberger (1992, 1995b: 221ff) produces an ethnological picture of ground spectators, detailing their social class, age, ethnicity, home locality within the city, cultural interests, and favourite players. These crowd characteristics are explicable according to the ground section favoured by particular supporters. For example, at Napoli's Stadio San Paolo, the *curva A* at one end comprised working-class *ultràs* from the poorer quarters of the city. *Ultràs* in the *curva B* were more diverse in age, home locality and class background, and included many students and secondary school children. More substantive results emerged from Marseille's Stade Vélodrome. Supporters from northern *arrondissements* favoured the ground's north end (and to a lesser extent the west stand's lower tier); southern inhabitants attended at the south end (and the middle tier of the east stand). The north end is also where the club's *ultràs* made their home, reflecting their localities' ethnic plurality, youthful vibrancy and behavioural freedom. The various ground sections also harboured strong and specific preferences for different players. In the mid-1980s, Bell, the flamboyant Cameroon goal-keeper was the hero of the ethnically mixed north end. The industrious midfield schemer Giresse was most appreciated by the lower middle classes (self-employed tradesmen or small businessmen) in the central terraces (Bromberger 1995a: 297).

One thinks here of how such affections are shaped by the sharing of common attitudes and personality characteristics within the football crowd, by its *habitus* to use the term of Elias (1978b) or Bourdieu (1984). In France, the quieter terraces or cheaper stands draw the older manual workers, who appreciate the congruent toughness of a resilient defender or midfield ball-winner. The traditional middle classes in the main stands may use their panoramic gaze in the manner of the defensive *libero* (who always has the play in front of him, and 'reads' it as an expert). Their lower middle-class companions may find a consanguine figure in the overtime worked by the productive midfield playmaker. The spectacular but unpredictable display of wingers and centre-forwards is most likely to dazzle the young working classes in the ends.

The player–spectator homology does make sense in class and masculinity terms. However, it may be a little reductive and underplay the social hetero-genesis of football's aesthetic codes. I argue in chapter 7 that the heterogeneity of playing styles is itself eroded by modern coaching and tactical thinking. Homogenization on the park may also relate to an equivalent process in the supporters' terrain. The modern football ground is sculpted to accommodate a less socially diverse and more bourgeois category of supporter. Crowd safety and crowd security issues underlie these fundamental architectural changes. Therefore, before going on to examine the social and cultural aspects of contemporary stadia, it is important to look at the historical background to these ground redevelopments. In the following two sections, I examine, first, the appalling record of disasters associated with football grounds; and, second, the specific events surrounding the 1989 Hillsborough disaster, which pressurized the football authorities at national and global level into standardizing ground facilities.

Football Ground Disasters: global and UK instances

All continents and social systems have experienced football stadium tragedies. The earliest on record are UK disasters, in Glasgow 1902 (25 killed, 517 injured) and Bolton 1946 (33 killed, 400 injured). After that, the major disasters have mainly occurred in the developing world and these may be classified by kind:

- Natural disasters are relatively rare in accounting for deaths. Nine were killed in 1962 at Libreville by a landslide; 70 died after an electrical storm provoked a sudden stampede.
- Poor facilities and overcrowding account for many more disasters. Forty-nine were killed in 1974 at Cairo by a collapsed wall, as were 15 in Ghana in 1978 and 18 in Colombia in 1981. A collapsed roof

killed 10 in Algiers in 1982; a collapsed stand (then stampede) killed 30 in Tripoli in 1988; in Bastia 15 died when a temporary stand collapsed. Eighty-one died in Guatemala in 1996 when forged tickets resulted in severe overcrowding in the cheapest sections.[3]

- Crowd stampedes killed 24 in Nigeria in 1979, then another 12 in 1989. Stampedes also killed 24 people in Greece in 1981, 40 in the Transvaal in 1991, and 9 in Zambia in 1996. In Mexico City 10 died in 1985 after an attempted forced entry by a large crowd went wrong; in 1982, two separate stampeding incidents saw 46 people killed in Cali. Later that year, 340 fans were reportedly killed on a stairway at Spartak Moscow's home UEFA Cup match against Haarlem of Holland.
- Most disturbingly, some of the greatest tragedies have been precipitated by those ostensibly employed to protect spectators from injury. In Lima in 1964, 318 fans died when a crowd fleeing from police failed to escape the stadium. Similar circumstances at a match in Buenos Aires in 1968 led to the death of 74 fans. In 1990, seven were killed when the presidential bodyguard in Ethiopia opened fire on an unruly crowd.

Tilly (1985: 171) argues that in the developing world, the state may operate as a form of organized crime by inflicting violence on the public and then making it pay taxes for protection. We may apply this notion of the protection racket to 'security' in football grounds. In the developing world, unnatural fatalities on the terraces are more commonly caused by police attempts to control 'violent' fans than by the violence of the supporters themselves. In the developed world, the illusion of security is more elaborately organized, so that police *in*action can be just as deadly. At Hillsborough, football fans perished through 'safety measures' introduced by the state ostensibly to protect supporters from their own excesses.

The UK has certainly the worst record on ground safety. The first disaster, at Ibrox in 1902, showed that early ground development could not match the pace of football's commercial expansion. During a packed Scotland–England international, one section of a high new wooden stand collapsed, killing 25 and injuring over 500. Wooden stands were discouraged subsequently, to be replaced by banking or reinforced concrete terraces. The huge, accident-free crowds at the 1923 Cup final forced the first Parliamentary report on safety a year later. It recommended the introduction of 'pens' inside ground sections to separate crowds and reduce their movement; major fixtures were to be made 'all-ticket' to control crowd sizes. The Bolton disaster of 1946, which killed 33 and injured hundreds more, occurred when trackside barriers collapsed under the pressure of overcrowding. A parliamentary report called for a more scientific approach in establishing stadia capacities. Still in Glasgow the tragedies continued: 1 death at Clyde's Shawfield ground in 1957; at Ibrox, 2 died and 44 were injured in 1961, with further casualties in 1967 and 1969 (Inglis 1987: 32; Forsyth 1990: 109).

In 1971, the second Ibrox disaster killed 66 and injured 145 fans. Rangers fans were leaving the ground in droves after the loss of what seemed a decisive, last minute goal to Celtic. An unlikely equalizer followed almost immediately; departing fans turned back into the descending crowd; scores were sent tumbling down the notorious Stairway 13. The subsequent Wheatley Report recommended tougher licensing of football grounds and paved the way for the 1975 Safety of Sports Grounds Act. Within a decade, Rangers had diverted their huge pools income to convert Ibrox into an all-seater stadium, but for the terracing at the front of the listed main stand. No other club in the UK could afford such refurbishment though a few – notably Aberdeen and Coventry City – converted their smaller grounds to all-seater status. More commonly, the dilapidated stands and terraces remained, in many cases barely touched since their construction during football's Edwardian boom-time.

In 1985, two disasters struck football on the same day. At Bradford's Valley Parade, 56 died as fire swept through the old wooden stand during a match against Lincoln City. The dropping of a single match or cigarette had ignited piles of rubbish below the seats. Most of the fans killed had sought to flee the blaze, but were effectively imprisoned by locked exit gates. Meanwhile, at Birmingham City's St Andrews, a man was killed by a collapsing wall after a match against Leeds that had been marred by crowd trouble.

By this point, an ecology of fear pervaded many English grounds, as topophobic venues of public disorder that threatened the supporter's safety. Up to one half of hard core club fans had experienced fear or anxiety over personal safety while attending 'away' fixtures (Bale 1989b: 7). Some grounds became footballing metonyms for hooliganism, yet it was in Europe that English fan violence struck its lethal nadir, at the 1985 European Cup final between Liverpool and Juventus in the Heysel Stadium, Brussels. Before kick-off, hundreds of Liverpool fans roamed across one unsegregated end inside the ground, chasing and assaulting their opposite numbers. Panicking Italian fans rushed to one side of the terracing, placing immense pressure on a weak side-wall that collapsed under the strain. Supporters at its foot were crushed under the pile of falling bodies; 39 were killed and 454 injured. It might be argued that none of the fatal injuries were inflicted directly by Liverpool fans. Criticisms might also be levied at the football authorities for their poor ticketing organization, inadequate policing by the gendarmerie, and the crumbling condition of the stadium. Yet there remains little doubt that the deaths remain primarily attributable to the Liverpool fans' reckless assault (Lewis 1989). UEFA and FIFA quickly banned English clubs from playing overseas. The measures might have contravened EC legislation on 'freedom of trade', but were accepted without protest by the FA (Evans 1986).

The Popplewell Report of 1986 provided safety recommendations on these disasters. Licensing restrictions on football grounds were toughened further; a ban on smoking in combustible stands stood out as *post hoc* wisdom. Popplewell's social philosophy reflected the prevailing Thatcherite *zeitgeist* that was lamentably out of touch with football's culture and infrastructural requirements. Future tragedies could be averted, it was assumed, by squeezing hooligans out of grounds. Closed-circuit television inside grounds was advocated at a time when Belgian police officers were already screening sixty hours of video-tape to find those responsible for Heysel (Virilio 1994: 44). Popplewell also favoured the partial introduction of the government's club membership scheme; perimeter fencing was retained, though gates were added. To pay for these modifications, the clubs set about wooing the 'family audience' in true Thatcherite style. Yet Popplewell failed to discuss the unsafe infrastructure of football grounds: the decaying terrace facilities and the unwieldy 'crowd control' barriers and fences still there to cage fans.

Hillsborough and Ground Redevelopment

Within three years of the Popplewell Report, English football had experienced its worst stadium disaster, in a situation entirely lacking in hooliganism. The Sheffield Hillsborough disaster of April 1989 began with crowd crushing inside the Liverpool end at an FA Cup semi-final against Nottingham Forest, and ended in ninety-six fatalities. Before kick-off, thousands of Liverpool fans, many of them without tickets, had packed outside the Leppings Lane end. Mounted police sought to alleviate congestion by opening the ground's external gates, allowing fans to pour inside. Most headed for the central terracing pen that was already full. As the match began, fans compressed at the perimeter fencing begged police to open the front gates, only to be told, ridiculously, to 'push back'. The commanding officers eventually ordered the opening of the gates and the full extent of the disaster gradually became known.

A quick appraisal of the tragedy's context inspires little confidence in Popplewell's foresight. It occurred within one of the UK's finest football theatres, described by a leading authority as 'a stadium, with all the grand connotations the term implies' (Inglis 1987: 97). The exact site of the tragedy, the West Stand, had been similarly praised for its 'excellent' view and facilities (1987). None of the fans were drinking inside the ground; as testimony to Popplewell's familial inclinations, the victims comprised females as well as males including, with macabre irony, two sisters. Most damningly of all, the ground boasted an excellent CCTV system, which had monitored the unfolding of the disaster from the very start. The commanding police officer had watched from the control room, his judgement clouded by the exaggerated danger of hooliganism and the stereotyped reputation of Liverpool fans. As the disaster unfolded before his very eyes, he steadfastly refused to ameliorate the suffering and open the perimeter gates, fearful that the fans might 'invade' the pitch and attack rival players or supporters. In these fatal moments, the political war on football hooliganism faced its denouement; the 'counter-measures' against hooliganism were shown to be far more deadly than their targets ever had been. An unsatisfactory inquest into the disaster returned verdicts of accidental death; the new Labour government rejected widespread appeals for a fresh inquiry.

A detailed study of the disaster criticized politicians, police, media commentators, academics and football authorities for exaggerating the importance of hooliganism 'at the expense of crowd management and safety' (Scraton et al. 1995: 17). The researchers attacked the sociologists John Williams, Kevin Young and Ian Taylor, who had published analyses of the disaster that falsely linked it to the English 'football lad' culture of drink, masculinity, tribalism and violence (1995: 294–300). The Hillsborough researchers argued that these commentators had based their analyses on 'sensationalist and unfounded allegations made by the press against Liverpool fans'.[4]

The disaster had more immediate and (in the main) very welcome impacts upon ground redevelopment. Unlike its predecessors, the 1990 Taylor Report into the disaster recommended that major structural changes be made to humanize 'football's ugly habitat' (Walvin 1994: 197). Lord Taylor noted that while modern grounds on the continent offered clean and user-friendly facilities, the old UK grounds had decayed into death traps. He recommended that clubs within the first two divisions in England and in the Scottish Premier Division should convert their stadia to all-seater status by the start of the 1994–5 season, a proposal later enacted by parliament. Standing terraces inside grounds were to be phased out over a four-year period. Taylor viewed the government's identity card scheme as inoperable; hence ministers quietly dropped the plan. To help meet the costs, the government announced a reduction of 2.5 per cent on the football betting levy; the £100 million savings went to the Football Trust for the purposes of club-by-club awards. A maximum of £2 million was available to each club; for most, this covered less than a quarter of total redevelopment costs. The ruling that lower division grounds should convert to all-seater status by August 1999 was relaxed in July 1992, thereby retaining some standing areas (Duke 1994: 131).

In implementing the report, the first measure adopted by all clubs had been the deconstruction of perimeter fencing. For Bale (1993a: 131), this architectural measure represented the beginnings of the 'post-modern stadium' in the UK. It signified also a small, if belated, victory for fans over club directors, police and political authorities, regarding control over ground space. A greater difficulty concerned how clubs should move towards all-seater status. Many clubs had an invidious choice between entering a groundshare agreement with another club, rebuilding their existing ground, or relocating to a newly built stadium (Black and Lloyd 1992, 1993, 1994). Frequently, their decision was a *fait accompli* determined by the club's particular circumstances. Most grounds were in a decrepit condition, but not incongruous to their surroundings of inner-city decay. At the height of *laissez-faire* Thatcherism, the government had absolved itself of responsibility for redeveloping these districts, leaving local authorities the task of somehow luring private investment. The plight of football clubs, in modernizing their grounds to meet the new requirements, therefore, represented a cultural epilogue to the painful renaissance of Britain's urban centres.

Only a few clubs, such as St Johnstone and Scunthorpe, were able to sell their existing ground to property developers and supermarkets, to pay for relocation. Latterly, television income allowed larger northern clubs like Bolton, Sunderland and Middlesborough to reflect their elitist aspirations by relocating. 'Ground-sharing' tended to be the least favoured option. If the ground truly was an emblem of the club and its surrounding community, then that socio-spiritual aspect would perish after moving. For example, in 1985, Charlton Athletic entered a ground-share agreement with Crystal Palace, but fan agitation saw their return to the Valley seven years later (Bale 1989a: 89–90; 1991b: 133–4). The most favoured option was to rebuild the ground on its existing site.

This task had no parallel overseas. Stadia in Germany and Italy, for example, were in far better condition and much younger, being on average still under 50 years old (48 and 43 years respectively) (Williams 1995: 221). The grand new stadia at Italia '90 had inspired football commentators and authorities, including Lord Justice Taylor, to argue for a more continental approach towards ground design. The post-Hillsborough period was part of a broader, more pro-European conjuncture in UK football and politics generally. Yet, it is important to note here that major differences existed within Italy, regarding the ideal theatre.

Some Italian stadia had all the architectural qualities of high modernism, in facilities, scale and shiny newness, but succumbed to the Fordist vices of soulessness and instrumentality. In Turin, Juventus abandoned their old Stadio Municipale to move to the Stadio Delle Alpi, constructed for the World Cup finals. The new ground boasted American-style landscaping, suburban location and a unique roof (Inglis 1990: 18–19), but neither players nor fans felt at home. It lacked intimacy while the authorities charged a high lease. Conveying their dissatisfaction, Juventus moved some of their home games to Milan's San Siro during the 1994–5 season (De Biasi 1996: 126). In contrast, the Stadio Luigi Ferraris in Genoa, shared by Genoa and Sampdoria, represents the more user-friendly stadium. The design explores post-modern style: four corner blocks painted in Pompeii red structure an edifice rooted in geometric minimalism (Inglis 1990: 25). Importantly, the stadium stands in central Genoa and reflects the architect Vittorio Gregotti's conviction that such buildings should be at the heart of urban geography, constructed with permanence and utility in mind. Fortunately for most British clubs, rebuilding (rather than relocating) their ground means they retain Gregotti's civic philosophy *de facto*, though they lack its aesthetic refinements.

An important fillip for the rebuilding programme was that the Home Nations would be free to bid for major football tournaments. These 'mega-events' help to legitimize public expenditure on stadia by boosting local and national economies through the 'multiplier effect'. Playing host to overseas fans for a few weeks or only a few hours can generate large hikes in tourist income from service industries, helping temporarily to reduce local unemployment (see Euchner 1993). Organizers of the 1994 World Cup finals claimed to have inflated the US economy by $4 billion (Lever 1995). Cities with poor international portfolios can refurbish their image. Conurbations known for deindustrialization, deprivation and crime (for example, Liverpool) may seek to ignite a 'cultural renaissance'. Tournament organizers may cultivate this new civic image, covering up or heavily policing slum areas and channelling foreign television crews towards positive background stories. One danger is that local people may feel excluded from the exposition (Hannigan 1995: 194–5).[5] Such sentiments of alienation and powerlessness over community events are not just encountered during major tournaments, but arise in more routine football contexts, such as street games and league matches.

The New Politics of Access to Football

In the contemporary football world, the most important spatio-political question concerns access to and control over playing spaces. The least powerful social groups increasingly lose this everyday battle over resources; young people's access to cheap recreation (most notably leisure spaces) is notoriously circumscribed. Urban redevelopment and housing projects reduce the number of designated football pitches (Fishwick 1989: 7). The remaining facilities continue under municipal control, commodified to extract payment from players, and leased out for league matches which are organized by adult clubs and committees. The quality of the facilities typically reflects low public expenditure on UK sports facilities, while the private sector is even less forthcoming. The late 1990s advertising campaigns by companies like Nike sought to elide the deep material inequalities between football's top professionals and park players. But hardly any of professional football's new wealth trickles down to improve the grassroots infrastructure. Meanwhile, the ubiquity of the car and the erection of 'No Ball Games' signs conspire to vitiate the informal association of street football.

A similar battle for resources is routinely fought out within the new, post-Hillsborough football stadium. Redevelopment work has significantly reduced ground capacities, both during and after its completion. Major clubs such as Manchester United, Liverpool, Everton, Arsenal, Tottenham and Celtic have, on occasion, seen their ground capacity limited to around 30,000 or less.[6] This has placed a premium on obtaining access to fixtures, particularly against the backdrop of football's post-1990 fashionability and its appeal to new markets. Clubs come to view seats as scarce resources, increasing the value of season tickets, and reducing the opportunity to pay at the gate. Some clubs, such as the northern renaissance ones like Newcastle United and Middlesborough, find themselves with season-ticket waiting lists. These price rises, and the sharpening of wealth inequalities courtesy of the Thatcher administration, ensure that major grounds are now increasingly unlikely to host their old working-class audience for top games (Horton 1997).

Right-wing figures within English football hold that the average ground's 'gentrification' and gilded prices have clear social benefits. Former England manager, Terry Venables (1996: 136), argues:

> Without wishing to sound snobbish or be disloyal to my own working-class background, the increase in admission prices is likely to exclude the sort of people who were giving English football a bad name. I am talking about the young men, mostly working-class, who terrorized football grounds, railway trains, cross-channel ferries and towns and cities throughout England and Europe.

Conversely, football's new social movements interpret the assumption that working-class fans are hooligans as a rhetorical smokescreen for further commodifying the game. Merrills (1997: ix), for example, claims the Taylor Report: 'threatened to sanitize the game to such an extent that the very reason for its existence – the entertainment of the people – was on the brink of being relegated to little more than an afterthought to be afforded cursory consideration by the money men who run the game'.

A key recommendation of the report, often forgotten by both sides, was that ground redevelopment should not be used to price out less wealthy supporters. Fan movements which attempt to redress this process find little support among their *prima facie* 'natural' allies. The Taylor Report received full cross-party support in the House of Commons, especially from opposition Labour MPs who revelled in its criticism of the government's membership scheme. For many political, social and academic commentators, the report crystallized a utopian vision for the 'regeneration' of English football. Purpose-built stadia were to rehost European fixtures, with business and television revenues enriching the playing staff and directors. The call from many ISAs, for the restoration of some football terracing, was stoically resisted by the new Labour government.

The market exclusion of many ordinary fans is, however, a feature of top professional football overseas. FIFA and UEFA inflated ticket prices for the World Cup finals and the European Championships, augmenting these tournaments' fantasy aspect by allowing corporate sponsors (who receive huge tranches of tickets) to give away some of these precious commodities in highly publicized competitions. The new ticketing 'policy' enables businessmen (whether in the black market or legally) to buy blocks of tickets for individual sale at several times their face value.[7] This perverse multiplication of the match ticket's exchange value makes a mockery of the football authorities' rhetoric

about 'fair play'. It promotes the attendance of wealthy, less passionate spectators at the expense of dedicated fans, and undermines the authorities' own
segregation and anti-hooligan strategies by stoking an unregulated market in
ticket dealing (see Giulianotti 1991, 1995a, 1996a, 1996b). Finally, a further
consequence of ground redevelopment has been the pacification of those supporters that do attend matches.

The Stadium and Social Control: the
Foucauldian aspects of football

To examine the downside of ground redevelopment, it is useful to look at the
theoretical insights provided by the French post-structuralist social theorist,
Michel Foucault. We may begin by exploring how the modern stadium accom-
modates the spectator's 'gaze'. The concept of the gaze was first used in its
full-blown form by Foucault (1975) in his 'archaeological' social history of the
clinic. The origins of clinical medicine begin with the new examination, or
'gaze', that its practitioners brought to bear on the bodies of their patients.
Medical experts came to 'study their subject' in both senses of the phrase.
Throughout the nineteenth century, other professions began to gaze upon their
subjects as a way of knowing and exercising power. Psychologists, criminolo-
gists, prison officers and factory owners utilized the gaze to observe and
regulate the bodies of others. Today, the gaze functions most proficiently at the
localist and interactional level, as people seek to know the identity, motives
and values of each other by gazing upon their face and body. Its disciplinary
aspect is not to be underestimated: 'our behaviour is regulated by the gaze of
others and by the gaze of our own self-reflection' (Rojek 1995: 61). Its practical sweep extends into consumer culture and leisure, among tourists, television
viewers, high-street shoppers and sports spectators.

Within the football stadium, the spectator's 'gaze' is satisfied technically
through an unobstructed view and panoramic 'sightlines', permitting the fullest knowledge of events on the park. Moreover, the 'gaze' enjoins the spectator
to adopt a 'critical distance' towards football, as found in bourgeois cultural
spaces like opera houses and theatres (Hargreaves 1986). The withdrawn,
objective perspective of the modern spectator comes to supplant the subjective
participation of traditional fandom. Football becomes less a process to interact
with, and more an event at which to gaze. Manchester United manager, Alex
Ferguson, noted while writing in the club's programme: 'The growing number
of hospitality packages has brought in a different type of audience. They sit and
admire the ground and can't wait to be entertained – just as if they were at a
theatre or musical' (Brick 1997: 30).[8]

Many early stadia failed to make the grade as venues for the gaze. Only the
main stands could guarantee authoritative vantage-points. The vast majority,
on the banked terraces, had obfuscated views of the match. More important,

however, was their participation in the terrace events: singing, chanting and flag-waving; or simply swaying inside the packed mass of humanity in accord with the distant, focal events on the pitch. Today, this topophilic experience is commonly banned inside the modern UK ground. Security staff will eject those who stand up out of their seats and obstruct the view of others. Fans who shout out at football matches may be charged with public order offences under recent legislation.

Bale (1993b: 155) locates the surfeit of new family ends at British grounds within Foucault's Kafkaesque world of surveillance and social control. The family is one of the most potent loci of social control, a crucial resource for reproducing labour and a key agency of socialization for the most passive and docile of bodies. The post-war 'leisure society' is now committed to the repro- duction of social consumption, with the family a key site for socializing chil- dren into future use of the culture industry (including sports events). Within football's family ground sections, parents may reproduce their control over children, while the 'family' of supervisors and stewards ensure that all main- tain pacified behavioural patterns. A silent, deathly atmosphere is inevitable, although the retail outlets within the ground do a booming trade. Additionally, we may note how the family ends contribute to the 'privatization of passion'. Giddens (1991: 162–4)) argues that, as Western societies industrialized and modernized, the release of intense emotion switched from the public arena of religious ceremonies, to the private family abode through sex with one's part- ner (see Foucault 1981). A parallel development has struck football, as the quieter, more personal or familial release of emotions in the stands has re- placed the old quasi-religious passion of crowd carnival across the terraces.

In the early nineteenth century, the utilitarian philosopher Jeremy Bentham forwarded the 'panopticon' model of surveillance as a utopian vision of social control. To improve the monitoring of prison inmates, Bentham argued that the building's architecture should maximize the visibility of inmates while minimiz- ing the labour of wardens. Ideally, prison interiors should be built in a circular shape. Rows of individualized prison cells were to line the circumference; the internal 'wall' to each cell should consist only of iron bars, rendering its occu- pant permanently visible. The observatory tower in the prison's centre would allow a handful of guards to scrutinize every activity of all inmates. In its perfect form, smoke-glass windows should encase the panopticon tower, so that inmates may never know if they are being observed by the guards. In the panopticon, vision is the resource of power, and 'visibility is a trap' (Foucault 1977: 200).

Since Foucault's use of Bentham, the panopticon has become a recurring metaphor for modern techniques of social control. Institutions controlled by the professions – such as education, health services, law – are typically housed within buildings where the bodies of the public are individualized and made available for examination. Moreover, the panopticon has been adapted to the control of public spaces. Since the late 1970s, the installation of surveillance cameras has moved from military installations, occupied territories and industrial plants, to the public high street, car parks and modern shopping malls. The UK alone will have over 500,000 CCTV cameras monitoring public streets by the year 2000.

The panoptical control of public space was first tested under 'normal conditions' in the football ground (Armstrong and Giulianotti 1998b). The 'hoolivan' emerged in the early 1980s, a large, rather conspicuous vehicle with blackened windows and a camera turret for filming the crowds. Football clubs and police units have also hired photographers to film passing crowds. Television camera operators have furnished police with film reels to help identify disorderly fans. Unsurprisingly, fans have attacked the film crews and photographers for the offence of turning in the people that feed them. More commonly, as football crowds arrive and disperse, police helicopters track their movement. On-deck search lights and video-cameras help to illuminate and zoom in on fans, recording their every action. As CCTV systems spread to public thoroughfares, football crowds are on camera many miles from the ground.

Inside the ground, surveillance technology is at the cutting edge. CCTV cameras are linked up to a central control unit equipped with numerous monitors. More advanced devices are enclosed within smoked-glass globes, making it impossible to know at whom the lens is gazing. Prior to the 1996 European Championships in England, the match venues took delivery of 'video faxes' that could transfer recorded film of football fans through ordinary telecommunications lines. In theory, recipients of the data at police headquarters would be able to compare filmed supporters with files on people already 'classified' by police intelligence (see Bale 1993a: 127). More recently, Watford, a tranquil English club playing in the First Division, took receipt of a new surveillance system that can by itself screen football crowds for those held on police file. It is only a matter of time before surveillance equipment screens the irises of fans at the entrances to UK grounds. Generally, then, the surveillance of football fans intensifies the nearer that they get to the football ground. Yet, fatally for this policing approach, football hooligan clashes are taking place well away from the ground, in a deliberate attempt to evade close scrutiny (Armstrong and Giulianotti 1995).[9] Perhaps the most disturbing aspect of such a surveillance strategy is that it has no equivalent overseas. In mainland Europe and Latin America, the spatial control of violent fans has tended to involve reactive policing on the ground. The military leaders of South America installed moats around the perimeter of pitches, to prevent supporters reaching the field of play; an aesthetically displeasing strategy, but one unlikely to result in mass asphyxia.

Towards a Post-modern Football Environment

In this chapter, I have discussed the major changes at football stadia, particularly at the more venerable structures found in the UK. From this discussion, it becomes possible to outline very generally the 'ideal type' characteristics of these grounds, according to their historical stage.

The 'traditional' ground was built before the First World War, with open terracing, stylized grandstand and easy access to public transport. As the UK modernized, this ground's locus became more central and acquired an increasingly symbolic or 'topophilic' importance for the surrounding community. In some contrast, the modern stadium sits in a suburban, greenfield site, with easy access to motorways. It features all-seater stands, multi-sport facilities and a functional, somewhat stereotyped design. The modern stadium is found mainly on the continent, constructed specifically for municipal use or to host major tournaments. The age and relative neglect of UK stadia meant that this model was rarely erected before Hillsborough. Instead, the piecemeal redevelopment of UK grounds adhered to this model haphazardly, with the added British emphasis on anti-hooliganism innovations (ground 'pens' or 'cages', segregation fences, television cameras).

In the post-Hillsborough period, UK grounds have come to resemble this model though often within incongruous, dilapidated inner cities. Rebuilding of 'traditional' grounds also allows for their 'post-modernization'. They might retain the old grandstand or introduce some fake gentrification of the new stands. Alternatively, the elliptical design of stands, as at Bolton or Huddersfield, can soften the sharp right-angles of standard, modern grounds.[10] An important aspect of this ground post-modernization involves the increased panoptical control of the football authorities over what supporters may and may not do inside. Accordingly, the uniformity of fan actions means that the old ethnological division of spectators, according to their location within the ground, may become meaningless.

There are other means through which the football authorities exercise a post-modern spatial control over fans. The 'mallification' of football grounds involves available ground spaces being commodified to sell merchandise. Hence, before matches or at half-time, the strolling spectator is no longer a social *flâneur* surveying the rest of the crowd; instead, he or she becomes a window shopper, studying club products. In Ajax's new Amsterdam ArenA, this process has been taken to new heights. Supporters inside the complex must purchase merchandise and refreshments with a special currency that is the only recognized tender. This fiscal arrangement inevitably inflates the profits inside the ground; exiting spectators may retain their unusual change, as a souvenir or 'for next time', while the club retains their Dutch currency. It also enhances the psycho-spatial divisions between the privileged inside the stadium and the greater numbers outside. A further aspect of this post-modernization involves the 'museumification' of grounds. Special museums are constructed within the ground for fans to visit, detailing the club's history, displaying old medals and trophies, and perhaps giving visitors some interactive experiences as well. Responsible parents will in future be able to take their children, to see or experience what an all-standing, packed terracing was 'really' like.

A provocative premonition of the post-modern ground is forwarded by Baudrillard (1993a: 79–80). In a regularly cited analysis, he foresees the occasion when 'hyperreal' football matches take place within the 'vacuums' of empty stadia. Likewise, the leading Italian football and media magnate, Silvio Berlusconi, has suggested football fans will prefer to watch matches live on television rather than in the stadium, hence the entry gates might have to be thrown open for free admission (Giulianotti and Armstrong 1997: 25). Television is, of course, not a neutral medium for watching football. It constructs a different viewing experience to that found in the stands, one aspect of which may involve withholding coverage of highly controversial or 'deviant' events that occur on the field of play (see Gruneau et al. 1988: 274).[11] Berlusconi's point also ignores the continuing commodification of football grounds in late 1990s Europe. The next stage of that process may see European football club owners viewing their cultural properties as potentially mobile sports 'franchises' as is the custom in North America. If the stadium is too small and the local authorities do not offer sufficient inducements to stay, the club might move from its original town or city to a larger, more profitable stadium, where another supporter base awaits.

In the longer term, to continue with Berlusconi's vision, there are trends in football culture which appear to privilege the aesthetics of the virtual (mediated) event over the 'real' (ground spectating) experience. First, the stadium's quality of facilities may be judged not against other models or concepts of public association, but according to the idealized, private leisure space of the family lounge. The armchair fan at the ground looks for the personalized seat, easy access to a diverse larder of hot snacks, quadraphonic music to relieve the tedium of half-time, and a quiet and unmolested viewing environment. The fan will also seek the creature comforts of a running commentary on the game via radio headsets, action replays on the giant screen for reviewing key moments in slow motion, or even enclosed spaces in 'executive boxes' that seal off the outside world (from these, the corporate spectator has direct access to a fully stocked bar).

Secondly, there is the match itself, always imperfect, full of uncertainties and human failings. The danger to live spectating comes when the viewer prefers a simulacrum of real football, something which is 'perfect' but 'unreal'. Televised sport has always produced its share of 'armchair athletes' who watch sports eagerly but never play them. Today, we are already at the threshold of 'hyperreality', where the psycho-spatial division of playing and spectating is disturbingly blurred. The 'pornography of football' entails multiple camera angles that enable us to see matches in minute but often useless detail (Baudrillard 1990: 31). Modern computer technology can simulate games by using old video footage of matches to 'create' new ones. More commonly, children 'play' football on television screens through their games consoles rather than in the streets. By the time of the European championships in 2008, fans will not need to travel to the tournament to enjoy the sensory pleasures of 'being there'. A combined headset and television decoder will enable the viewer to partake in an interactive experience, 'as if' they are there in the stadium (*World Soccer*, February 1997). The 'paradoxical logic' of this new technology has a disorientating effect on the senses (Virilio 1994: 63). With a post-modern circularity, football does indeed 'come home'.

5

The Price of Victory: Football Finance and the Television Revolution

Since Italia '90, world football has experienced unprecedented financial growth. In late 1994, the President of FIFA João Havelange boasted that football generated $225 billion annually (Galeano 1997: 147). He later claimed that his successor would inherit contracts worth $4 billion in 1998. By the summer of 1997, the European football industry was reckoned to be worth $10 billion. The London financial analysts Deloitte and Touche placed five European clubs comfortably inside an elite with annual turnover exceeding £40 million. Bayern Munich, AC Milan, Juventus and Barcelona were all headed by Manchester United and its budget of over £50 million (which grew to some £90 million a year later). They have since been joined by many more of Europe's premier clubs, such as Borussia Dortmund, Internazionale and Atlético Madrid.

In this chapter, I examine some of the key social and economic dynamics fuelling this football boom. I begin by noting some of the traditional administrative and business differences between UK, European and Latin American clubs. Football's globalization, and the international circulation of sports capital, have eroded many of these cultural peculiarities. The growth of football merchandising within clubs was a relatively early post-war form of commodification, but major financial and cultural changes have been inspired by television, most notably the rise of satellite broadcasting and the potential of pay-per-view. Europe's leading clubs have transformed their business arrangements by raising equity through entry to stock markets. I conclude by exploring one consistent downside to this commodification, namely, the corrupt practices of match-fixing and illegal transfer dealing.

Traditional Club Frameworks: general
international comparisons

In the UK, football was one of the last major industries to experience a move from the 'family business' model of the nineteenth and early twentieth century, in which owners and controllers are identical, to the subsequent 'joint-stock' model, in which ownership and control are separated. Towards the end of the nineteenth century, football's spectator appeal had encouraged club directors to turn their recreational activity into a more profitable investment. The new Companies Act enabled the 'companification' of sports clubs, converting from private associations into limited companies (Birley 1995a: 39). Shareholdings were created and distributed among investing directors and supporters within a pyramid framework. Large share-holdings were retained by individuals or families whose control over the clubs was confirmed by the share-based support of other board members; a large collective of investors divided the outstanding minority of shares. Only rarely did the board of directors delegate everyday power within the club by appointing a professional chief executive. Such a hands-on, familial corporate structure is found in few other industries. One exception may be the mass media, though even here it is explained by the industry's exceptional receptivity to entrepreneurship and expansionism; market philosophies that are not traditionally found among football club owners. Until recently, the major shareholders did not expect to profit greatly from football, though their social status was enhanced by their public influence over a major popular cultural institution.[1]

In most European nations, football clubs are privately owned organizations in which a small number of large shareholders control the boardroom. However, in Iberia and Latin America, clubs are organized as private sports associations, controlled by the *socios* ('members') who pay a monthly or annual subscription. The clubs thereby maintain a strong if archaic tradition of economic and political democracy. The *socios* elect club officials (including the president) every one or two years, and depose those unwilling to meet their demands. Hence, clubs rarely benefit from the large personal investments made by owners under other systems. Instead, the elected officials frequently use their club position as a populist springboard into more conventional political elections.

In the old state socialist systems of Eastern Europe, prior to the 1989 revolutions, clubs were usually controlled by major state-run institutions, such as the army, security forces or railways. Football success was often assisted by club patrons high in the party machine. In the Soviet Union, Stalin's close colleagues (most notably his son, Vasillii, and security chief, Beria) were apt to influence results: matches were forcibly replayed; players sent to the gulag; and the most popular team, Spartak Moscow, was regularly persecuted (Edelman 1993: 64–5, 83–5). In Romania, the son of the despotic President Nicolae

Ceausescu intervened in the 1986 Cup final in a bid to prevent his side, Steaua
Bucharest, from losing to the Dinamo team.

The globalization of capital, and the fall of alternative kinds of social system, mean that it is increasingly difficult to resist the 'privatization' of football
clubs on the open market. Some top East European clubs have already been
bought by local entrepreneurs or Western businesses. In Brazil and Argentina,
legislation is being framed to permit clubs to follow suit.[2] The financial revolution in most nations is driven by the rapid rise in worldwide merchandise and
television revenues. Televised football's globalization is reflected in the reach
of Eurosport, the pan-European channel, which was broadcasting in 12 lan-
guages to over 170 million viewers in 43 countries during the 1996 European
Championships. Smaller football nations struggle within the new business
environment. Local players are sold to *nouveau riche* foreign clubs; attendances for league fixtures fall as viewers switch on at home to watch superior
players and teams. Before discussing television's recent impact on football's
political economy, it is important to examine the first wave of football's modern commodification, specifically the rise in club sponsorship and merchandising.

Merchandising and the New Modernity of Football

Since the 1960s, football's political economy has undergone rapid modernization as its star players and clubs have been incorporated more deeply within the
wider commodification of popular culture. The football experience became
increasingly synonymous with track-side advertising, shirt sponsorship, television commercials, league and cup sponsorship and the merchandising of club
paraphernalia. Towards the end of the 1980s, most professional clubs in the
UK were aiming to earn more money from their off-field activities than from
gate money paid by the average supporter. Executive boxes were carved into
stands to attract the patronage of local businesses. Some towns had grown and
prospered largely through a single employer in the locality, which backed the
local football team as part of its cultural investment. In France, Sochaux have
enjoyed a lengthy patronage by the local Peugeot car company. In Germany,
the promoted VfL Wolfsburg club received £8 million from the local
Volkswagen HQ. Latterly, the Uerdingen and Leverkusen clubs have benefited
from their ownership by the multi-national Bayer pharmaceuticals company;
both clubs have the 'Bayer' prefix in their official names and players are listed
as 'company employees' (Merkel 1998). Most famously, in Italy, the small
Parma club was transformed when the dairy product multi-national, Parmalat,
took charge. Usually, however, this company–town option was not immediately available to European clubs. To improve off-field earnings, club directors
introduced an extra tier of business management, creating 'marketing depart-
ments' and appointing chief executives.

Except for the Catalonian club Barcelona (who refuse any shirt sponsorship), all modern professional clubs have sought such backing. While divisions existed inevitably in the monies accrued (with top clubs now attracting over £1 million annually from shirt sponsors), further differences lay in the kind of product advertised. Shirt and trackside displays for technological products have multiplied and serve to link football to a rapid modernity (Métoudi 1987). There are key differences between clubs that say something about the market habitus of their supporters. English clubs with 'national publics', such as Arsenal or Manchester United, advertise global, technology-based companies, like Sharp or JVC. Smaller clubs advertise more parochial and less modern companies, for example West Ham United (Dagenham Motors). In Scotland, advertisements for local car dealers, building companies or brewers abound, with alcohol featuring strongly in the sponsorship of major competitions. Even the erstwhile European players, Glasgow Rangers, have long worn an advert for a Scottish lager, reflecting the national game's symbiosis with serious drinking. The manufacture of the team kit has become an increasingly prized source of revenue for clubs. In 1996, Manchester United signed a five-year deal with Umbro worth £10 million annually. In July 1997, Real Madrid secured a similar, ten-year kit deal with Adidas. Nike's ten-year kit deal with the Brazilian national team is reported to be worth £250 million. These arrangements are highly profitable for the transnational manufacturer; clubs like Real Madrid and Manchester United are global commodity signs, recognized and consumed on a universal basis. Meanwhile, the manufacturer will design several new shirts to be worn each season by the team, forcing 'brand loyal' fans to pay inflated prices for each one.

The increasing importance of sponsorship provokes deeper conflicts between players, clubs and nations. Until recently, players were little more than 'advertising sandwich-board men' for hawking the products of club sponsors (Brohm 1978: 176). The body's commodification intensified when the world's biggest sports merchandise company, Nike, entered football. Nike's sales base and financial power have mushroomed through endorsement deals with American sports personalities, notably Michael Jordan, Tiger Woods and Pete Sampras. Nike had been confident that basketball would dislodge soccer's global supremacy after the American 'Dream Team' of basketball players had starred at the 1992 Barcelona Olympics (Katz 1994: 29). The event failed to make any great sales impact, so Nike turned instead to buying into local soccer markets (1994: 203). Inevitably, the company were at the centre of major speculation when it signed Ronaldo of Brazil as its prize football asset in 1996. The deal earned Ronaldo a minimum £10 million over ten years and, reportedly, £120 million throughout his post-football life. It also left the player in immediate market conflict with his then employers, Barcelona (sponsored by Kappa), and his prospective employers at Lazio (sponsored by Umbro). Eventually, Ronaldo signed for Internazionale, who conveniently took on Nike as their shirt sponsors. Internazionale then sold 35,000 Ronaldo replica shirts within ten days of the transfer, thereby recouping part of his £19 million fee. The question of who 'owned' the player, Inter or Nike, had been temporarily fudged rather than directly answered. Later, a global controversy centred on why Ronaldo had played in the 1998 World Cup final against France, only hours after suffering a fit and receiving sedative medication. Some Brazilian players suggested that the secret deal between Nike and the Brazilian football authorities contained a clause stipulating that the company's prize asset must play the full ninety minutes in every international.

Other sponsorship conflicts have emerged between individual players and the national team. In the build-up to the 1998 World Cup Finals in France, the French Football Federation signed a boot deal with Adidas until 2002, stipulating that all players must use the company's footwear. Over half of the French football squad at that time held endorsement deals with other companies (*Independent on Sunday* 1 June 1997). Similarly, prior to the 1994 finals, Ireland's players, managers and football association held conflicting endorsement deals with a range of companies, most notably banking institutions. Neither case resolved the issue of control over sponsorship.

The global financescape of contemporary club football is also producing international conflicts of interest. Notoriously, factory workers in the developing world are paid poverty-line wages to manufacture football merchandise for the developed world. In May 1996, the International Confederation of Free Trade Unions reported that child labour was manufacturing match footballs in Pakistan and other Asian nations, embarrassing FIFA into formulating anti-slavery policies. Sponsorship of football sides in the developing world is equally skewed towards Western interests. For example, Parmalat have been one of the major players in the transnationalization of football sponsorship. By the mid-1980s, Parmalat had established themselves as southern Europe's major dairy products company, with an annual turnover of $1 billion. In 1987, the company bought the local club Parma, bankrolling it to the tune of $66 million within ten years. Meanwhile, Parmalat had also turned their attention to international sponsorship deals. Most money (around $24 million) went to Palmeiras of São Paulo, while further deals with Peñarol (Uruguay), Boca Juniors (Argentina), Santa Cruz and Juventude (Brazil), Benfica (Portugal), Moscow Dinamo (Russia), Parmalat (formerly named Videoton, of Hungary) and latterly Atletico Chacao (Venezuela) took Parmalat's outlay to over $100 million in eight years of football involvement (*World Soccer*, November 1995). These recipients have regarded Parmalat's investment as commercially inspired, to familiarize distant markets with the company's brand name. However, Parmalat's benefaction may come with strings attached. For example, the company attempted to use its influence at Palmeiras to ease the sale of two players to Parma, the jewel in its footballing crown.

A case of more long-sighted cultural imperialism appears to have unfolded between Brazil and Japan. The Brazilian legend Zico is the owner of a rising club team in Rio de Janeiro, which is sponsored by his former Japanese club,

Kashima Antlers. The arrangement allows for players to move between the two clubs. The net benefit can only favour the Japanese club as its Brazilian partner is transformed into a glorified training camp. Young Japanese players will benefit from playing with Brazilian players and coaches. But Kashima Antlers may have the pick of all top players at the club: Zico's status in Brazil guarantees that millions of young players will aspire to join him. A more sinister situation obtains in West Africa. One Italian football agent has founded a Ghanaian club for recruiting young players who can then be sold to Europe when they reach sixteen, a system denounced by the Italian football authorities as 'slavery' (Broere and van der Drift 1997: 94–7). Western involvement in sports development in the Third World therefore tends to mask cases of classic imperialism, the athlete becoming a commodity akin to the coffee bean or banana. Western agents erect training camps to refine the rich, raw material of sports talent that avails itself locally. The finest products are sent for consumption by the affluent Western market; the inferior residue is left for the local populace (see Klein 1991). These deep inequalities are certain to grow as television money inflates the financial power of Western clubs.

UK Football and the Television Revolution

The marriage of football and television has not always been a passionate one. Club directors in the UK were long mistrustful of televised live football, wary that it might adversely affect match attendance figures, especially as fans' leisure options multiplied from the 1960s onwards (Hargreaves 1986. 116, Crisell 1997: 155). Nevertheless, by the late 1970s, the directors had become reassured that regular, controlled television helped the game's public appeal. Research from the United States agreed that televised sport increased gate receipts by enhancing team recognition and loyalty (Horowitz 1974). Others contended that the foundation of any modern sports league depended upon a broadcasting deal (Scully 1995: 28–9).

The football associations in England and Scotland tended to enjoy a cosy relationship with the British Broadcasting Corporation (BBC) and Independent Television (ITV) who shared football highlights (Szymanski and Smith 1997: 150). Television fees for matches were also markedly low. In 1978, the BBC signed a four-year television deal with the Football League for a mere £9.8 million (Cameron 1997). Five years later, the first contract to show live English league football involved the modest sum of £2.6 million. The 'duopsony' ended during the late 1980s when UK satellite television emerged with three channels devoted to sport (Whannel 1992: 59). The major player soon became British Sky Broadcasting (BSkyB), a subscription satellite company born from the merger of the rival BSB and Sky TV companies. Its *de facto* controller is Rupert Murdoch, whose transnational media empire, News Corporation, owns 40 per cent of BSkyB (Fynn and Guest 1994: 63).

In May 1992, BSkyB and the BBC agreed a £304 million, five-year deal with the new English Premiership. BSkyB paid £191.5 million to screen sixty live matches each season; the BBC paid £22.5 million for regular match highlights; the remaining £90 million came from sponsorship and overseas TV rights. The deal effectively excluded ITV from covering major domestic fixtures, except the Champions League matches in which British clubs consistently failed. In response, in November 1995 ITV signed a £60 million deal to cover live FA Cup matches for four seasons from 1997. BSkyB were again a major partner, paying £55 million for live matches except the final, with the BBC restricted to a £15 million highlights package. Seven months later, BSkyB announced a new £670 million deal with the English Premiership for live match coverage over four seasons. Significantly, the agreement included a pay-per-view provision. The BBC remained the junior partner, paying a further £73 million for recorded highlights (*The Observer*, 4 May 1997). ITV were again excluded. Some chief executives at top English clubs criticized the deal for selling their product short.

Technological breakthroughs in satellite broadcasting were vital, but the new social and political environment of English football was critically important in enabling these huge deals. BSkyB's vast initial outlay was effectively subsidized by diverting profits from other operations inside News International, most notably the newspaper empire that included top tabloids the *Sun* and the *News of the World*. Since then, BSkyB's football and other satellite services have enjoyed huge profits (£314 million in 1997), enabling News Corporation to initiate a newspaper price war against rival titles.

Meanwhile, the FA had capitalized on inequalities between English League clubs by formulating a 'Blueprint for the Future of Football'. The document proposed the foundation of a breakaway, 18-team Premier League which would retain total television income, rather than have it filter through to all 92 senior clubs. The new league started business in August 1992. It was favoured particularly by clubs outside of the elite 'Big Five', who had struggled to gain much coverage from terrestrial television, while sides such as Arsenal and Liverpool had earned £1 million annually from heavily televised trackside advertising. The new BSkyB deal guaranteed a more balanced share of television revenues, and thus followed the principles established in other large European nations, such as Italy.[3]

Pay-Per-View in the Global Game

The long-term inducement for football bodies to sign satellite deals is pay-per-view (PPV) television. Under this system, television subscribers pay for an individual sports event (such as a single football match) rather than subscribe to a sports channel for a monthly or annual fee. Theoretically, viewers may make a single payment of perhaps £10 per match; previously, a monthly fee of

£30 would have covered the same fixture and perhaps nine others. PPV is certainly most popular (and profitable) where the event involves top athletes: championship boxing, especially heavyweight, has been its main income source in the United States and UK.

A 1996 Harris survey of UK television viewers found that PPV could charge £10 per English club match, netting the Premier League £2.5 billion annually. Top clubs like Manchester United would accrue up to £380 million. Understandably, economists greeted these ambitious projections with some scepticism. Alternative figures pointed to an annual income of £700 million; uncertainty also remained over the elasticity of demand relative to the PPV fee (Cameron 1997). Nevertheless, PPV will certainly add to, rather than diminish, the gross income of top English clubs.

PPV for football matches was first introduced by the French company Canal Satellite in September 1997. Viewers were offered any French First Division match for 50 francs; all games would be screened for a further 25 francs while a season ticket of games would cost 1000 francs. The revolutionary role of the French was not accidental, as television already contributed more to the domestic game's income than did gate receipts (Guest and Law 1997). Although its quality fell well below the status of rival continental leagues, the French PPV built up a core of 500,000 subscribers within a year of launch. Later in the same season, Italian television company Telepiù 2+ took the same road to covering all Serie A games through digital transmissions.

Underlying the dynamics of PPV are the national and transnational dimensions of potential audience share. In large television markets, such as England, Italy, Germany, France and Spain, highly profitable audience figures are guaranteed, even if these constitute only 2 per cent of all viewers.[4] Smaller television markets, such as Holland, Scotland, Portugal, Belgium and Sweden, cannot hope to match these revenues. Yet these nations also contain at least one or two clubs with major European aspirations. Their predicament is perhaps most succinctly illustrated by Glasgow Rangers, Scotland's biggest club with a turnover of over £30 million, trapped inside a domestic league that accrues only £4 million from television rights. South of the border, far smaller English clubs find their income is multiplied by television revenues that Rangers cannot touch. To rectify their stunted financial growth, clubs such as Rangers will shift their attention towards more consistent European competition, to the extent that participation in the domestic league becomes a secondary matter.

One possible outcome is an upgraded European League as Europe follows the South American model, through its television-driven obsession with subcontinental rather than national tournaments.[5] A *rapprochement* may be reached here between the biggest clubs in the larger television markets as their domestic football associations struggle to satisfy these clubs' demands for greater shares of the television windfall. In August 1998, UEFA acted to head off a proposed breakaway European League by revamping the existing continental competitions to increase the television income of the major European clubs. A second alternative is the creation of new tournaments involving bordering nations. Possibilities include the oft-proposed British Cup or British League, or the more concrete bid by Belgium and Holland to share a league tournament. While football remains in this transitional stage between the national and the global, the leading football players find that there are exaggerated demands on their labour. The introduction of a world club league and numerous new tournaments (such as the Confederation Cup) may inflate the television income of FIFA and the national associations, but players struggle to enjoy any break for recuperation. Meanwhile, club versus country conflicts emerge as these highly paid superstars are ordered to miss domestic league games to lend credence to these international charades.

Football's governing bodies have *eo ipso* encouraged these television-based deconstructions of national boundaries. A key principle at UEFA had been that the national associations were empowered to decide how much football from other countries could be shown on television. For example, the Scottish FA would complain of lowered attendances at small league games that were played at exactly the time when BSkyB were beaming English matches live into Scotland. However, in line with governmental deregulation of the media, that principle has been discarded, so that in the UK, several matches played in other countries can be watched while English or Scottish teams are playing. Second, the allocation of tournament finals has also deconstructed national boundaries. UEFA have awarded the European Championship finals for the year 2000 to Holland and Belgium, and considered a joint Nordic nations bid for the 2008 tournament.[6] To smooth ruffled political feathers, FIFA awarded the 2002 World Cup finals to Japan and South Korea, before struggling to persuade future bidders that no more joint applications would be entertained.

In Western Europe, two factors had guaranteed that network stations dominated the televising of international football tournaments. First, the governing bodies were publicly committed to reaching the maximum number of viewers. Second, the European Broadcasting Union (EBU), made up of the major national television stations, was able to pay enough to UEFA and FIFA to ensure they did not reconsider their democratic posture. However, the proliferation of new subscription channels has multiplied the bidding power of rivals to the EBU and found the price of the governing bodies' semiotic democracy. The global deal for France '98 brought in no more than £120 million with the EBU winning European rights. The rights to the next two finals in 2002 and 2006 have been won by a joint bid from the German Kirsch group and ISL (FIFA's marketing agents, based in Lucerne), valued at £1.45 billion. Notably, the EBU failed with a bid for similar rights that topped £1 billion. Although FIFA maintain that everyone should see the finals free of charge, they have effectively sold the right to implement this policy; with the necessary changes, pay-per-view for major matches is inevitable.

Critical Responses to the Television Revolution

Opposition to the growing influence of television has centred on its perceivably negative effects on football. The most regular criticism is that football will come to resemble American sport, whereby television 'controls the tempo and timing of the game' (Brailsford 1991: 156). The football calendar might be corrupted to fit television schedules and the match itself fragmented to allow for advertising slots (see Hoch 1973). More seriously, it is argued, television will hasten the transformation of fan from club 'member' to 'consumer' (Critcher 1971: 116–17). The new spectator may elect to 'shop around' the football marketplace to find the team with winning traits (Alt 1983: 100). The supporter base of small football clubs will be eroded irrevocably. Second or Third Division clubs will disappear in much the same way as the locality's dialect or accent. The next generation of rootless football fans may come to practise placeless forms of language and fandom that are promoted through the spectacular television coverage of the top teams.

A related criticism here is the threat posed by television to one of football's major attractions: 'uncertainty of outcome'. Professional football has always been skewed economically in favour of large clubs which can afford to buy and pay the best players. This has become even more obvious since the abolition of the old 'retain and transfer system'. Some economists have suggested that football should follow the 'reverse draft' model of player recruitment operated in American football, but the game's poor structural integration with the education system precludes this option (see Leifer 1990: 658).[7] The unequal distribution of television fees between clubs must result in an even greater concentration of financial wealth and footballing success. PPV will hasten this process, but other broadcasting developments may contribute. Some clubs, notably Manchester United, have introduced their own subscription television channels, allowing for the marketing of club products and the reproduction of fan loyalties through the showing of old matches and youth team games.

In the longer term, a television channel would encourage the club to retain copyright on *all* its matches. Major clubs would receive by far the largest royalties through the demise of collective television deals and the fragmentation of live and highlights transmission packages. In Holland in 1997 the top four clubs (PSV, Ajax, Feyenoord and Vitesse Arnhem) broke from their national league association by signing a separate television deal with Canal Plus. Though other Dutch clubs started legal action, the agreement was lent support by EU commissioner Karel van Miert on the grounds of free-market competition. The resultant televisual power of these small cartels may be over-determined by processes of vertical integration as television companies begin to buy into football clubs. In September 1998, BSkyB's £623 million bid for Manchester United prompted a frenzy of negotiations involving English clubs and satellite broadcasters.[8] Successful bidders may sit at both sides of the table when the clubs and television stations come to negotiate new deals. UEFA and FIFA may find their constitutional powers challenged by the broadcasting interests of the major clubs *qua* satellites of the satellite stations.

At the national level, there is the suspicion that match results may be directly influenced by television's interests. In Latin America, this may have already occurred. The Argentinian company Torneos y Competencias (T y C) has exclusive rights to screen live club fixtures in Argentina, Uruguay, Paraguay and Chile. Its deal with the Argentinian FA runs until an improbable 2011, enabling T y C to screen four league matches live each weekend, from Friday to Monday. This arouses public concern that television's pursuit of viewers will bias it in favour of the top clubs and undermine the integrity of competition. In 1993, in a move that was at best unethical and at worst corrupting, T y C intervened in the final week of the league championship. With top club River Plate a single victory ahead of Velez Sarsfield, T y C moved to buy the best player of River's final game opponents, Argentinos Juniors, and sold him to River – who duly won their match, and were confirmed as champions. In Mexico, the Televisa company has dominated the domestic game since 1969 (see Orozco 1994, quoted in Arbena 1998), and was instrumental in attracting the 1986 World Cup finals there (Glanville 1997: 271). Televisa controls three of the nation's top teams, holds the rights to the national side's matches and owns the Aztec Stadium. By the mid-1990s, it was thought that the national team had become a company pawn. The Mexican team manager, Bora Milutinovic, was favoured by Televisa; the affinity was repaid in part by his curious refusal to select the nation's top scorer (Hermosillo) – who played for a club owned by a rival network.

The trend towards a decline in 'uncertainty of outcome' appears to contravene the dramatic interests of television, since armchair audiences prefer competitive matches. Soccer's free market in television coverage will hasten the movement of top players to the most prestigious clubs, destabilizing the game's competitive *raison d'être*. As this contradiction is realized through the routine triumph of superclubs over weakened domestic rivals, so television is likely to respond by focusing more on how the top clubs may arrange themselves internationally, to regenerate some uncertainty of outcome. Cartel competitions involving top continental clubs will have increasing appeal for television companies which are themselves locked into a network of international deals to control the development of digital television. The promised FIFA–Adidas World League, initially scheduled to begin in 2008, promises to be the major club-centred televisual attraction.

One possible danger to the television revolution is the political argument, concerning the social justice of accessing premier sports events on television. In short, making viewers pay more to watch football only emphasizes the inequalities of access to these leisure products. There is nothing within the economic logic of PPV or subscription television to prevent the vast majority of viewers missing out on something they would gladly watch free of additional charge.

Behind these protocols for a semiotic democracy stands a reassertion of the 'national interest'. Satellite television's acquisition of major sports competitions has attracted UK parliamentary scrutiny, on the need to ensure that 'blue ribbon' sports events of national importance remain available on terrestrial television. Listed events include not only the football Cup Finals, but the Derby horse race, the Wimbledon tennis championships, the Olympic Games and the World Cup finals (Hargreaves 1986: 199). All of these are deeply symbolic, political rituals, when emblems of nationhood (flags, anthems, political leaders, the aristocracy) are on open display. The takeover of these sports events by subscription television may be viewed as an attack on citizens' cultural rights to experience them freely. The sudden exclusivity of top sports also threatens to fragment the unifying dimension that these events have with regard to national identity.[9]

Paradoxically, parliamentary legislation will not safeguard the terrestrial televising of more than a few top UK football matches. The major political parties clearly favour media deregulation. Governments attempt to demonstrate their public concern on football's commodification, but absolve themselves of the political responsibility to act. The creation of a football 'task force' in August 1997 has been indicative. Although the 'task force' is intended to represent the views of fans in particular, it is headed by the controversial former Conservative MP, David Mellor. In Habermas's (1987b) terms, the 'task force' is oriented towards 'strategic' rather than 'communicative' action. It facilitates a defensive governmental policy towards football, shaped more by 'technical' choices and solutions than by political or moral debate. Ideally, it should facilitate the fair and frank exchange of ideas and views that are held by all in the football community. Its goal should be to enable an 'intersubjective understanding' and consensus between all sides. In reality, it is concerned with winning technical 'results'; cost–benefit strategies take centre stage, with the most powerful operators inside football (especially satellite television) flexing their muscles.

Alternatively, one of the most insightful analyses of football's future has come from Mark Perryman (1997) in a thoughtful pamphlet for the Fabian Society. Perryman maps out some radical social policies for the contemporary game, calling for clubs to adopt a more communitarian strategy. He argues that they should become much more involved in charity work and contribute more fully to sports education and community exercise projects. Critically, he calls for the creation of a football regulator to safeguard fans' interests in the way that other monopolized industries are monitored and regulated.

Football Clubs and the Equity Market: France, the UK and beyond

European club football's commodification has been 'overdetermined by a number of post-modern conjunctural factors. The prospective profits of satellite / PPV television have coincided with the rising fashionability of football in the post-1990 epoch, thus exciting attention in the financial markets. In this section, I discuss the important financial developments within the post-modern football market.

We should begin by noting that football has experienced previous 'boom and bust' periods. The financial roller-coaster of French football during the 1980s provides a salutary illustration. Rapid growth was based on financial quicksand. French football's subsequent slump became a spectacular moral lesson on the corrupt, destabilizing free-market policies then propounded by right-wing Western regimes, including President Mitterrand and his colourless socialist administration. To bolster France's cultural industries, the socialists had introduced *laissez-faire* tax policies for top earners, inspiring French clubs to attract crack foreign players by paying some of Europe's highest wages. Greater television revenues were forthcoming (though nowhere near the scale of PPV), while the national game's financial future seemed secure after winning the right to stage the 1998 World Cup finals. Most importantly, several charismatic businessmen took control of the top clubs. Bernard Tapie arrived at Marseille, Jean-Luc Lagardère at Racing Matra of Paris, and Claude Bez at Bordeaux; Prince Rainier's heavy investment in Monaco is also noteworthy. Between 1977 and 1988, revenues in French football catapulted from FF37 million to FF870 million. The corporate structure of French clubs shifted from the traditional to the brashly modern. During the late 1960s and 1970s, St Etienne had been France's most successful club, reaching the European Cup final in 1976. It was owned by a local company and run according to the family business ethics of discipline, hard work and continuity of labour. St Etienne's decline coincided with the ascendancy of Marseille during the late 1980s under the control of Bernard Tapie, owner of the Adidas sports chain. At Marseille, Tapie introduced his starkly modernist business formula. Ailing firms were bought at rock-bottom prices; the entire enterprise was audited, the deadwood cleared; pure professionals were hired for instant results, in a blaze of manu-factured publicity (Raspaud 1994).

The sudden financial expansion of French football had no real cultural or economic referent. French 'supporterism' was fickle, characterized by low attendances and merchandise expenditure. Boardroom graft and match-fixing scandals rocked Marseille, Toulon and Bordeaux. Racing Matra were wound up amidst mountainous debts. Huge deficits were reported by Bordeaux (FF242 million), Brest (FF80 million), Toulon (FF70 million), Niort (FF47 million) and Laval (FF9 million) (Broussard 1991). By 1991, the game's income had risen to FF1,200 million, but the deficit stood at FF800 million. Marseille and Bordeaux were forcibly relegated and French football entered its post-expansionist phase of rapid 'downsizing'. Small clubs founded on tight business principles and strong youth teams, such as Nantes and Auxerre, emerged to compete successfully against larger survivors like Monaco and PSG. Notably, with the partial exception of PSG, all French clubs are now firmly repositioned on the supply-side of Europe's market in top players.

English football had struggled through periods of modern austerity in the 1970s and 1980s. Its supporter base and watchfulness towards club debts ensured that the French experience was rarely repeated. By the mid-1990s, UK clubs were under severe pressure from the Taylor Report, rising transfer fees and player wages. To augment their working capital, many turned to an expansion of share ownership and membership of the London Stock Exchange. By early 1997, nineteen clubs had raised over £2 billion through the main stock market or its smaller derivatives (Sloane 1997). The majority enjoyed share price rises of over 200 per cent; clubs like Aston Villa, Liverpool and Glasgow Rangers topped 500 per cent of their original value. These spectacular profits were underwritten by extreme shareholder loyalty: many small investors were fans with an emotional commitment to the club, precluding the quick, profit-taking sale of shares (McMaster 1997). City institutions were lured into share-buying by football's growing off-field potential and soon acquired the greater proportion of shares.

However, playing results will impact upon all share prices. During the 1996–7 season, Millwall were forced to call in the administrators and sack over twenty club employees, following a poor run of form. Sheffield United's market value fell 31 per cent (over £9 million) when the team lost its final promotion play-off match (*Independent*, 28 May 1997). Moreover, City enthusiasm for football shares was sobered by reports from Coopers and Lybrand in the New Year of 1997 that the football sector was overvalued by £1 billion. Throughout 1998, many listed UK clubs lost between one-third and one-half of their original value, but the momentum was soon recovered after BSkyB's astronomical bid for Manchester United.

Prior to the late 1990s boom, football's business people had run local clubs for emotional and social rather than financial rewards. However, capitalization has multiplied their original share investment. In Scotland, David Murray's £6 million investment in Glasgow Rangers became a £100 million holding within a decade. Fergus McCann's £13 million investment in Glasgow Celtic in 1994 was worth over £50 million three years later. Profits at England's major clubs have been equally high. Sir John Hall paid £8 million for Newcastle United in 1991; post-flotation in April 1997, this became worth over £100 million. Over the same period, Alan Sugar's £2.7 million investment in Tottenham could be revalued at over £50 million. Doug Ellis held a fortune valued at over £50 million in Aston Villa, based on his meagre investment of £500,000 in 1982. Most spectacularly of all, Martin Edwards was set to earn over £100 million from a gradual sale of all equity in Manchester United, less than a decade after agreeing to sell his interest for £10 million to a proposed buyer who could not find the money (Sloane 1997). In all of these cases, 'going public' did not mean any real loss of executive control over the club.

Football's capitalization has not been restricted to the UK. The international 'financescape' positively encourages continental clubs to explore their options in other stock markets. Several Spanish clubs have opened negotiations with fund managers in London, including Real Betis, Deportivo and Atlético Madrid (*Independent on Sunday*, 30 August 1997). The legal status of German clubs has been re-examined with a view to facilitating capitalization. At least six top Italian clubs have exercised financial austerity to satisfy legal requirements prior to going public. Lazio's flotation in the summer of 1998 enabled them to purchase major international stars like Vieri, Salas, de la Peña, Mihajlovic and Stankovic. Seven Norwegian clubs have capitalized, generating income of around £11 million. Leading Danish clubs have ignored the lesson from Brondby's disastrous flotation in the early 1980s by declaring their stock market intentions.

The frenzy of capitalization has attracted some top business institutions to invest in different foreign clubs. For example the English National Investment Company (ENIC) holds a controlling interest in AEK Athens and Slavia Prague and large minority holdings in the Italian side Vicenza and Glasgow Rangers. One of the earliest regulations in UK football had barred individuals from investing in more than one club, to prevent conflicts of interest and possible match-fixing. These old dangers seem to re-emerge, but with greater acuity as the 'sibling' clubs may clash in high-stakes European competition. In the concluding section, I continue on this theme to explore the unlicensed or corrupting dimensions of the football marketplace.

Illicit Gains: the corrupt side of contemporary football

Essentially, there are two dimensions of corrupt practice within football. First, most traditional activity involves fixing match results; the second concerns illegal activity within the football marketplace, especially player transfers.

Match-fixing has two categorical motivations: satisfaction of emotional attachments by ensuring the favoured side wins, or securing of financial gain from the result. Often, the two motives are interlinked. Europe's largest corruption case involved Bernard Tapie's Marseille, a French inquiry finding that many matches were fixed throughout 1993 as the club won the French League and European Cup. Tapie was eventually jailed, while Marseille were forcibly relegated in 1994 and placed in receivership soon after, with debts of $48 million.

Many European match-fixing scandals have centred on Italian clubs, particularly during the 1970s. After one major inquiry, AC Milan were relegated for match-fixing; their president and goal-keeper were banned *sine die*, as was one Lazio player. Eight other players were banned for between three and five years, including Paolo Rossi, whose minimum term was reduced to two years, to allow him to play decisively in the 1982 World Cup finals. Internazionale, Milan and Juventus were among those at the centre of other UEFA inquiries during the 1960s and 1970s. Latterly, compelling evidence emerged in 1983 that Inter had approached Groningen of Holland to throw a tie. AS Roma were accused of 'tapping' officials following their victory over Dundee United in the 1984 European Cup semi-final; and Torino were alleged to have hired prostitutes to act as 'interpreters' for European match officials.

Other European rigging scandals have centred on Belgium, Hungary, Portugal and Romania *inter alia*. In 1983, the top Belgian internationalist, Eric Gerets, was among 16 players and officials to be banned for fixing a Standard Liège–Waterschei match. A year later Anderlecht bribed the referee to beat Nottingham Forest in the UEFA Cup semi-final. Their admission in 1997 encouraged former Forest players to seek over £1.5 million in damages through the Belgian courts. During the mid-1980s, the chronic state of corruption in Hungary was investigated by the national FA: 260 players and 14 referees were suspended and 75 convicted later in the courts. In Portugal, FC Porto were accused of bribing the Romanian referee for their 1984 European Cup-Winners' Cup semi-final win against Aberdeen. In Romania itself, the national FA accept that match-fixing is endemic, as big clubs buy results from smaller ones unable to pay their wage bills. A special commission was set up in Yugoslavia to investigate similar problems.

In future, as the football economy expands and institutional arrangements become more complex, direct illegal payments to players will come to be regarded as unsophisticated and inefficient. Major club shareholders will also be major players in other areas of the entertainments industry, such as television, radio, newspapers and magazine publishing or in public relations. They may offer plenty of opportunities to players to augment their football income, by opening a shopping store or doing a paid interview. Instead of delivering cash directly to corrupt opponents, there are now countless sinecure roles available within these industries for passing on bribes indirectly.

According to the traditionalist ethics of football, corruption of match officials is probably more shocking than that of the players. The notion that the referee and his assistants are 'impartial' is the cornerstone of any game. The introduction of referees to modern football reflected bourgeois thinking on the general position of umpires in sport regarding 'neutrality' and the preservation of 'fair play' and sporting conduct between each side. The match officials themselves are drawn disproportionately from classic middle-class and lower middle-class professions, such as law, accountancy, banking, teaching and middle management. Traditionally, the referee's 'professional' status has been treated with some scepticism by football supporters, an attitude that has since hardened into deep suspicion as part of the wider demythologizing of other middle-class 'professions'. If the football crowd is strongly partisan, the referee becomes 'only human', and unable to withstand the emotional pressure in making key decisions. If a local club is playing, personal ties and childhood support will be seen as influencing the referee. Popular stories about biased referees are recycled throughout the football culture and acquire a mythological potency.[10]

Referees are also regularly caught up in the turmoil of their wider social and economic context. In Colombia, referees have been shot for refusing to accept bribes or heed the threats of drug gangs which invest heavily in clubs and 'gamble' on results (Oliver 1992: 650; Vélez 1995, quoted in Arbena 1998). In Brazil, evidence has surfaced of direct bribes changing hands, but the perception remains that referees are generally 'neutral'. However, the payment system for referees clearly undermines their impartiality. Instead of receiving a standard match fee, Brazilian referees are paid a percentage of a match's gate money, encouraging them to avoid alienating the best supported clubs. Big clubs typically win controversial decisions in matches against small teams. Where two major rivals meet, the referee will struggle to appear even-handed and thus 'balance' any disadvantages encountered during games. For example, if a player is sent off, the opposing side becomes highly likely to lose a player for the most minor of offences, so that neither team gains a lengthy advantage over the other.

Evidence of bribery and corruption at international matches is rather harder to identify. These fixtures tend to be scrutinized more closely by football authorities and supporters; there are also few internationals in which a potentially tight game is 'meaningless' for one team and so more easily 'bought'. Moreover, those in charge of national football associations have a more administrative and less interactive position than club presidents or chairpersons. The strongest suspicions fell on a 1978 World Cup fixture in Argentina, when the home side needed to beat a useful Peruvian team by at least four clear goals to reach the final. Before the match, Argentina shipped 35,000 tons of free grain to the Peruvian junta and released $50 million in bank credit. These arrangements were made by Argentina's World Cup organizer, who was also a vice-president of FIFA. Argentina went on to win 6–0 after the Peruvians fielded four reserves and missed several easy chances (Kuper 1994: 175–6; see Arbena 1990).

A major problem here was that Argentina knew exactly what result they needed to qualify ahead of opponents who had played earlier. Four years later, at the Spanish World Cup, the friendly football nations of Germany and Austria visibly contrived to allow a 1–0 German victory, enabling both to qualify at the expense of Algeria, who had earlier played their final group match. To combat these scandalous arrangements, FIFA decreed that the final round of group matches in all tournaments should be played simultaneously.

Hence, the fixing of international games is now more likely to be rooted in gambling. In all football cultures, the value of clubs is outstripped by their associated gaming industries. In 1997, the UK football pools industry alone drew in £427 million, its revenues having reached £823 million before the National Lottery.[11] In Italy, the state-sponsored Totocalcio still attracts more money than any rival lottery (Lanfranchi 1994: 142). Further bets are taken on the time of the first corner-kick, free-kick, substitution or throw-in, all of which can be easily fixed without exciting curiosity. Illegal gambling is particularly corrupting and at its most pervasive in the Far East. To undermine illegal betting cartels (and help pay for the new national league), the government of Singapore legalized gambling on matches. Nevertheless, concerns remain that football's globalization inevitably brings it into contact with the huge gambling cartels in the Far East. Emissaries of these cartels have almost certainly travelled to Europe to fix matches by bribing professional players.

The globalization of football capital has also facilitated a second class of corruption involving off-the-field activities that has become more complex and less controllable. The professional transfer market is notoriously shady, where informal chats, anonymous tip-offs and secret meetings are vital to securing deals. After newspaper revelations that large, undeclared sums were paid as transfer sweeteners to club officials, the English FA instigated an inquiry into the background to several transfers. Its most interesting finding concerned the complexity of foreign transfers, highlighting a potential conflict of interest among some club officials. Previously, transfers may have taken place with three key participants – the two club managers and the player himself. Today, market relationships are more complex; agents mediate for players, while assistant managers or chief scouts may represent the club in negotiations. Sometimes, the position of the parties can become rather confused. For example, a major agent for Scandinavian players developed a financial relationship with the chief scout at Arsenal, who then became instrumental in 'introducing' these professionals to English managers. As football's division of labour becomes ever more complex, intermediaries with specialist knowledge and contacts are able to secure income from both parties to the 'bargain'. The scope for corrupt practice is self-evident.

Player agents became increasingly important during the 1970s and 1980s. Foreign transfers came to the fore and difficulties arose around the role of agents in agreeing deals with different clubs. To exercise some control over this development, FIFA required all agents to obtain 'licences' by lodging bonds of £100,000 with them and passing an interview with the relevant national federation. By the start of the 1997 season there were 286 registered agents, but licensing evasions were commonplace. Players often retained their original agents as 'accountants' or 'lawyers', so avoiding any FIFA sanctions. Meanwhile, these *de facto* agents could ignore FIFA's rules by speaking to different clubs while the player was under long-term contract with another club.

Football and Business Strategy: towards the millennium

In conclusion, we may say that football's business development has been through traditional, modern and post-modern phases in each nation. In the UK, following 'companification', the 'traditional' arrangement would see the board of directors owning a decisive number of club shares. Off-field earnings became increasingly important in the modern, post-war era. A wider division of ownership and control emerged, although key decisions rested with club chairmen and their acolytes. Since Italia '90, the European football industry has entered a distinctive, post-modern phase. Income from television has revolutionized the game's political economy, enabling clubs to seek out new, wealthier supporters to sit in comfortable, reconstructed stadia. Club directors have amassed phenomenal personal fortunes after capitalization, while retaining their majority shareholding. Latterly, modern, national boundaries have been threatened through continuing proposals for a European Super League, independent of the recognized football bodies, and involving up to eighty clubs. Again, television revenues provide the inspiration for such breakaway projects, with up to £20 million guaranteed to each club (*The Australian*, 7 August 1998).

Other aspects of the football business, such as player–club relations and match-fixing, have continued through this process. I discuss the position of player–club relations more fully in the next chapter. However, here it is sufficient to point out that, traditionally, players were effectively 'owned' by the clubs. Greater freedom of contract was won gradually in Europe from the 1960s as a process of labour market modernization. However, the club's predominance in its relationship with players was reflected in the fact that it used players to advertise the products of club sponsors. Latterly, a new, post-modern period has been signified by the tendency of sports manufacturers to hire the player to advertise their commodity, often against the business commitments of the club. Importantly, the player is considered to be a more potent and reliable commodity sign than his club. Similarly, in relation to match-fixing, there have always been traditional suspicions about the apparent fallibility of referees and the rigging of results. Revelations during the 1970s and 1980s showed the practice to be sophisticated, modern and widespread. Gambling regulations have helped to keep this under check within nations. However, in football's global, post-modern epoch, the easy circulation of capital and international gambling cartels undermine this control.

The post-modern financial turn is reflected in the commodification of football's cultural 'heritage'. Alienated fans may turn to the 'authenticity' of the past, but still cannot avoid consuming a commodified simulation. 'Classic' football shirts, from the days before sponsorship names were emblazoned on the front, are available by mail order. Old matches are recycled through 'retro' shows on subscription television. Football museums introduce the next generation of supporters to old-style terrace fandom, through simulated, interactive models.

Some new commentators have argued that the television-enhanced commodification of football can be resisted. Their central premise is that football fans do not switch their allegiance, and so cannot be defined as 'consumers' or 'customers'. Such a naive assertion requires an education in the basic sociological imagination. No football supporter is hermetically sealed off from the new marketing system. The complexity of football's economic relationships means that all 'fans' are tied into this commodification process. Anyone who pays for satellite television (directly, at home, or indirectly, by buying a drink in a pub to watch it), is putting money towards the clubs that are being shown, no matter whom he or she supports. Fans who buy merchandise from their club may be contributing financially to their favoured team. They are also putting money in the hands of Umbro, Adidas or Nike, which can be used to sign bigger merchandising deals with rival clubs. Any Manchester United fan who bought a pint of Carlsberg in 1996 was effectively paying money into Liverpool via that club's shirt sponsor. Moreover, many football fans who retain a lifelong affection for a small club are also likely to favour at least one large club. From the latter relationship, money is still extracted, for club merchandise, satellite subscription, watching on television (thus helping with the sale price of club trackside advertising), and so on.[12]

There is certainly a class dimension to this process. Television and merchandising companies have successfully targeted a new, young, middle-class audience whose club affiliations are the most plastic of all. Even the champion of 'true' middle-class fans, Nick Hornby (1992), shows how especially fickle this fandom can be. Although claiming to be a staunch Arsenal fan, Hornby rarely travelled outside London to watch matches; at university he switched his allegiances to Cambridge United. More broadly, the class culture aspect of this post-modern fandom is nicely encapsulated by Hannerz's (1990) opposition of the 'local' and the 'cosmopolitan'. The working classes and lower middle classes are tied to 'local' cultural practices and identities (including the community football team). The middle and upper classes tend to be more geographically and intellectually mobile, and 'cosmopolitan' in their cultural commitments, favouring an interest in big football teams, but moving on to other sides (or sports) when it suits.

Indeed, the biggest danger for football's new marketeers is that this new, cosmopolitan fan may abandon the game as quickly as he or she arrived in it. The clubs and the mass media are experimenting with all kinds of 'spectacular' entertainment to hold transitional viewers. Yet ultimately, it may be that only the most spectacular kinds of play will sustain interest. In this sense, attacking rather than defensive tactics may come to have more than an aesthetic value for football purists. They may also improve the club's level of 'customer periodicity' (among live spectators and television viewers) and thus reflect favourably on its stock market price.

The more pessimistic scenario emerges when this new class, as a large football shareholder, puts greater emphasis upon financial rather than emotional dividends. Will they allow the club to become indebted by buying players needed for the team? There have been signs at Newcastle United and Juventus that the business wing of the club (with one eye on its market value) can come into direct conflict with the long-term football strategy (in terms of heavy investment in the transfer market). Players are sold without replacements being found, while dividends filter money permanently out of the game.

In the post-modern football world, top players earn more, directors and share-holders profit, and media stations generate new markets. A new class of disenfranchised fans appears, missing out on the club's profitability, unable to afford entry to grounds, and reduced to watching the spectacular game on pub television. That is the privilege of the 'core' football markets. Smaller European nations on the semi-periphery will struggle to break in. Peripheral nations (including the Latin American leagues) will be increasingly bedevilled by the export of their most precious playing commodities, sowing the seeds for future under-development of their old 'national' game.

6

Football's Players: from Local Heroes to International Stars

In this chapter I turn to examine the historical and cultural position of football players. A genealogical approach continues to be valuable in tracing the economic and industrial emancipation of players. Football's 'traditional' period of labour relations must be regarded as its 'amateur' one. In the UK, amateurism finished in the late nineteenth century but the debate rumbled on until the 1930s. The transition from amateurism to the early modernity of paid players reflected an obdurate social structure within football: the aristocracy and upper middle class tending to the rules; middle-class businessmen controlling the clubs; working-class professionals playing the game.

Professionalism offered working-class players a route towards social recognition within a meritocratic environment, and life-chance opportunities that were denied elsewhere, in politics, commerce, and higher education (Baker 1988: 126). Yet, like their siblings in industry, professional players had little control over their labour power. Football's labour relations struggled to emerge from an 'early modernity' that lasted until the early 1960s; throughout, players were tied to the club, worked within the confines of a maximum wage, and had few prospects upon retirement. Prior to the First World War, the UK's 6,000 or so professionals were in a 'quasi-feudal market and work situation' comparable only to that found in the military (Hargreaves 1986: 69). The Association Football Players' Union bluntly claimed that 'the professional player is the slave of his club and they can do practically what they like with him'. Collective bargaining was blighted by the failure of up to 90 per cent of players to join the union (Vamplew 1988: 255).

This oppressive industrial atmosphere continued well into the post-war period. Club directors were like local factory owners, austere and untrusting in dealing with players and managers. The bosses' contempt was reflected by Football League supremo, Alan Hardaker, when he stated in 1961 that he 'wouldn't hang a dog on the word of a professional football player' (Fynn and

Guest 1994: 31). As a labour market, the football world was a disturbingly one-sided affair (Dabscheck 1979: 232).

In the UK, the later 'modern' period of football's labour relations was signalled by the gradual industrial emancipation of players. The maximum wage was abolished in 1960–1, while the 'retain and transfer' system was adjudged to be an 'unreasonable restraint of trade' for the 1963–4 season. Slow modernization meant that clubs remained permanently in control of their players' destiny until the 1977–8 season. The 'freedom of contract' principle then entitled out-of-contract players to negotiate their transfer. The players' former club would receive financial compensation, set by a special arbitration committee with jurisdiction in each Home Nation (Thomas 1996: 21). Latterly, in Europe, football's 'post-modern' era of labour relations was heralded when the Bosman case was fought and won through the European courts.

Football Players and the Industrial Experience: maximizing body capital

Early sociological studies of football's labour relations drew heavily upon a Marxist perspective. Objectively, professional football was viewed as a capitalist enterprise, hence the player became a worker alienated from his productive labour. The club extracts surplus value (profit) from his productive labour. In football, as in industry, the worker fits into the division of labour, performing his or her allotted role continuously, to facilitate the team's playing system. 'Every description of the position contains a catalogue of characteristics which imply a prescribed pattern of behaviour for the individual player' (Rigauer 1987: 51). Like machines, football players are programmed by their trainers to perform only predetermined moves rather than to play creatively without rehearsal (Vinnai 1973: 38). Football trainers seek an absolute influence over their employees, signing players with the 'right mentality' who have a stunted personality and obedient respect for authority. This obsession with controlled and directed action is part of the *unfreiheit* of sport (Adorno 1967), the rise of technical 'purposive-rational action' over consensual 'communicative action' (Habermas 1970). In football, this means planning to avoid defeat rather than debating how the game should be played. Players are denied the opportunity to outperform their individual opponents; the higher goal of team success, by following the coach's instructions, takes priority (Overman 1997: 197). Meanwhile, 'commodity fetishism' afflicts the best paid players, as they become known and appreciated for their 'price tag' value rather than their technical qualities or intrinsic worth (see Marx 1963: 183).

This interpretation of player–club relations has strong parallels with those of Foucault and Bourdieu on body subjugation and discipline. Though highly rewarded for their labour, leading professionals still experience top clubs as carceral organizations. In these settings, the individual is removed from routine social relations and relocated within a confined space. The body is subjected to new and rigid disciplines, and examined by 'experts' or other figures of scientific authority (Foucault 1977; Goffman 1961). The diet and fitness of players are constantly monitored. Sexual relations are prohibited in the days before matches; some clubs remove players from the family home and place them in special training camps. During training, players are put through a complete regimen of repetitive exercises day after day; failure to arrive on time or finish the drill results in their downgrading. The manager's corporeal control over the football institution mirrors that of the governor inside prison, the headteacher within school or the sergeant inside the barracks. Empowered to construct an elaborate surveillance system, he delegates responsibilities to his subordinates: reserve and youth team coaches, the 'kit manager', club 'scouts' or even (for younger players) the landlady. In the UK, until the early 1960s, conscription or national service ensured players held first-hand experience of this total institutionalization. Disciplinarian managers like Bill Struth at Glasgow Rangers, or Stan Cullis and Major Buckley at Wolves, were surrogate commandants to their young conscripts.[1] Managers continue to favour obedient, 'true professionals' who practise careful dieting, fitness training and other 'technologies of the self' off the field.

According to Wacquant's (1995: 66–7) interpretation, the player is an entrepreneur in bodily capital, a young man self-employed through his feet. Yet the physical capital of players is central to their productive relationship with the club. Fail the medical examination, and no contract is proffered. In pre-season training, the body is refined from a plastic commodity into footballing capital. During the season, it is fine tuned by training and the ascetics of sacrifice. When describing the late stages of a fixture, or of a professional's career, the body is thought of as a machine, a 'dead labour' asset with a finite existence. Players with 'big engines' keep running until the final whistle; those visibly slowing have 'nothing left in the tank'. These mechanical metaphors foretell a fatal and irresistible conclusion: 'A machine either works or it does not. Thus the biological machine is either dead or alive' (Baudrillard 1993b: 159). The constant creation of new football tournaments at continental and global level places greater pressure on the players' bodies and minds, while the various football institutions extract the maximum surplus value from these employees.

While the clubs impress upon their employees the necessity of obtaining results, the players find themselves facing the legal and physical consequences of faithfully applying these instructions (see Wickham 1992: 227). Combative football carries the risk of sanctions from match officials and the football authorities; bookings and red cards accumulate, leading to periods of suspension. The club may fine the player for his indiscretions without pausing to consider the irony; match bonuses evaporate while the replacement player secures the vacant first-team place. In more exceptional circumstances, the football authorities may penalize the player further, through additional fines, extended suspensions or a *sine die* ban. Tackles that result in serious injuries are increasingly likely to attract criminal and civil law suits against one or more players (Redhead 1986a; Evans 1989: 8). Conversely, the club's control over the player's body can put him at risk of injury and permanent physical impairment. Italian researchers found that boys who played football regularly were likely to have weaker reproductive powers after puberty, particularly in terms of lowered sperm counts. Most players at all levels are socialized into accepting that exposure to injury is integral to the game. Attempts to minimize these risks are said to contravene the masculine aesthetics of the sport, jeopardize the team cause, and must inevitably reflect badly on the individual's moral character (see Young et al. 1994). Some players are effectively instructed that their body is a weapon, for stopping opponents, winning possession or scoring goals. And, as Messner (1990: 211) points out, 'the body-as-weapon ultimately results in violence against one's own body'.

An aggressive, occupational psychology increases the likelihood of injuries. Being out of the game is the biggest single fear of the professional; sudden injuries highlight the physical fragility on which his career is built. Pickering's (1994: 158) suggestion that fifty players retire every year through injury is almost certainly an underestimate for England alone. During periods of recuperation, players encounter added dangers in the pressure to return to 'match fitness'. 'Pain-killing injections' allow players to complete matches, so proving beneficial to the club, but perhaps with serious long-term personal damage. During the early 1960s, Allan McGraw was a star striker for Morton in Scotland, but pre-match injections crippled him in perpetual agony before he was thirty. Marco van Basten played his last game in 1993 because of an ankle injury that the best medical treatment could not cure. He insisted afterwards that a surgeon had inflicted the greatest physical damage in the bid to get him match fit again. Routinely, football leaves players with chronic injuries that undermine their future mobility and quality of life. Bad tackles weaken leg joints from the knee below; knee cartilages are shredded by constant running and twisting; goal-keepers retire with gnarled hands and weakened ribs; brain injuries and senility result from heading footballs, particularly in wet conditions. Drugs like erythropoietin (EPO), creatine and even strychnine may be administered to the player to improve performance or to help with mental relaxation between games. Muscle development and bodily growth may be enhanced through a regular course of anabolic steroids, most famously in the case of the adolescent Zico. Yet here, again, 'dope tests' are used against the professional to re-establish the football authorities' corporeal control. Players convicted of substance abuse are banned for several years or find that their career goes into free-fall, for example, the French internationalists Patrick Guerin and Bernard Lama.

A final point here concerns body capital and its relationship to the footballing identity of players. The muscular-skeletal structure of players sees them stacked into playing positions on the basis of football's traditional, corporeal assumptions. The defensive centre of the team (goal-keeper and centre-backs) is typically dominated by players in the region of two metres tall. Full-backs require pace rather than height. Midfielders tend to require good body strength, to move around continuously and tussle for the ball. More exceptionally in recent years, the 'play-maker' may be a physically lighter player, who dances round tackles and passes the ball intelligently and accurately. Centre-forwards typically require an exceptional asset, such as power or accuracy in shooting, good height for winning the ball in the air, or speed across short distances to go past defenders. On the wings, players may be smaller and lighter, with pace again an important asset.

While these 'natural' body shapes may influence the physical possibilities of play, the 'cultural' contribution cannot be underestimated. Nations often differ over which physical build fits a particular position. Players may also transform their body shape, through adopting different training routines and pinpointing particular muscle areas for development. Critically, there is the question of how the player 'learns' his or her position from colleagues and coaches, and what skills are conscientiously shaped. The honing of this body capital can enhance the professional's off-field earnings. Live television sports contests (most especially football) have greatly increased the visibility of the body and the time spent by viewers and voyeurs in gazing at its specific qualities and blemishes (Kirk 1994: 174). Physically attractive players are recruited by fashion houses, businesses and the mass media to perform in modelling work, public relations exercises and light entertainment shows.

Nevertheless, football's popular culture continues to celebrate those players that do not conform to a stereotyped, highly athletic body shape. The little Scottish international Gordon Strachan, who masterminded the successes of Aberdeen, Manchester United and Leeds United throughout the 1980s and early 1990s, was regarded as a 'visionary' play-maker, but is partially blind in one eye. The gait of Stanley Matthews, with his slight build and knobbly knees, signified a physical vulnerability which, coupled to his exquisite skills, endeared him to a national audience (Mason 1989b: 15). The great Austrian player of the interwar period, Mathias Sindelar, was known as *der Papierene*, for his remarkably flimsy frame. Most famously, the brilliant Brazilian winger Garrincha dazzled opposing defenders despite a childhood bout of polio that had left him with a twisted right leg. The mythology that evolves around these great players, of innate talent that triumphs determinedly over physical infirmity, certainly belongs to the realm of the heroic. It also signifies to the football fan the very ordinariness of these players, and that he himself, with his equally incongruous body shape, may have been able to join this pantheon. These 'deviant' bodies provide irrefutable proof that no matter how hard the club may try, the exceptional skills of football cannot be instructed by rote.

Missing Strikers: football and industrial conflict

The bodily subjugation of professional players reflects their long history of industrial weakness. Individual players rarely succeed in defending their interests against employers. Disputes within clubs commonly arise, but are usually resolved by 'dropping' or 'disciplining' the player, or selling him to another club. Players may see the demise of a manager that has 'lost the dressing-room', but the directors may reinforce order by appointing a disciplinarian as successor.

Collectively, professionals do have the option of withdrawing their labour through an industrial strike. English players were pondering this strategy as early as 1909, with the redoubtable Billy Meredith a key protagonist in the dispute (Birley 1995a: 39). Since then, strikes have been considered with a surprising infrequency given the players' irreplaceable industrial skills and high level of public sympathy. The most recent strike threat from the Professional Footballers' Association (PFA) won its members their desired share from future television deals from 1992 onwards. Strike action certainly threatens the football and sports authorities with loss of gate money, but it also stems income from television and gambling taxes. In March 1996 a one-week strike by Italian players saw the loss of £33 million in pools revenues to the state-run Italian Olympic Committee.

The aversion of professional players to syndicalist action might be explained by their internal divisions. The English PFA represents elite players in the top division and far more who struggle to earn a living at the lower end. Little changed for this latter group when the 'maximum wage' was abolished and greater 'freedom-of-contract' arrived (Polley 1998: 116–17). Autobiographies of 'journeyman' players testify to the financial, physical and emotional insecurities that they continue to experience.[2] Elite and average professional players may unite within the union, but they are employed by clubs with incommensurable economic interests. Top clubs endeavour to monopolize football income (much of this going on higher salaries); small clubs seek to survive (and pay their players some wages) by maintaining a share of television fees, pools money and other revenues. The division may be ameliorated by the PFA winning more power within the FA and Football League, or securing better pension schemes for members. A protracted struggle with the employers saw the PFA win better accident insurance for its members during the mid-1960s (Dabscheck 1979: 236–7). But, there is little chance of it securing strike action by elite players to save a debt-ridden club at the foot of the league.

While the English PFA has made some advances for members, its Scottish equivalent has failed to attract sufficient membership interest from players (Morgan 1996). Not only is the economic 'pie' in Scottish football far smaller than its southern equivalent, the financial differences between the top clubs (and players) and the rest are far starker. Old Firm players do sometimes participate in testimonial matches for lower-league players; but they would far rather set up private pension plans than have their investment diluted within a national player fund.

At the more global level, football recapitulates the fundamental differences in labour relations between the West and the developing world. Strikes during the 1940s and 1950s rocked football in Argentina and Uruguay, triggering the migration to Europe of leading players such as Di Stefano, and the creation of the Di Mayor rebel league in Colombia.[3] In Argentina, players struck in 1997 after the Argentinian Football Association (AFA) had extended the season beyond the duration of many contracts. Presidential intervention brought a speedy resolution as it had done to a previous dispute in 1931 (Mason 1995b: 76). Elsewhere, in contractual matters, the clubs effectively own the players. Brazil's tortured history of slave trading and feudal servitude is replicated within professional football. Young players wishing to carve a career in professional football must give up their *passe* (labour market pass) to the club, effectively removing all their wage bargaining and transfer rights until they reach thirty years of age and again become free agents. Players who challenge the *passe* system are shunned by other clubs and ignored when selecting the national team. The *passe* provides players with few financial securities during difficult times. Those failing to play to the expected standard or suffering debilitating injuries have their *passe* returned by the club, and are thus discarded as exhausted labour power.

Given this scale of player inequalities that are found within each nation and between different societies, it is understandable that the new world professional players' union has failed to make much headway. It may have contributed towards a positive resolution of the Bosman case in Europe (discussed later). But it has been unable to establish a set of universal rights regarding working conditions and labour relations, in the same way that FIFA, for example, has belatedly standardized the safety facilities at grounds. The union has certainly failed to follow other sports like tennis or golf, in seizing the initiative for professionals within the sport.

True Professionals: the occupational subculture of players

While their class consciousness is notably limited, players do share sufficient commonalities for them to constitute an 'occupational sports subculture'. First team players are usually aged from their late teens to early thirties. A strong and active heterosexual culture prevails: players are either single men regularly in contact with single women, or 'family men' with dutiful and attractive wives. Since the 1960s, leading professionals have acquired a 'leisure class' status, characterized by high disposable income, plenty of free time and a penchant for conspicuous consumption (see Kerr et al. 1973; Veblen 1925). In the UK, professional players have common occupational routines, rising for training in the morning, having the afternoon free for recreational sport and leisure, then socializing more widely at night (though still within a particular network of relationships). The highly competitive, often violent ethos of professional football is accepted as 'part of the game'. Friendships and senses of empathy exist among players at different clubs, but when the match starts, such sentiments 'go out the window' for the 'true professional'.[4] Some deviation is tolerated, but players who do not 'fit in' with the dressing-room banter are socially marginalized. Players tend to have the same limited educational background, conservative social values, and codes of communication that are 'restricted' in meaning to fellow professionals (such as in their shared sense of humour). UK players employ a limited repertoire of dead metaphors and clichés during media interviews, reinforcing the occupational subculture while curtailing public understanding of it. Moreover, the subculture is reproduced across time and space. Players experience common career patterns and share similar professional goals. They regularly move between clubs, and find that managers constantly seek to inculcate camaraderie within the team.

The creation of the modern occupational sub-culture contains within it an ironic tension for the club. Fostering a collective *esprit de corps* can establish discipline, but may undermine the individuality of players and their ability to react to unplanned events on and off the pitch. This paradox throws particular attention on the process of player recruitment, and how it relates to wider cultural values about player individuality and identity.

Until the 1970s, most top clubs used a fairly traditional system of information-gathering for recruiting young players. An informal scouting network monitored the progress of young players at youth and junior levels. Famous clubs still expect schoolboys to join upon invitation; signatures might be sweetened by giving the parents some household furniture or a car. In the UK, this traditional arrangement was modernized by the gradual emancipation of players in the 1960s and the foundation of the national and international transfer markets. Wealthier clubs negated the lottery aspect of youth recruitment by buying up the talent available at poorer clubs. Players recruited through the youth ranks would struggle to displace the purchased talent or find some other career outwith football for which they were ill prepared.

European clubs gradually modernized their youth recruitment. The Dutch club Ajax have been at the vanguard, winning three consecutive European Cups in the early 1970s with a pool of players hand picked in their childhood and crafted to professional excellence. Ajax's clinical evaluation of child players now involves an annual testing session of several thousand boys from across Holland by the club's youth coaches. Only a handful are asked to return. The Ajax success has continued with victory in the 1995 European Champions' Cup and defeat in the final a year later.

The Ajax system looks like an economical *fait accompli*. Dutch football finances cannot match the salaries offered by leading European clubs. Importantly, however, the Ajax system succeeds because it benefits from the Dutch educational system, which produces rounded and polyglot young citizens receptive to other cultures. Internazionale of Milan have extended Ajax's highly modern approach. Forty 'Inter Camps' have been founded across Italy, through which the club can organize and monitor the football skills of 6,000 boys aged twelve and under. The process lasts a maximum of twelve years for the best few players who are signed by Inter professionally. The scheme costs around £1 million annually, over half of it coming from kit sponsors (*Sunday Telegraph*, 2 February 1997). Like the Ajax system, the key to Inter's scheme lies in its harmonization with indigenous cultural values. Inter claim to preach a trinity of virtues: schooling, family life and club success, in that order of importance. Wealth and prestige otherwise guarantee Inter a healthy position in the player market. But the team's long-term fabric requires player continuity and commitment. There are signs that UK clubs are following suit by establishing formal relationships with local schools for educating promising young players.

Inter's foresight is vindicated by football history. The old modernist strategy, of using basic wealth to recruit players, has regularly been shown to be insufficient for cultivating a winning team. Modernist coaching techniques presume that the club is responsible only for teaching the player football skills, thus tolerating his personal failure in elementary social skills. Conversely, the more post-modern coaching techniques of Ajax (latterly) and Inter adopt a holistic educational strategy, cultivating a more rounded and cerebral individuality within each player. They also produce results and are highly cost-effective. For example, in 1997, the multi-million pound Glasgow Rangers team were easily beaten by the part-time Swedish side Gothenburg in the Champions' Cup pre-qualifying round. Afterwards, the leading Swedish coach, Peter Keeling, argued that British clubs still were readily seduced into signing expensive players for their image rather than their team utility, retarding their social development with pernicious effects on the park:

> Because players in Sweden are only part-time, they are well aware of what goes on in the world outside football. They are used to making decisions for themselves in their everyday life and they take that into their football. Players in Britain are cosseted. At some clubs they don't even have to bother looking after their own passports. When they finish at 32 and 33 they may have plenty of experience of night clubs but no real experience of the outside world.
>
> (*Independent*, 29 August 1997)

A post-modern, holistic educational strategy prepares players for life outside of football. Research undertaken by Lüschen (1984; and Rütter 1991) confirms the utility of this strategy. Lüschen examined the 'status crystallization' of sports athletes as a way of measuring their failure to generate balanced social identities. Status crystallization (also known as 'status congruence' or 'consistency') refers to the relative social prestige of individuals across a number of status pursuits, such as education, income, occupation, sports activities, community participation and voluntary associations. Lüschen found that status crystallization was inversely proportional to the level of sports achievement. Those with poor status crystallization in other areas of social life tended to immerse themselves in sports like football as a form of compensation. Athletes at the peak of their careers (aged 27 to 32) had the lowest levels of status congruence in other areas of social life like education or community involvement. The imbalance points to the fact that modernist coaching techniques store up problems not only on and off the park. Severe psycho-social problems are encountered by players when they are forced out of football, either through injury, contract termination or retirement. [5]

To summarize, we may note that the occupational subculture of players emerges from their common industrial, social and cultural characteristics. The recruitment and educational practices of clubs contribute towards this occupational subculture. Traditionally, most UK clubs mixed the recruitment of youth players with buying older players from other clubs. The latter approach increased in importance as the modern transfer market came into place. Modern UK clubs viewed their employees exclusively as footballers, ignoring the other educational needs of these young men, in contrast to some continental clubs. More post-modern, holistic educational techniques have proved successful in gaining results and helping players prepare for life outside football. Towards the end of this chapter I elaborate this issue by examing the twilight of players' careers. Before doing so, we need to assess two possible buffers which may protect players from the downside of retirement. The first relates to the changing cultural status of professionals; the second concerns the new legal and financial freedoms that top players now enjoy.

From Heroes to Stars: football players and modern consumer culture

Undoubtedly, the financial position of the best British football players changed dramatically during the 1960s. In England, the maximum wage had been £20 a week in the early 1960s; by its close, its star player George Best was turning down £250,000 in advertising work (Wagg 1984: 143). The real debate lies in what structural factors underlay these transformations. Leftist sociologists like Critcher (1979) and Taylor (1970, 1971) have pointed towards the effects of the economic emancipation of players, ushered in by the Eastham case that ended the maximum wage for English professionals in 1963 (Evans 1989: 9). Large transfer fees and salaries promoted greater mobility, dislocating players from their local, working-class contexts. Famously, players like Stanley Matthews had sustained a close social and symbolic attachment to their working class audience, personifying the virtues of the craftsman and the artisan (see Hopcraft 1988: 28–30; Mason 1989b: 15). Higher income catapulted players into uncharted territory. The process was exaggerated by the migrant superstars of each generation: from Aberdeen to Huddersfield to Manchester to Turin (Denis Law); from Scunthorpe to Liverpool to Hamburg (Kevin Keegan); from Gateshead to London to Rome to Glasgow (Paul Gascoigne). Critcher (1979: 167–8) argues that one side-effect of this new stardom was a rise in gamesmanship, dissent and flagrant rule-breaking.

In some contrast, historians have argued that the changes in players' fortunes (economic and social) have been primarily quantitative rather than qualitative (Walvin 1994; Vamplew 1988). Before the First World War, top footballers were supplementing their wages by endorsing products and having press articles ghost written. As the UK's post-war austerity came to an end with the consumer culture of the 1960s, so the players' sign value (in sterling and status) multiplied constantly. In 1951 Stanley Matthews received around £1,000 per year in boot sponsorship (Walvin 1994: 177). In 1996 the injury-ravaged Diego Maradona signed a $7.2 million deal with Puma to use their footwear for two years. A year later, David Beckham signed a £7 million boot deal. Even the claim that the game became 'dirtier' in the 1960s is questioned. Walvin (1994: 136) observes that, as early as the 1930s, the emergence of 'an unwelcome sense of gamesmanship' was explained according to the new sense of 'professional determination' among players.

Certainly, player sponsorship and advertising are not entirely new. However, the kind of relationship that exists between players and their audiences remains to be explained. Players like Matthews had a far different public persona from Gascoigne or Maradona. Matthews may have been a working-class 'hero', but Law, Best, Gascoigne and Beckham are international media 'stars'. This transformation must be located within a wider cultural context. Featherstone (1995), for example, notes how the social role and perceived attributes of famous people have changed over the century. Traditionally, *heroes* embodied eternal qualities and extraordinary goals; 'the quest for virtue, glory and fame, which contrasts with the lesser everyday pursuit of wealth, property and earthly love' (1995: 58–9). Here, the heroic is intrinsic, a part of the individual's moral character, and thus acquired through fate. The greatest football heroes include the graceful 'natural players', such as Puskás and Di Stéfano; or the honest and glorious leaders, such as Charles and Blanchflower.

Heroic players personified the values of the milieu in which they excelled. In Edwardian times, 'the players were local heroes representing the local community against all comers'; they were 'essentially decent, steady, long-lasting and respectable, ordinary men with one extraordinary talent' (Mason 1996: 84). Lanfranchi and Wahl (1996), for example, discuss two heroic post-war French footballers, Raymond Kopa and Rachid Mekloufi, who represented the wider social values of their times. During the 1950s, Kopa symbolized social mobility, integration of immigrants, social harmony with a hint of rebelliousness; a little later, Mekloufi became a symbol of Algerian nationalism and international sportsmanship.

Inglis (1977) points up the traditional sporting heroes' relationship to the ageing process, arguing that they retained their dignity as men upon retirement. True heroes are vulnerable to defeat in battle; nature too impacts upon their powers. When thus challenged, the hero must be allowed to depart the stage and reclaim his privacy, as someone who 'will not simply feed on his past' (1997: 89). Within this romantic mythology, the adventure and pursuit of glory can end in a Wagnerian disaster that still serves to augment the hero's status through a virtuous circularity. Premature deaths 'stimulate the creation of myths and legends by future generations, elevating the deceased to the rank of immortal and unimpeachable heroes' (Horak and Maderthaner 1996: 152). In football, thoughts turn here to those brave talents cut short in their prime, to be sustained in memory and valediction. The list of air disasters takes a heavy toll on footballing heroes: Valentino Mazzola and the Torino team killed in 1949; Duncan Edwards and the Manchester United players killed at Munich in 1958; the Alianza Lima team killed in 1987; and the Zambian national team that perished in 1993.

In contrast, the more modern variant of *celebrity* status is extrinsic, being located in personality (not character), and in the practising and honing of an attractive and colourful self before the evaluative gaze of others. The role of the media in promoting stardom and celebrity status is critical and reciprocal; for the biggest medium of all, 'Personalities are central to the institution of television' (Lusted 1991: 251). In an early paper, Critcher (1971: 117) sensed the transformation taking place in British football culture through the inevitable medium, George Best. An hour-long television documentary on Best devoted a mere three minutes to his sublime talent. 'The attempt was to transform a hero into a celebrity: the legitimacy was no longer that of unique human achievement, but of stereotyped lifestyle.' At the same time, Chelsea emerged as the first 'glamour' club in West London, supported by showbiz celebrities and fashioned by the nearby King's Road (Taylor and Ward 1995: 176–87).

Football celebrities have joined the young stars in other culture industries, notably television or popular music. As C. Wright Mills remarked of American sports and Hollywood personalities in the mid-1950s: 'All the stars of any other sphere of endeavour are drawn toward the new star and he toward them ... to populate the world of the celebrity' (Mills 1956: 74). The creative productivity of these *declassé* entertainers is commodified and repackaged as a fantastic cultural asset for purchase by any consumer (see Tolleneer 1986). Advertising and popular media present their lifestyles as 'glamorous'. Consumers receive paradoxical messages; young superstars are both ordinary yet exceptional, accessible yet distant, down-to-earth yet colourful. They enjoy public adulation and rewards that are both attainable ('He came from nowhere', 'He's an ordinary lad') yet intangible ('Never in his wildest dreams did he think') (Featherstone 1991a). These subtle, contradictory messages broaden the star's public appeal. The cultural illusion is fostered that, one day, the 'ordinary but special' individual consumer may realize his or her unique qualities, and join the ever-changing pantheon of celebrities. Sport has a particularly potent role to play within this ideological formation. It is presented as intrinsically fair and meritocratic, where talent and dedication make such stardom appear far more attainable than in other avenues of social mobility where class inequalities are known to count (Ehrenberg 1991).

Unlike the eternal and fateful attributes of heroes, celebrities live in danger of having other aspects of their persona exposed as mundane or ordinary. The problem for the image-making industries is that football stardom is also a precarious and elusive resource. Players are liable to lose that 'star quality' on the park, by going off-form or incurring long-term injuries. Some may fail to qualify or win selection for major international tournaments that are watched by the largest audiences. Off the field, players must also strike a careful balance between the charismatic and morally upright. Their private lives are monitored incessantly by the mass media. Reports of excessive behaviour, such as drinking, fighting or sex, can tarnish their market relations with the 'family audience'. Conversely, if players fail to appear regularly in the 'nightlife' pages of tabloids and magazines, they may acquire a 'boring' public persona, vitiating the sale of endorsed products.

A central problem here concerns the opposing loyalties of the football star and the journalist writing about him. Both share an underlying materialistic commitment to sustaining public interest in their sport. They must establish a mutual rapport to cement their professional standings. The player has a problem with management, agents, sponsors and fans, if he struggles to communicate through the medium that reaches his markets. The journalist has a problem if he cannot reach the primary sources that are available to rival media. The common bond that subsequently develops between player and journalist may become quite strong within the private realm, as they mix in nightclubs, casinos, private parties, golf clubs and holiday retreats. Yet questions of trust bedevil their relationships. The journalist must win and retain the trust of his source, without being seen as excessively sympathetic by readers or employers. The player must remain wary that the journalist may prioritize the interests of readers or employers, and so present him in a bad light (Bourgeois 1995: 197). This watchfulness is premised on the knowledge that for tabloid journalists 'the best downmarket story is a negative story about a star performer' (Tunstall 1996: 188).

The creation and marketing of a certain public identity can be clearly at odds with the self-conscious, private identity that the famous individual may seek to preserve (Chaney 1993: 143–4). Modern football players may film commercials or endorse products that unrealistically emphasize a single personal dimension (such as their 'tough', 'zany' or 'honest' qualities), only to be roundly stigmatized for any public deviation from this role. Additionally, players recognize that their celebrity status may emerge through the caprice of reporters and media people or via unforgettable moments of footballing disaster. No one actively pursues a pathetic role as the player forever associated with a decisive own goal, a missed vital penalty, or a goal-keeping blunder. Yet these lapses establish a deviant identity for the player which more than negates the positive, professional self that he may have spent many years in constructing (Schmitt and Leonard 1986: 1097–8).

Nevertheless, the expanding sports media may afford future employment and security to modern players. Media bosses are attracted to ex-players for the simple reason that, 'Celebrity represents. Fame lends authority' (Inglis 1995: 2).[6] The famed exploits and 'inside knowledge' of former players buttress their arguments (see Hargreaves 1986: 145). Occasionally, the difference between footballing and discursive skills are too severe. Players may possess an intuitive 'practical consciousness' to perform on the park; after matches, they can struggle to match this through a 'discursive consciousness' of eloquent words (see Giddens 1984: 41–5).

There are signs of a post-modern turn within this social construction of the player *qua* celebrity. Post-modernity enables actors to be more reflexive about the pitfalls and risks of modernity. Clubs, players, mass media and fans may adopt new strategies to counteract the deleterious aspects of modern football. Many clubs put their young players through short educational courses on how to present themselves effectively and without controversy in their media dealings. The club management may fight hard to shield these protégés from premature public scrutiny (for example, Alex Ferguson's 'minding' of Ryan Giggs at Manchester United, or Jorge Valdano's protection of Raul at Real Madrid). The tumultuous careers of George Best, Tanju Çolak, Diego Maradona and others represent reference points for the club's management when it takes the role of 'moral entrepreneur'. These players are depicted as 'wild men' or 'bad boys', self-destructive and liable to bring shame upon family and friends (see Wagg 1984: 144). The personal stress which results may push the player into a more rapid process of decline, as witnessed by Maradona's drug addiction, Best's alcoholism and Çolak's imprisonment in Turkey for auto theft (see Blake 1996: 153).

Alternatively, some deviants who offend the sanctimonious face of authority have always been tolerated or quietly admired by working-class fans (Hargreaves 1986: 147). There are signs that the mass media have come to acknowledge this popularity by adopting a less pious and condemnatory stance towards 'controversial' players like Paul Gascoigne, Eric Cantona and Vinnie Jones. In Argentina, Maradona's complex and reversible treatment in the national press is explained by popular beliefs regarding the qualities of star players: that they must possess *aguante*, a kind of endurance of spirit or a capacity to survive, traditionally expressed through the debilitating working-class vices of drink, sex, gambling, turbulent social relationships and latterly drug abuse. While fuelling a whole industry of media comment throughout his career, Maradona is still able to do all the media and public relations work that he wants (see Burns 1996; Archetti 1997a).

Football's post-modern 'retro' culture allows players to continue reproducing their great moments in the game, long after they are physically able to play professionally. The more famous players keep themselves in shape, remaining available for 'replays' of classic fixtures that were originally played years earlier.[7] High attendances are never likely, although sponsors and television can show interest. Unlike golf's senior players, whose declining powers are camouflaged by technological advances in equipment, footballers cannot disguise the loss of pace, touch, stamina and balance. More regularly, footballers live on in retro culture through the eternal images of their excellence, in photographs and films. To fill the gaps in enlarged television schedules, a wealth of football memorabilia is regularly mined from broadcasting archives and screened again, so that these forgotten talents may recapture their moments of past glory. Yet these nostalgic encounters also serve to darken the lustre of early stars. The original spatial and ideological distances between supporter on the terraces and player on the turf are reduced. The ageing process alone confirms a common bond between the two. Identical moments in football are recalled; first experienced from different standpoints but remembered with more equal sentimentality in the shared position of aged television viewer.

Finally, a fourth strategy becomes available to top players on their retirement: the 'disappearance' of the media-created celebrity. In the past, this sink into obscurity had all kinds of negative financial and social status connotations. The *Bosman* case now enables the very best European players to enjoy the financial protection that truly prepares them for life outside football, without the need for spin-off media work.

The Post-Modern Era of Player Mobility: the Bosman case and beyond

In December 1995, the European transfer system was revolutionized when the European Court of Justice supported Jean-Marc Bosman's case against the Belgian FA.[8] The exact background to the case is complex, although it subsequently gave rise to a simple civil action over Bosman's freedom of movement as a European worker. Bosman had been a mediocre player employed by the Belgian first division side RC Liège, his contract expiring in June 1990. He was offered a new contract at the minimum rate permitted by the Belgian FA, effectively reducing his salary by 75 per cent. He refused and contacted US Dunkerque, a French Second Division club, who then agreed the framework for a loan or transfer deal with Bosman and RC Liège. However, Liège became suspicious about Dunkerque's financial position, cancelled the arrangement and suspended the player. In response, Bosman turned to the courts, demanding monthly payments from Liège and the removal of his transfer price-tag while he sought a new club. The Belgian courts referred his case to the European Courts, setting in motion the legal endgame for the European transfer system.

Bosman submitted that European transfer regulations contravened Article

48 of the Treaty of Rome which secured the freedom of movement of all EU workers against any discrimination based on nationality. The court ruled in his favour.[9] It also backed his contention that UEFA's '3+2 rule' on foreign players was illegal.[10] UEFA had no option but to scrap the '3+2 rule' and all existing regulations on the international transfer of European Union players who were out-of-contract. *Bosman*'s free-market principles were soon applied to player transfers *within* EU nations. Indeed, some football associations had been working within this framework for a long period of time.[11]

Bosman has had three essential impacts. First, the mobility of players has increased immensely, especially on a European scale. Most top European clubs have several foreign stars on their books. New patterns of labour migration have emerged; for example, Italian players now leave Italy for clubs in the UK, France and Spain. Second, the balance of power within European football has tilted increasingly towards the richest clubs who have unfettered access to the best professional labour. Third, the income of top players has increased greatly, although huge gulfs in wages still exist between players in the top European divisions.[12] Clubs signing players through *Bosman* are willing to sacrifice some of their booming off-field earnings for higher signing fees and salaries. By the late 1990s, the best players at top clubs were typically on an annual income of over £1 million. Economists and legal analysts have suggested two solutions to spiralling player wages (Campbell and Sloane 1997). First, a 'salary cap', as found in some sports in the United States and Australia would put a basic ceiling on player earnings. Second, more equal gate sharing would spread match income between clubs, reducing differences in bargaining power and so depressing inflationary pressures in wage negotiation. However, neither measure would be favoured by the more powerful clubs who thrive on economic inequalities. Moreover, if either measure was introduced in some European nations, additional problems would follow. The best players would still maximize their rewards by moving to clubs in the freer markets.

Locally, the exact economic impact of *Bosman* has been difficult to calculate. Most clubs have become anxious about evaluating the real worth of contracted players since large slices of this human capital may disappear without recompense. Some clubs such as Tottenham Hotspur have included players as assets in their annual financial statements. A major problem here is that, whereas accounting procedure relies on objectivity and verifiability, player valuations rely upon subjective estimates (Morrow 1992: 19). Another incalculable aspect of 'free agentry' concerns its impact on supporter attendance. Free agentry is more established in American baseball; economists have estimated that the loss of an average player costs the ball club around 4–5 per cent of total attendances, and $500,000 annually. New players can attract followings of their own, help teams to win games and draw in fans. Nevertheless, researchers maintain that if the 'roster' or squad of players remains stable throughout the season, average attendances can rise by up to 20 per cent (*Washington Post*, 6 January 1997).

To combat the free market, long-term contracts may be employed to tie the player to the club (Simmons 1997: 17). These arrangements guarantee profes-sionals their high wages against loss of form or injury, and entitle the club to a fee in the event of sale. In Spain, several clubs have handcuffed their human assets by inserting huge 'buyout clauses' into lucrative contracts.[13] Neverthe-less, between nations there are serious inequalities regarding the impact of *Bosman*. Most clubs expect that *Bosman* will simply emphasize the importance of the transfer market over home-grown players, although its 'post-modern' aspect here is felt in the new internationalization of transfers. For the top clubs, it provides an opportunity for 'flexible accumulation', by hiring players for one or two years to do specific jobs without the need to offer long-term security (see Harvey 1989). Accordingly, top Italian clubs such as AC Milan and Juventus have scrapped their youth teams. Conversely, nations with a strong history of home-grown domestic talent have struggled. France and Spain considered them-selves to be among the worst affected in the post-*Bosman* era. Top Spanish clubs have started hiring foreign stars rather than grooming their own. Smaller clubs like Sporting Gijon, Athletic Bilbao, Nantes and Metz had profited in the past by refining young talent for sale to larger clubs, but *Bosman* terminated that lifeline.[14] To alleviate this difficulty, French clubs may continue to expand their rich heritage of hiring foreign players from Eastern Europe or former colonies (see Guttmann 1994: 52). In Spain, the problem is complicated by the large number of *canarinhos* (Brazilians) and other South Americans recruited by clubs like Deportivo La Coruña. These 'foreigners' acquire dual nationality after two years in Spain, and no longer count in calculations aimed at limiting the number of non-EU players in each team. All of these pressures militate against the retention of local youth training programmes and reduce the range of choices available to the national team manager.

Nevertheless, we may identify some positive, deeper features of *Bosman* that fit with the holistic coaching and recruiting techniques of clubs. The players' legal freedoms are worthless if they cannot adjust to unfamiliar sur-roundings. A holistic learning process encourages this adaptability to change. From the national team's point of view, mobile players are able to assimilate more knowledge of technical skills and playing styles. Players from small Scandinavian nations like Sweden and Denmark are groomed to play abroad, bringing that cosmopolitanism to full benefit with the international team (see Andersson and Radmann 1998). From the club's point of view, the best strat-egy is to hire 'essential' players on long-term contracts, while regularly releas-ing the less-valued players into the open market.

At the End of Play: stardom or a return to obscurity?

The economic and cultural advances won by professional players represent a long revolution. During professional football's long, 'early modern' period, players may have been paid for their labour, but their feudal relationship to the club was inescapable. This situation still obtains in many advanced football nations in the developing world, particularly Brazil, with reforms being staunchly resisted by domestic football authorities. In the UK, top players supplemented their controlled income through product endorsement, but their status as local or national 'heroes' meant that they tended to fall back into obscurity after retirement. The fully 'modern' age for football players was signalled in the 1960s by the abolition of the maximum wage; greater freedom of transfer gradually emerged. Top professionals became dislocated from their natural environment; they acquired an international celebrity status as 'stars' of the wider entertainment industry, with the new mass media and surrounding consumer culture adding to their lustre. Post-retirement careers opened up within the media and in public relations activities. The 'post-modern' era for players is signalled by the *Bosman* case, the free-market benefits of higher income and the potential for international mobility, and the growing awareness that football celebrity has its own pitfalls.

These advances by players have been earned in spite of a collective reluctance to flex their industrial muscles. Strikes are relatively rare, although industrial action is highly expensive to the sports industry as a whole. Players certainly represent an occupational sub-culture, but it is one that tends to be defined by club interests. A critical sociological perspective highlights how clubs retain control over their labour power, emphasizing performance to the extent of jeopardizing the player's body capital, through match suspensions or injury. Moreover, 'modern' recruitment and coaching practices do little to nurture the social skills of players or soften the blow of retirement. European clubs have shown the way in terms of more holistic approaches towards player recruitment and education.

I will conclude here by making some points on the nature of the post-football phase for players. No matter how professional the club is in preparing players for that moment, the actual experience of retirement can be akin to a form of public death. Hanging up the boots may grant the privacy and mental relaxation that the player had earlier craved. More commonly, it ushers in the end of an institutionalized camaraderie with team-mates, and the shattering of a public looking-glass self in which he had become so positively familiar (see Gearing 1997). For the majority, the gilded option of moving into management, coaching or media work is not available. Even if it was, the existential sensations of playing would no longer be there. The novelist and football writer Brian Glanville (1976: 21) captures the despair of retirement through one of his fictional players.

> While I walk and jog along and run, I play through matches; I'm at Wembley again, in Rome and Liverpool and Budapest. There's no substitute for playing; don't let anybody fool you. Once you've been as good as I am, once you've got the taste for success, you never lose it. The day I packed up I cried; I mean it. Sat there in the dressing-room and blubbered like a baby.

This public 'death' of the retired player is given added piquancy by the sense of loss that spectators feel. Football supporters pass on their personalized memories to younger peers, famously slipping into nostalgia as the past becomes romanticized before the mundaneness of the present. The subjects of such mythologies meanwhile slide into public obscurity. Often, the announcement of the death of leading former players leads to a fuller reassessment of the collective memory that must immortalize glorious careers. In some instances, the sentiments of loss also harbour feelings of guilt and complicity. The once adulatory public may realize the failure to recompense their memories through finance and affection during the rest of their heroes' lives.

In England, the death of Bobby Moore brought with it some astonishment that a truly heroic figure who had delivered the 1966 World Cup could flirt with insolvency and a mediocre celebrity role to which he was not suited (*The Observer*, 26 February 1993). A more palpable lamentation followed the death of Garrincha, the heroic, crippled figure, a product of Rio's *favelas* and factories, and the dribbling mestizo fulcrum of Brazil's World Cup winning teams of 1958 and 1962 (Leite Lopes and Maresca 1987; Leite Lopes 1997). The 'third age' of retirement saw Garrincha fall headlong into a fatal alcoholism. Yet his death heralded a popular clamour for a final ceremony to celebrate his presence and memory. His body was taken to lie in state at his 'home', the Maracanã stadium, before being buried in his home town.

In death, therefore, the symbolic value of these heroes expands incalculably and enters the realm of mythology. The social meaning of the dead becomes problematic and open to renegotiation. Returning Garrincha to the Maracanã concludes the problem by converting him into a mythical symbol. It represents a way of reclaiming his memory for Brazil *qua* nation of football. More deeply, it also delivers him to Brazil *qua* religion of football, to the spiritual home of the national game, in preparation for leaving the earthly (as alcoholic former genius) to enter the eternal (as mythical national symbol). Hobbs (1993) writes similarly in his obituary to Bobby Moore, former idol of London's East End team, West Ham. Moore's retirement from football in the mid-1970s symbolized the death of the mythical old East End, reflected in the migration of its white working class. 'It meant that the 1960s were over, the docks were shut and nothing really belonged to us any more. So we all moved to Essex.' Only with the death of Moore does this process become fully reflexive, something that demands reflection and interpretation in mythological terms. Only now 'Bobby Moore' becomes part of a semiological system (the docks, the team, the streets, the local eccentrics, the playing style) that no longer has any material presence, save for its provocation of a seductive nostalgia.

It is increasingly unlikely that the greatest contemporary professionals will elicit this localized sense of loss when they die. Stardom, the transfer system and media involvement serve to uproot players, transforming them instead into international signifiers, sharing an occupational sub-culture with other transnational celebrities. At the national and international level, they will certainly be mourned. But, it will not be a lamentation for the heroic individual and the era that made him. Instead, the public will mourn the passing of a simulation, the end of a televisual life, as occurred on a rather more grandiose scale with the death of Princess Diana in August 1997.

7

The Goal of Winning? Football, Science, Tactics and Aesthetics

Beyond the Functional: football aesthetics

Having discussed the social and economic background of players, I seek in this chapter to consider the various historical and cultural aspects of football play. My first point is that academics have contributed relatively little to our understanding of football's playing styles and techniques. The sporting body has attracted much attention, but sociologists and anthropologists have rather ignored its tactical and aesthetic dimensions. Exceptionally, Norbert Elias employed a football metaphor to elaborate upon his 'process sociological' perspective. The unfolding match between team-mates and opponents illustrated the nature of all social life: the interdependency of human beings, and the 'flexible lattice-work of tensions' generated through their social bonds. Power flows fluidly between players jockeying for possession and moving between attack and defence (Elias 1978b: 130–1).

Perhaps Elias was too much of a sociological maverick for this metaphor to be explored more fully. Yet, for any sociologist, football does illustrate how the ontological tension between social action and structure is dramatized eternally. Players are locked into structured relationships which emphasize the collective over the individual: divided into teams, with their own division of labour (playing positions), and preprogrammed into maintaining this 'shape'. Even in receiving the ball, players pursue the collective interest and follow procedure, 'clearing the danger' in defence or passing to team-mates. Yet, in doing so, the 'actor' is required to select from a number of options – who exactly to pass to, at what speed or angle, and with what accompanying instructions. Occasionally breaking from his 'set position' may also benefit the team, but again the decision remains with how the player reads the game, and his willingness to shape its pattern. The agency aspect of play offers a theoretical antidote to the oppressive Marxist view discussed in chapter 6, that players'

actions are predetermined by coaches. Yet even its most individualistic exponents are caught up within the collective; their 'free' creativity should be
directed to help the team cause.

In football management, a similar interdependency exists between inspired
decision-making and strong social networks. The UK's most successful managers (Alex Ferguson, Bill Shankley, Matt Busby and Jock Stein) were reared
in the Scottish mining and ship-building heartlands, where a rich seam of
pragmatic, 'communitarian' values existed *avant la lettre*. The Calvinistic
culture dictated that individuals should exploit their talents, especially in sport,
to enlarge their constrictive horizons. Liverpool managers Bob Paisley and
Kenny Dalglish were raised in similar circumstances in Tyneside and Glasgow
respectively. The charismatic status of these football heroes may suggest that
their managerial masterstrokes were purely instinctive. But, their blending of
players or adaptation of playing styles was rooted in their early socialization,
when they had learned how specific characters respond to different treatment
and how particular personalities mix most effectively.

This balance of individual and collective, action and structure, suggests a
further sociological problem in explaining playing styles and techniques. On
one hand, the aesthetic perspective appreciates that football generates its own
panoply of actions, styles and productive creativity. On the other hand, the
more functional position views football culture as a straightforward reproduction of wider social relations. Here, I am at pains to tread a path between these
two positions. Football is certainly shaped by and within the broader society,
but it produces its own universe of power relations, meanings, discourses and
aesthetic styles (see Wren-Lewis and Clarke 1983). I am therefore at odds with
one strain of cultural studies that explains the popular culture of the lower
classes in terms of its functional necessity rather than its aesthetic content
(Willis 1990; Fiske 1992, 1993). (A similar problem is apparent in the work of
sociologists like Lash (1990) who in writing on post-modernity, privilege the
middle classes with an aesthetic sensibility that is intangible to other classes.)
This kind of critical functionalism identifies a latent connection between the
practising of popular culture and the material conditions of exploitation and
oppression. Watching a soap opera or playing in a rock band does not really
involve an exercising of critical distance, aesthetic appreciation or acquired
'taste'. Instead, the viewer or popular musician is merely 'grounding' culture
according to his or her 'objective' conditions. The problem with this perspective is its haughty tone and privileged epistemology. As Banck (1995) and
other anthropologists have argued, the cultural studies position reclines on the
indefensible assertion that (the) 'common people' are somehow incapable of
producing or appreciating an aesthetic within their cultural practices.[1] For
those of us who have grown up with football, the game is replete with aspects
of beauty and grace.

In examining football's technical and aesthetic development, we find that
body culture and social environment are closely related. Football skills emerge

from a 'bio-psycho-sociological complex of body techniques' (Loy et al. 1993: 72). Technique in this sense is based on the Maussian definition, that is, the array of 'traditionally efficacious acts' which are physiologically enabled, culturally defined and (re)produced through socialization. Similarly, football's aesthetic dimension is not ahistorically given, but instead derives its meaning from the wider socio-historical context. As Walter Pater noted in 1873, 'The aesthetic critic will remember always that, beauty exists in many forms. To him all periods, types, schools of taste, are in themselves equal. The question he asks is always: in whom did the stir, the genius, the sentiment of the period find itself?' (quoted in Lambourne 1996: 12). Sociologically, we must add that the aesthetic will reflect the political struggles and ideological interests of dominant and subaltern social groups: young against old, scientists against artists, middle classes against working classes, the old world versus the new world. The aesthetics of football are both a medium of ideological control and a weapon for resisting such domination. In short, they are 'an eminently contradictory phenomenon' (Eagleton 1990: 3).

In this discussion, therefore, I begin with a historical study of football's aesthetic and tactical changes. In the process, I seek to periodize these changes into 'traditional', 'modern' and 'post-modern' phases. Some of the major problems underlying this historiography are explored, particularly those relating to team formation; individual stylistic developments are less problematic. Football's globalization ensured the rapid spread of tactical and aesthetic innovations, although it initially dramatized cultural differences. The final two sections discuss the impacts of other sports on football: first, in terms of football tactics; second, more organizationally, with regard to rule changes and the management of new technology. My overall intention is to generate debate among football academics, since playing techniques, styles and their aesthetic appreciation have been notably absent from scholarly work.

From 'Kick and Rush' to WM: the transformation of UK football style

Football's earliest playing styles reflected the game's middle-class imprimateur in favouring the rather entrepreneurial values of risky, individualistic attack. Until the 1880s, English football was predisposed aesthetically to the exhibition of each player's unique skill, notably by flamboyant dribblers who left the pack behind. As football became a working-class passion, the crowd's favour soon switched from middle-class pseudo-artistry to professionally earned victories (Walvin 1994: 74–5). A more successful, rationalized form of play – the 'passing game' – gained ascendancy, featuring a more advanced division of labour in which players were allocated spatial positions to perform their allotted tasks. Only gradually did this playing style influence football in England, where the more atavistic, 'kick and rush' approach predominated. The passing game did display a strong symmetry to the industrial experience of its Scottish, working-class proponents, but it was also enabled by the sudden popularity of football itself. More and more young players were learning the rudiments of ball control and passing, skills that were essential for the passing game to survive and become aesthetically meaningful. Hence, this 'traditional' period established a trinity of tactical and aesthetic virtues: teamwork, technical skills and final results.

The attacking manoeuvre remained football's principal tactical and aesthetic concern, although more prescient teams paid increasing attention to defence. Ayrshire football in Scotland had already established the four defenders and six attackers model by the 1880s.[2] In late Victorian England, the eight forwards were gradually reduced to seven then six, to bolster the defence and midfield. After the First World War, as the clubs sought again to increase attendances and thus profitability, attention turned to the apparently widening gap between attacking popular aesthetics and defensive pragmatism. To rectify the situation, club directors sought to alter football's playing structure, to 'spectacularize' the game. Specifically, the 'offside game' of defenders was held up as a major problem, although continental observers argued that only English forwards could not counteract it (Meisl 1955). In 1925, FIFA accepted English submissions and instituted the new rule; players were now offside if fewer than two opponents stood between them and the goal (previously it had been three opponents).

The rule change provided a new framework for team organization, coinciding with a global receptivity to tactical and stylistic diversity. Many football coaches, born in the UK but exiled abroad, had managed to win the favour of their host clubs and nations. Foreign tours and international fixtures allowed them to test their innovative playing systems. Meanwhile, in the UK, football club directors were gradually learning the benefits of devolving greater powers to team coaches.

In England, the new offside rule brought further defensive modifications. The centre half dropped back from midfield to become the 'stopper', a kind of third 'full-back'. The new 'pivot' robustly repelled attacks; the distance between attackers and defenders increased. No longer were teams beseeched to attack in sheer numbers, like soldiers pouring out from the trenches, in waves of five forwards and three half-backs. Instead, as the attackers stayed upfield, so the full-backs patrolled the defences.

The first genuine form of early modernization came from Herbert Chapman, who won five championships and two FA cups as Arsenal manager during the 1920s and 1930s. Chapman founded the 'WM' formation: three forwards and two attacking half-backs were buttressed by two defensive half-backs and a final line of three full-backs (including the 'stopper'). Chapman was football's arch-Fordist and first modern manager. 'In his view, every device used by the industrialist to speed up the production of goods could be used equally well to speed up the production of goals' (Davies 1992: 30). He established his managerial autonomy at the club, spent heavily in the transfer market and shaped his team to exploit the new laws. He fed off the extended publicity given over to managers in the popular press, skilfully marketing the club and its players to the general public (Holt 1989: 311).[3] A hallmark of Arsenal's playing style was their composure in defence, relaxed in the knowledge that their devastating counter-attack would probably win them the game. In this way, Chapman relied heavily upon the unsophistication of Arsenal's opponents, who felt obliged to attack in the old style, gallantly but recklessly.

In southern Europe, leading clubs under the tutelage of Danubian coaches developed similar responses to the rule change. During the 1930s, Spanish and Italian teams introduced three obdurate defenders, led by the destructive 'stopper'. The tense, replayed World Cup semi-final between the two national sides in 1934 provided the fullest illustration of this new tactical thinking on the park, Italy winning 1–0 after the first game had finished 1–1 (Lanfranchi 1995: 133). In Italy, this system became known as *il metodo* ('the method'). Differences with English play centred on the prevailing fascistic notion, that footballers were the nation's warriors without armour, that individual skill remained aesthetically and practically important (De Biasi and Lanfranchi 1997: 89). Some Italian clubs continued to play *sistemo*, keeping the 'centre-half' as a genuine midfield player (Meisl 1955: 27). The tactical debate continued until the early 1940s, when Fiorentina and Genoa borrowed the 'WM' system from England and *il metodo* won out. By that stage, football had established its own global 'ideoscape' for the circulation of tactical plans and aesthetic statements. Often, WM would be creolized to fit the local conditions. During the 1940s, it was significantly embellished by Russian tactical thinking. Iakushin, the coach of Moscow Dinamo, introduced greater flexibility to this 'bourgeois' system of play. He encouraged his five attacking players to change positions constantly during the game, and so unsettle opponents. The strategy was a notable success during the UK tour in November 1945, though it has left football analysts struggling to explain it tactically. Some argued that Iakushin anticipated the 4–2–4 formation later popularized by Brazil (Edelman 1993: 91); alternatively, I would suggest the great mobility of players presages the Dutch 'total football' model of the 1970s.

Post-war UK Decline and Modern Football Tactics

The major post-war tactical and aesthetic innovations came from outside the UK, reflecting its declining stock in world football. Under the tutelage of Karl Rappan, the Swiss side of the 1950s added a further, defensive variation to 'WM'. The resulting 'Swiss Bolt' system was exceptionally fluid and difficult to describe geometrically. Two central defenders (with one 'sweeping') were supported by attacking full-backs; two proto-midfielders controlled the centre while the two attackers were assisted by wingers. Players were never statically situated in three playing lines, but were instead to advance or retreat according to the game's flow, thus demanding high levels of tactical intelligence.

The Swiss Bolt's enduring influence was its creation of the 'sweeper', which the *catenaccio* system developed further. *Catenaccio* was founded by Helenio Herrera, initially at Barcelona, then with Internazionale throughout the 1960s, and dominated the technical and aesthetic principles of Italian football for over two decades.[4] Herrera's system was rooted in the ultra-professionalism of football's full modernity: discipline, concentration, regimental training, careful planning, and an astute use of possession. But it was also a hybrid form, exploring the aesthetic and technical capabilities of defensive players, demanding fuller use of their intellectual and creative capabilities. The *libero* ('free man') swept behind the defence, reading the play guilefully to spot and extinguish danger before it could spread. The first *libero* was Armando Picchi who played for Internazionale during the early 1960s (Wolstenholme 1992: 307–9). Its greatest exponent was perhaps the late Gaetano Scirea of Juventus and Italy. However, one should avoid overlooking the *libero*'s colleagues in defence, the 'man-markers' employed to stop strikers by tracking them all over the pitch. These defenders read the play of their opponents, knew how to psyche them out of games, and were highly judicious in timing and weighting their tackles. *Catenaccio*'s emergence reflected the growth of football's commerce and status during the 1960s, in which anxiety about defeat had supplanted the old aesthetic reference to attack. The early post-war flood of goals was reduced to a trickle. More broadly, *catenaccio* actuated the cultural politics of the Cold War, the phoney war of attrition, with bluff-calling and nerveless deception played out before huge defensive stockpiles.

Two other playing strategies were advanced with notable success during the 1950s and 1960s. The first was the adventurous 4–2–4 system made famous by Brazil's 1958 World Cup winning side. This style symbolized the survival of football's aesthetic commitment to attack and goal-scoring within the modern age. Although its pragmatism should not be underestimated, given the illustrious forwards who were at its spearhead, this attacking Brazilian style is still looked upon throughout the world as the purest and most pleasing form of football as the game's own specimen of 'high modernity'. Although the Brazilians gradually accommodated one forward in midfield, the attacking fluency remained. Its zenith came at the 1970 World Cup in Mexico with the 4–1 dismantling of Italy in the final. Significantly, colour television coverage brought, for the first time, the full spectacle to millions of television viewers in Europe and the Americas, with the game's first global superstar, Pelé, at its epicentre. Constant television replays of the Brazilian triumph provide a crucial referent for the mythologizing of football's ultimate team.

The second playing strategy was the 4–3–3, 'Wingless Wonders' system devised by Alf Ramsey as manager of England's 1966 World Cup side. Ramsey's study in Anglo-Saxon empiricism dispensed with individualistic players in preference for the 'sweat and versatility' of midfield workers (Critcher

1994: 83). His philosophy resembled the equally scientistic, ill-fated rhetoric of Harold Wilson on the 'white heat' technology that would save the nation's economy. Although Ramsey's champions were trounced at Wembley a year later by an exuberant Scotland side, his artless heritage was extended by his successors. Don Revie's highly Fordist managerial style took the reproduction of knowledge to new lengths when preparing for key matches in the mid-1970s. Squads of professionals (sometimes over fifty in number) would gather for meetings. Thesis-sized dossiers on opposing teams would be circulated among young England players, many of whom had failed to complete their secondary education. Meanwhile, a rich lineage of gifted ball-players and wing craftsmen was increasingly passed over for the number 7 and 10 shirts.

At this time, 'scientific' approaches dominated modern football. The FA coaching supremo, Charles Hughes, was promulgating the functional purity of 'direct football' (see Macdonald and Batty 1971; Batty 1980). Through the simplified method of management by objectives (MBO), teams were instructed to play the 'long ball' as data analysis 'proved' that up to 90 per cent of goals came from less than five passes (see Wilkinson 1988: 93, 107). This Taylorist aesthetic eroded working differentials between players who filled different positions; collectively, it amounted to industrial deskilling (see Braverman 1974). It said nothing about the other goal-less 88 minutes of matches (Taylor and Ward 1995: 295–7); nor could it explain its disastrous effect on the English national team during the 1970s and 1980s; or how teams like Glasgow Celtic were able to triumph in Europe by playing fluent, attacking football. Nevertheless, off the park, even Brazil were influenced: for their doomed World Cup campaign of 1966, they spent £300,000 on 'scientific preparation', including a four-month training camp for players who were monitored by two hundred medical staff. Across the world, psychologists started to research players' habits; some were hired to do pre-match team-talks, although the players retained a jokey disdain for the resulting psychobabble (see Yaffé 1974; Sik 1996).[5]

During the late 1960s and 1970s, the Dutch side Ajax fashioned 'total football', a more fluid and attacking style of play. All team players needed to be highly adaptable and capable of playing in most outfield positions. Total football's industrial philosophy was nearer to an 'enskilling' than a 'deskilling' model. It resembled Japanese labour practices (then beginning to impact upon global markets) which required all factory managers to be adept on assembly lines, while workers contributed new ideas for improving productivity. Its superiority to English 'science' was rooted in the mature relationship between Dutch players and coaches, compared to the antediluvian class distinctions between the British 'Boss' and his 'lads'. Although the Dutch produced some 'crack' players (notably Cruyff), the majority acquired a basic technical virtuosity that enabled them to play anywhere. The resulting style of constant movement and positional realignment was strikingly similar to the 'style of the future' predicted by Willy Meisl (1955) over a decade earlier. Meisl's 'Whirl' style had been envisioned to 'rotate on individuality rooted in all-round capacity'. For it to be executed as a 'non-stop switch' during games, the Whirl needed 'all-round' players; 'every man-jack must be able to tackle anybody else's job temporarily without any ado' (1995: 189).

Notwithstanding the appeal of the Dutch model, by the mid-1980s most club and international teams had become Taylorist in their suspicion of wing players' productive worth. Tactical variations involved tinkering with defensive strength: whether to play a sweeper/ *libero* or a 'flat back four'; whether to play one winger (two would be profligate) or an extra man in midfield. Football's late modernity saw the 4–4–2 system predominate, particularly in England, from which the British colonial squads of Liverpool, Nottingham Forest and Aston Villa won a procession of European Cups. In an era of deskilling and the erosion of craft differentials, the overlapping full-back could double as a winger, while play-makers were forced to do some labouring by tackling.

By the late 1980s, the baton of European football club power had passed on to Italy. There, the *catenaccio* system had met its nemesis in the *zona* style, favoured by Arrigo Sacchi at Parma and AC Milan. The *zona* game borrowed the late modern English flat back four and added a rigorous midfield 'pressing' tactic against opponents in possession. It abandoned *catenaccio*'s skills of craft, subtlety and situational psychology, and despatched players to patrol specific spaces on the park. Sacchi's idyll foresees players fitting into the system (rather than the other way round). They learn an exhaustive series of actions and manoeuvres through simple repetition. According to one of his fiercest critics, the former Italian manager Enzo Bearzot, the robotic players are caught, not in real football, but in 'virtual football, based on a geometric scheme'.[6]

Post-Modern Football Styles: a return to creativity?

In the early 1990s, European football underwent a period of tactical *perestroika* for several conjunctural reasons. Following the defensive dourness of the 1990 World Cup, FIFA were convinced that a more attacking, flowing game was needed to conquer new sports markets in North America and the Far East. Referees were instructed to get tough on the most mundane of 'professional' offences (see Blake 1996: 209).[7] Meanwhile, coaches began to deconstruct the fixed Fordist 4–4–2 model, to create a more flexible, post-Fordist system of play, to suit specific match circumstances. Again, attention turned to the team's defensive formation. In some, the addition of a third centre-back (playing as a *libero*) allowed the full-backs to attack more consistently. Italy's Maldini has been the leading exponent of the new *fluidificanti* position; others have included the late Fortunato of Juventus, Romania's Petrescu and the Brazilians Jorginho (of Bayern Munich) and Roberto Carlos (of Real Madrid). In the UK, the term 'wing-back' is affectedly employed to designate this new specialism, although the team formation is often indistinguishable from the old 4–4–2 with overlapping full-backs. Introducing wing-backs is not necessarily an attacking tactic, as they can overcrowd the midfield. In playing 3–5–2, managers must decide where their advantages lie, by choosing between players brought up as traditional full-backs or orthodox wingers.

In Italy, since the late 1980s, the post-modern solution has been found in attack. Much has been made of the role of the *mezzopunta* who plays a creative role between midfield and attack. Usually, the *mezzopunta* has the exceptional vision, ball-control and dribbling skills of the classic inside-forward. He receives the ball early and in some space, facing the opposition rather than with his back to goal. Defenders face uncertain choices when confronted with this anomalous player, who is like matter 'out of place', being neither forward (to be marked closely) nor midfielder (to be left to midfield colleagues). Great *mezzopunta* players include the gifted Italians of the 1990s, such as Mancini, Baggio and Zola; all learned their position at a time when the peerless Maradona was reinventing Napoli. The *mezzopunta*'s influence is now inscribed in the numerical geometry of football tactics, as coaches and fans alike speak of teams playing in four digit formations, just as they had done with WM.

However, perhaps the strongest split between modern and post-modern tactical thinking involves a post-modernist scepticism towards the scientific predictability of team coaching and management. Contemporary coaches are resigned to the fact that, ultimately, the result is out of their control. The Argentinian coach and football *penseur*, Jorge Valdano, captures this mood well: 'No coach can guarantee results, the best you can do is guarantee a way of playing; results are in the hands of fate' (quoted in King and Kelly 1997: 1).

To summarize, we may note that football's aesthetic and tactical development has contained 'traditional', 'modern' and 'post-modern' stages. The traditional game mixed individualism, the teamwork of passing and endeavour, and the pressure for results. In England, it was manifested by an emphasis on strength, particularly the 'kick and rush' game, while in Scotland the teamwork of smaller players was important. The early modern period is signified by the offside rule-change of 1925, the creation of the WM tactical system to take advantage, and by the new homogeneity in playing styles across Europe, manifested especially by moving the old centre-half into the defence. The full 'modernity' of post-war football introduced scientific approaches to the game, though cultural differences remained important. In Italy, *catenaccio* was the science of defence, rooted in an unbreakable will to win. In England, flairless 'direct football' held sway in tandem with the late modern, productive reliability of 4–4–2. The skills-centred philosophy of 'total football' was eclipsed by the earlier, more attacking, but equally efficacious Brazilian system of 4–2–4, which remains football's aesthetic form of 'high modernity'. Later, 'post-modern' styles have slackened the scientific shackles through their 'post-Fordist' flexibility. Once again, key players are those in 'marginal' positions, either between midfield and attack or playing along the flanks. Usually, these players need exceptional attributes, such as great technical skill or pace, but they still need to be 'team-players' in the old modern sense, by tackling, running hard and organizing colleagues.

Writing the Histories of Football Styles:
some analytical problems

To this historical narrative, I would append some analytical caveats. First, besides the tactical or aesthetic style that is formulated, there are also the circumstances and demands of the match to consider. A key question here is whether it helps to play 'aggressively' or to take the sting out of the game. Research suggests the answer lies in which side is playing at home. Early studies found that teams tended to play aggressively away from home (as they felt themselves to be in a hostile environment), and when positioned low in the league (due to their inferior skills and more desperate circumstances) (Yaffé 1974). Yet, aggressive play seems to backfire on the away team. Research from North American ice hockey found aggression was efficacious, especially when deployed early in matches (Widmeyer and Birch 1984). Subsequent studies indicated that home teams were particularly advantaged; aggressive play drew local fans into greater participation, to the detriment of visiting sides (McGuire et al. 1992). Hence, while a playing system is crucial for structuring the team, the social psychology of the players (notably, their 'attitude') will greatly influence their results.

Secondly, there is the availability of playing resources to take into account. Only the best football nations or richest clubs can afford the luxurious selection between 'total football', 4–4–2, 3–5–2 or 4–2–4. Football's harsh economics mean the majority of managers must operate as *bricoleurs*, tailoring their aesthetics and tactics to fit the players available. Most valued are 'utility' players, who fit in as full-backs for one game and as inside-forwards for the next. The most perceptive managers may detect a latent talent in a player's poise or touch, and successfully convert him, for example, from a centre-half to a centre-forward.

While the finest managerial *bricoleurs* cannot be easily copied, they have no way of disguising the tactical changes that they introduce. Unlike other 'knowledge' industries, there is no patent on innovative playing styles. The greatest compliment may lie in imitation, but managers run the risk of losing to their original style, and then finding that the victor claims the credit for innovation. Gilles Deleuze (1995: 132) noted that 'sporting bodies show remarkable ingratitude toward the inventors'. As in other forms of history, football's is written by the victorious against the vanquished.

A notable victim of this process is the small South American nation of Paraguay. In 1926, while competing in the South American championship in Chile, the Paraguayans introduced the notion of the 'third defender' as part of a 3–2–5 team formation. This system soon became much discussed throughout the world, but Paraguay's contribution was ignored. More momentously, the Paraguayans innovated further in the South American championship of 1953, by introducing the 4–2–4 formation to defeat Brazil in the final. Brazil's manager, Feora, adopted the system for his 1958 World Cup-winning side, to much misdirected tactical acclaim (Giulianotti 1997b).

Hence, my third point is that the exact origins of most cultural paradigms or genres are very difficult to establish. Football's status as one of the first truly transnational cultural practices means that pinning a particular style down in time and space is a hazardous exercise. Roy Hodgson, cosmopolitan manager of Blackburn Rovers and formerly of Internazionale, saw the *mezzopunta* position first played by Eric Gates at Ipswich Town in the 1970s (*World Soccer*, June 1997). Others point to the mesmeric Hungarian side of the 1950s as first demonstrating the arts of the deep-lying forward (Duke 1995: 98). This clashes with the argument that Puskás, Kocsis et al. inspired not the *mezzopunta* but the 4–2–4 system of Brazil (Taylor 1996). And this latter claim, of course, goes against my point on the innovative Paraguayans (whom Brazil encountered far more frequently than Hungary).

One difficulty here is that a legendary team's 'system' of play cannot be easily classified according to modern categories. The attempt to do so becomes an exercise in a historical kind of ethnocentricity. We begin to expect players and managers to have shaped up to geometrical and tactical notions that are 'common sense' in the contemporary game, but which were then unknown or unrecognized. We might rationalize these styles in quasi-scientific terms, reifying their historical inevitability. But the greatness of these teams and their players lies in their immediate *creativity*, their capacity to traverse the barriers of what was considered possible within football, and take it off in new directions.

This leads us to ponder how some playing styles come to be seen as better than others. Thomas Kuhn's (1962) model of scientific 'paradigms' has strong currency here. Applying this model, we may argue that football people at any one time are brought up to value one or two 'traditional' playing styles. A 'revolution' occurs in this footballing community when the dominant tradition loses power to a new model. The community of followers, once seated firmly in the old tradition, experiences an epiphanic 'gestalt shift' and deserts to the new style. This perspective helps to explain sudden changes in football styles. It also illuminates how nations or clubs can deliberately forsake their playing traditions, and attempt to harmonize their tactics and aesthetic viewpoints with those that are successful elsewhere, for example, Brazil's switch from *futebol arte* to the rugged *futebol forca* in the early 1970s (Helal 1994: 9), or Italy's switch from *catenaccio* to *zona* defence in the 1980s.

Significantly, we may speak with far greater conviction about the individual origins of particular playing skills. Two of the great innovations in striking the dead ball came from Brazil, reflecting the deep cultural emphasis on individual skill and its public display. During the 1950s, the Brazilian forward Didì developed the art of the curved shot or 'banana kick'. A generation of compatriots, notably Rivelino, showcased this skill at international tournaments, and it became a standard weapon in the attacking artillery of most sides. In the late 1970s, the Brazilian forward Zico added a second aerodynamic movement to the ball. Zico's shot combined a swerving horizontal movement with a dipping or rising lateral one. To achieve this extraordinary feat, Zico would strike over and across the ball in the manner of a tennis player rather than a standard footballer. Direct free-kicks became a disorientating experience for uninitiated goal-keepers. In a Brazil–Scotland friendly in Rio in 1977, for example, Alan Rough stood dumbfounded as a Zico shot that seemed certain to miss veered back into his net.[8] Since then Zico's double banana shot has become a new technique to learn and master for free-kick specialists.[9]

Some commentators have argued that the kick would not be possible without the new, synthetic football which is more receptive to variations in strike. At about the same time, the football world had been stunned by the spectacular, long-distance goals scored with this new ball at the 1978 World Cup finals. No similar number of such goals had been amassed in the heights of Mexico eight years earlier. As Zico's shot became established in world football circles, it was perfected by dead ball specialists such as Maradona and the Brazilians Branco and Roberto Carlos. While Branco went primarily for power, Roberto Carlos combined velocity with swerve. Following his spectacular goal at a France–Brazil friendly in June 1996, it was noted that he typically places the ball to strike its air-valve, thus exaggerating the swerve. Yet, it would be churlish to emphasize the weight or texture of the ball in explaining this lineage of Brazilian innovation. All of these master craftsmen bring to bear their considerable physiological capabilities (in power, direction and timing), acquired through insightful tuition and endless practice. To this, they add their willingness to challenge the cultural and historical parameters that initially confront them when striking the standard football.

Aesthetics and Modernity: playing the other

The globalization of football information and knowledge may obscure the origins of particular playing styles, while simultaneously enabling their circulation. Yet, different localities and societies do generate distinctive understandings of football style, tactics and aesthetics. Globalization enables clubs, nations and continents to experience this exotic dimension of football, that is, the encounter with decidedly 'other' approaches and philosophies. In discussing these different styles, we often find a fine line between celebrating diversity and reimposing old racial stereotypes. Sociologists routinely attack the national media for racializing foreign athletes, but academics too may slip into this lexicon.[10]

Historically, serious encounters with the most exotic 'others' have often reflected the limited cultural empathy between the sides. The great Uruguayan team of the interwar period had a particularly violent tour of Europe in 1936; then there is the battle of Highbury in 1934 between England and Italy, and the many violent World Cup matches during the 1930s, 1950s and 1960s. Since the 1960s, football's rising number of international competitions may have been cloaked in the marketable discourse of international fraternity and cultural exchange. But, events on the park have often transmuted from the physical clashing of playing styles into illustrations of Orwell's famous refrain, that sport is 'war minus the shooting'. Curiously, the most aggrieved (and injured) parties from these encounters have often been Scottish players. One thinks here of the 1968 World Club Championship match between Glasgow Celtic and Racing Club of Argentina; the 1974 European Cup semi-final between Celtic and Atlético Madrid; the 1986 Scotland v. Uruguay World Cup match in Mexico. Matches played in North America between European and South American club sides as part of the North American Soccer League (NASL) in the 1960s and 1970s were regularly peppered with undisguised violence (Murray 1994: 267–8).

These clashes demonstrate that football carries very different social and symbolic meanings for the opposing sides and their cultures. From the Western viewpoint, it is easy to fulminate against southern European and Latin American sides for their 'violent' or 'cheating' play. Yet, in the latter societies, the meaning of football is bound up within an ensemble of core Mediterranean values involving localist chauvinisms, masculinity, honour and shame (Goddard, Llobera and Shore 1995: 4–11). Football is but one cultural medium through which these values are dramatized; folksongs and bullfights are two others. Indeed, we may add that the 'brutal' *futbol da muerte* practised by Atlético Madrid and other Latin sides represents a rich fusion of football and bullfighting. To the Western eye, the bullfight is a savage and sickening event, overly real in its representation of death. But, to the Spaniard or the Mexican, the *corrida* has many ritual qualities and functions, through which personal fear of death may be confronted and controlled. It dramatizes the natural fragility of masculine power and virility, and imagines the mortal consequences of competitive social relationships (see Pitt-Rivers 1984; Zurcher and Meadow 1967). Turning some of these aspects of the *corrida* back onto an analysis of football may help to explain more empathetically the cultural rationale and aesthetic beliefs surrounding physical Latin playing styles.

Neither popular nor sociological discourses are fully equipped to formulate a neutral yet celebratory, cross-cultural but non-racial discussion of football styles and social identities. For this to be possible, analysis must focus more fully on the construction of racial and national identities. 'Discourse analysis' is a useful methodological tool in this regard, and has been employed to excavate the narrative frameworks which are common to most international sports media (Blain, Boyle and O'Donnell 1993). A strong relationship exists between the geo-political locations of nations and their sports typologies. The more powerful, 'core' nations are deemed to have peoples of sound morality, character and temperament; peripheral nationals are the opposite. Northern nations (Scandinavia, the UK, Germany) produce calm, reliable, cultured individuals. The further south one goes, the more this stereo-type changes. Southern Europeans are 'emotional'; South Americans are 'fiery'; Africans are 'magical' and 'irrational'. While it is possible to highlight the contradictions or anomalies within these international discourses, the stereo-types remain impervious to fundamental change (O'Donnell 1994).[11]

Of all the social disciplines, anthropology has produced the most sophisticated readings of football traditions within clubs or nations. In the Mediterranean, Bromberger (1993: 120) found that, aesthetically, 'the styles of Olympique Marseille and Juventus are strongly opposed, each reflecting a particular vision of the world, of mankind, of the city". He discusses at length the value system of Juventus as symbolized in the three Ss: simplicity, seriousness, sobriety. *La Vecchia Signora* (the Old Lady) are committed to the industrial rigour and discipline espoused by the Agnelli family who own the club and the Fiat motor empire (Bromberger 1995b: 148–53). This Juventus style has been embodied in the endeavour of Cabrini and Tardelli and, most famously of all, the graceful power of Charles.

In South America, Archetti (1996, 1997a) has written perceptively of the symbolic importance of football players who refuse to fit into the professionalism of positional play and tactical systems. Players such as Maradona, Valderrama and Romario are lauded as *pibes* ('boys') by the fans, not only for their sublime skills, but also for their carefree and joyous play, which kindles personal memories of childhood games and formative experiences, uncluttered by the burdens of adult life. The poor origins of such players also help confirm the collectively held myth that football genius is most readily found and cultivated in the urban *potreros* (wastelands) and slums of Buenos Aires or Rio de Janeiro. Archetti's thesis finds ready evidence in the UK through the adulation of street-kid geniuses such as Paul Gascoigne, George Best and Jimmy Johnstone (see Inglis 1977: 122–3). Indeed, it is often said, as a kind of counter-myth to explain the sudden disappearance of such players, that the natural habitat for their rearing, the inner-city backstreet, has long since gone.

Within Brazilian football folklore, the relationship of severe urban deprivation and fantastic football style is embodied by the *malandro*, another mythological figure. The *malandro*'s qualities are found in his indefatigability, his ability as a streetwise trickster, skilled at surviving by fooling fortune and authority alike.

> If you go to a *favela* . . . you will see a woman – there is no man in the house – who takes care of her five or six boys. The smartest of these boys, who can flee from the police if he needs to, who can put up a fight, is a good football player. He can dribble past life's difficulties. He can provide food for his mother. There

is a deep connection between tricking defenders on the football field and being a smart boy in real life. This boy is a *malandro*.

(Prof. Muniz Sodre, quoted by Kuper 1994: 197–8)

Yet the vast economic, social and geo-climatic differences in Brazil mean that the *malandro*'s position in the cultural imaginary is cross-cut by other regional traditions. Rio's teams are true pioneers of the South American aesthetic, through play that is flamboyant and rhythmic, flowing between careful build-up and sudden attack. In the urban sprawl of São Paulo, the football is more industrious, routinized and geometrically fixed. Pôrto Alegre's teams employ a more 'Uruguayan' approach, playing without stars and often with a violent determination to win, regardless of the means.[12]

Moreover, just as Spanish football interleaves with the *corrida*, so the Latin American game sits within an ensemble of other popular cultural practices, most notably national dance. Brazil's *carioca* rhythm is an extension of samba music. The Colombian striker, Faustino Asprilla, is a renowned fan of salsa and other gyrating forms of body culture. During the 1978 World Cup finals, the balletic skills of Oswaldo Ardiles were likened to those of a tango dancer by the foreign media. Indeed, a deeper understanding of the complexity of Argentinian football style is provided through a closer appreciation of the tango. According to Archetti (1993, 1994), one of the corporeal poetics of the tango centres upon a ritual drama of masculine honour. The *compadrito* is a young male, a ready seducer of women, with a criminal past, strong and potentially violent, but with a willingness to cheat if necessary. In keeping his woman, and beating off the attention of rivals, the *compadrito* may find himself confronted by a humiliating loss of honour, and 'the choice between courage and death or pardon'. Hence, while a bourgeois audience might be wooed by the grace of the dancer's poise, the violent semiotics of his movements remain equally instructive. Within this idiom, a violent tackle on a dangerous opponent is just as redolent of the tango as a dextrous turn on the ball, and deemed to be equally suitable by the crowd.

In marking out the 'traditions' of these styles, we must, of course, avoid assuming that they say something essential about the relevant nation. The flowering of football traditions in Brazil and Argentina owes a great debt to international pollination, particularly by early UK sides and the 1960s exploration of European 'science'. Perhaps this process is most visible in a relatively small nation such as Sweden, which has reached the last four of the World Cup finals on three occasions, and won the Olympic final in 1948. Swedish football places a decidedly Nordic, collectivist emphasis on *esprit de corps*, thereby extending the early national sports culture and the regimen of gymnastics long taught in the educational system (Levine and Vinten-Johansen 1981: 24). But, in the early post-war period, large numbers of Swedish players played abroad under different tactical systems. The Swedish FA adopted the English coaching style from the 1960s onwards, and acquired the German defensive habit of close marking with a *libero*. English coaches working in Swedish club football developed the zonal game in the late 1970s, before Sven Goran Eriksson at IFK Göteborg encouraged players to perform more creatively (Peterson 1994). The Swedes' success would therefore seem to rest on an adaptability and openness to outside influences, a pragmatic football strategy which also represents a remarkably honest intellectual assessment of their national position within a global setting.

Style in Post-Modernity: sports globalization and football's response

The globalization of football therefore has long involved the inter-penetration of sporting aesthetics, techniques and tactics. Such hybridity can only expand as we enter the post-modern milieu of increased labour migration, television coverage and international competition. Yet it may be that the post-modernization of football's aesthetics is most acutely experienced within the structural relations of the game to other sports. In chapter 1, I discussed the common genus of association football and many other ball sports. In true modernist fashion, from the mid-nineteenth century onwards, football and other sports became increasingly differentiated and specialized, in terms of rules, playing positions, tactics and body technique. The cultural integrity of every modern sport was protected by the assumption that each was *sui generis*.

Nevertheless, the differentiation of these 'modern' sports was always incomplete. Football players have tended to share the same age and fitness levels as other sports performers; indeed, it has been argued that modernity homogenizes these sports further, by demanding particular 'performance levels' and athletic body shape from the professionals. Spatially, with the exception of pre-industrial cricket, most outdoor team sports share the same approximate size and rectangular shape of playing field. Temporally, English sports follow calendars designed to fit with other popular sports.

There are several models employed by sociologists to explain the globalization of sports. An important one is 'Americanization' and this certainly has ramifications for football. Some cities or nations are highly receptive to the incursion of American and other sports. This is particularly apparent where the status of professional football teams has declined markedly or is unable to compete effectively with more powerful opponents. In Greece, for example, basketball has virtually displaced football as the national sport, primarily because of the latter's poor international standing; a similar situation obtains in Poland (Andrews and Mazur 1995). In Argentina, the dominance of Buenos Aires clubs has encouraged cities from the interior to adopt other sports at which they can be more competitive.[13] As European football also becomes increasingly dominated by a select elite, it may be that supporters of smaller clubs, invariably to be found in the provinces, will also follow suit.

Yet, the Americanization of global sports need not be an oppositional one for football. In the late 1980s and early 1990s, Nike transferred their National Basketball Association (NBA) marketing strategies to football, which were soon adopted by more established football companies like Reebok and Adidas. Most European leagues have adopted the American practice of numbering players at each club as part of their squad (or roster), rather than for individual games. Hence, one of the most coveted shirts for young players is no longer the number 10 (immortalized by Pelé) or number 14 (of Cruyff), but is instead the number 23 (retired by Michael Jordan at the Chicago Bulls).

More substantively, it is argued by some coaches that a close tactical relationship exists now between football and other sports. For example, the Irish national team's attritional style during the late 1980s and 1990s may have replicated England's 'direct football', but it also drew heavily on the hard tackling and kicking skills found in Gaelic football or hurling (Giulianotti 1996b). In southern Europe and the Americas, it is thought that basketball has significantly influenced football techniques and tactics. The relative warmth serves to promote the popularity of small-team games, such as five-a-side, which is played indoors, on the beach or on small, multi-sport floodlit pitches during cooler evenings. Players find themselves operating within the same kind of spatial and competitive parameters as basketball, the indoor sport *par excellence*. The pitch area is the same size, marking tends to be tight, the teams have five members including a guard / keeper minding the hoop / goal, while play moves repeatedly from end to end. In the search for skills and strategies that will defeat opponents, it seems quite logical to look to another sport where solutions to similar problems are much more evolved. Today, the more obvious examples of basketball's influence would seem to include triangular or diamond shaped passing patterns, to hold possession or maintain attacks; zonal defensive systems; and the use of cross-field passing during fast counter-attacks.

Football has sought to curtail the appeal of American sports by going on the offensive itself in terms of 'Americanizing' the game's aesthetic and technical principles to attract new audiences (especially American ones). In doing so, FIFA has tended to be stuck in the old modernist, Taylorist mode of thinking, which assumes that the aesthetic aspects of football can be measured and made more efficient in terms of time and motion. Productivity on the park is deemed essential: time-wasting and feigning injury have been attacked; the old pass-backs to goal-keepers are banned; injury time often runs into five or six minutes; several match balls placed around the pitch keep up the tempo. The rule changes have altered football's geometry and temporal pattern, but contribute little to the pleasure of playing or watching. The increase in the effective time of play has primarily confirmed football's emphasis on player fitness and the standardization of playing patterns. The new pressure on players to keep the game moving has given them less time, either to think before passing the ball, or to gain some respite during breaks in play. Further changes have been mooted along similar lines: replacing 'throw-ins' with 'kick-ins' and banning any form of tackling. The latter measure would destroy one of football's most elementary skills and part of its aesthetic attraction for all but the most inexperienced of spectators.

Rule changes such as these are aimed at Taylor-making the aesthetics of football to fit with the fast entertainment typically favoured by passive television consumers. Some innovations have proven successful already: specifically, the digital clocks in Italy showing how much injury time the referee is playing, and the time-outs employed in Brazil for advertising space and for coaches to intercede among their players. Yet football's highest authorities have some major problems in limiting the political impact of television and new media technology upon the game. Slow motion action replays are almost as old as televised football itself and have long concentrated on crucial refereeing decisions over goal-line saves, penalties, fouls, corners and throw-ins. Inevitably, many have been shown to be wrong, but 'human fallibility' was accepted by most associations as a natural hazard of the game. However, some associations (including FIFA and UEFA) have come to accept videotaped evidence as part of any enquiry into matches, thereby implying that television should be used for making crucial decisions during games. Since 1994, the German Football Association (DFB) has ordered three league matches to be replayed because of refereeing mistakes that came to light from television evidence. The DFB's actions brought them into direct conflict with FIFA who remain committed to the pre-television principle that the referee's decisions are final and irrevocable. Some leagues have experimented with a 'second referee' in the stands, using television consoles to adjudicate on key incidents. FIFA's refereeing experts have been reluctant to support such changes, fearing that it would create a two-tier game (where aids were available at most professional games, but not semi-professional or amateur level), and effectively institutionalize the belief that problems in matches originate with the referee rather than the players. Moreover, a 'humanist' view has been put forward by some coaches, notably Javier Clemente, that technology would destroy the interpretive soul of football, ending the debates and arguments over player actions and refereeing responses. Ironically, Clemente's empathy towards referees has been undermined by FIFA's authoritarian ruling, that giant screens inside stadia cannot replay controversial decisions for spectators. New computer software is already shifting the argument further against FIFA's position. One recent innovation is the computer simulator which traces and projects the exact timing and path of shots or passes, and is used by television stations in match post-mortems. The device measures the speed and angle of shots, but also determines the veracity of offside decisions from oblique viewing angles by simulating the likely path of the ball.

For the spectator, the relationship of television to the aesthetics of football can underline class inequalities. Football players or matches exude a certain 'aura' that cannot be reproduced by photography, television or any other medium (see Benjamin 1975, 1979). This auratic element of football involves a 'strange weave of time and space'; close and immediate proximity is essential to experiencing it. The 'aura' of playing cannot be replicated by watching on the sidelines, which is why so few ex-professionals attend matches. The 'aura' of 'being there', at the match, cannot be replicated by watching at home, no matter how advanced the technology. Yet, as I noted in the conclusion to chapter 4, access to this fundamental aesthetic of spectating is increasingly controlled by commercial interests. The claim to have 'been there' is restricted increasingly to the wealthy. Even the finest simulations of 'aura', as afforded by leading televisual technology, still necessitates a sizeable financial outlay. For those who struggle to afford entry, the 'anti-auratic' medium of ordinary television cannot come near to the 'auratic' match. Little wonder, then, that so many disenfranchised fans seek to bridge the gap by watching their club's players during mid-week training sessions. In this at least, the aesthetics of football may be imagined or studied in their studio production, although public display of the completed work remains a commodified experience. I turn to examine more fully the role of these contemporary class distinctions in chapter 8.

8

The Cultural Politics of Play: Ethnicity, Gender and the 'Post-fan' Mentality

In this chapter, I examine how the cultural politics of class, gender and ethnicity are reshaping football's social condition. In discussing the 'class' dimension, emphasis is placed on the changing nature of general football fandom in the UK, particularly in England, but also in other Home Nations. Historically, UK football culture has been uniquely embedded within the modern, urban working classes. The new post-industrial society and the remarkable commodification of top professional football underpin the possible realignment of the game's class identity. The notion of the 'post-fan' is an important heuristic here; this new supporter category has white-collar employment, and shows a greater reflexivity and critical distance when engaging with popular culture.

A more global perspective is employed to discuss the cultural politics of ethnicity and gender within football. The major problems of sexism and racism lie within the mainstream of football culture, among ordinary supporters, coaches and officials. Prejudicial assumptions remain influential in determining the role to be played by women and non-whites within football cultures in the UK and overseas. The major historical contribution of women and non-whites to football tends to be submerged. The new football cultures, such as the USA, do seem to promote female participation, but at the expense of a genuinely 'multi-cultural' game. I conclude the discussion by arguing that recent, heavily publicized anti-sexism and anti-racism drives in UK football are reflective of football's class transformation rather than any structural revolution along the lines of gender or ethnicity.

Football and Social Class: introductory remarks

In previous chapters, I noted regularly that social class is an important theme in football's historical and structural development. Generally, football's modern and urban character ensures that its social meaning has been heavily influenced by the processes of nation-building, industrialization and the creation of a large working class. In southern England and South America, the old upper middle-class elites still exercise substantial control over the game, though their cultural influence was greatly diluted by football's 'massification' throughout the twentieth century. Conversely, southern European football always possessed a relatively classless character, although the working classes remained the most sizeable contributor. Class issues and football's bourgeoisification received substantial critical analysis by sociologists during the 1970s and early 1980s.[1] I am therefore committed to avoiding a straightforward recapitulation of this body of work. My concern instead is to assess the key changes in football's class culture within the context of the game's recent economic boom.

Since 1990, the structural nexus of football and the working classes has been strongly undermined. Football clubs and the police are less tolerant of expressive forms of support. Ground redevelopment has replaced the old terraces with more expensive, family-friendly stands. Those locked out must forfeit a hefty subscription fee to watch on television. Merchandising and share issues mean that clubs pursue wealthier, national fan groups rather than satisfy local supporters. On the park, the local one-club heroes have become peripatetic national or international 'celebrities', drawn increasingly from affluent suburbs rather than poor housing estates.

Concomitantly, the working class itself has undergone major structural changes since the 1970s. Deindustrialization and the rise of the service-sector economy have reduced the industrial working class and expanded the white-collar workforce. The structural boundaries between the old lower middle classes and the affluent upper working classes have become very blurred. A dispossessed underclass is sedimented at the base of the new class hierarchy. In the post-modern era, this underclass and the class strata just above are most visibly excluded from football's brave new world. UK football's new target audiences include family groups, the first generation middle classes and the young metropolitan elite. These developments have certainly enlivened the cultural politics of football. The new middle classes have contributed particularly to the UK game's fashionability throughout the 1990s. It is to an analysis of this new class and its material culture that I now turn.

The Post-fans: class and cultural properties

To open this discussion it is useful to consider the changing culture of football fandom in the UK. This relates specifically to the emergence of a new category of football spectator, which I have previously termed the 'post-fans' (Giulianotti 1993).[2] The concept of the 'post-fan' is derived from my re-application of John Urry's (1990) notion of the 'post-tourist' to a football context. According to Urry, 'post-tourists' are distinguished from mere 'tourists' by their reflexivity, experience and irony. They are highly knowledgeable about the constructed and artificial nature of tourist experiences. Behind the façade of an 'authentic tourist encounter' with another culture lies a large commercial organization which manufactures the host society to fit with the stereo-typed expectations of Westerners. Post-tourists are conscious that tourism carries its downside for their 'friendly hosts': it places the locals in a dependency relationship with the West, undermines the indigenous culture, and has a disastrous effect on local ecosystems. Post-tourists acknowledge that, within the multi-million dollar tourism industry, their capacity to generate meaningful change is rather limited. Nevertheless, post-tourists pursue alternative travel strategies: staying off the beaten track, signing up for 'green' holidays or educational tours.

Football's 'post-fans' share this reflexivity, irony and participatory outlook. They represent an epistemic break from older forms of fandom, in particular the passivity of the 'supporter'. Post-fans are cognizant of the constructed nature of fan reputations, and the vagaries of the media in exaggerating or inventing such identities. They adopt a reflexive approach in interpreting the relative power positions of their players and club within the political structures of domestic and international football. They maintain an ironic and critical stance towards the apologetic propaganda emanating from their board of directors, and against the generally sympathetic relationship that exists between the latter and the mass media. The comments of post-fans on their favoured club and players often slip into parody or hostility. They are at the epicentre of supporter movements which militate to change club policy on the players, manager or directors. Nevertheless, post-fans recognize their influence remains very limited within football's corridors of power.

Crucially, Urry (1990) argues that 'post-tourists' emerged from important changes in the class structures of post-industrial Western societies. Specifically, 'post-tourists' hail from the 'new middle class' of white-collar workers (see Bourdieu 1984). Many received further education, particularly in the liberal arts and social sciences; they tend to be employed in the new 'knowledge industries', such as sales, media and market research. Unlike the traditional bourgeoisie, this new class embraces rather than rejects popular culture, often mixing football or rock music with an interest in literature and the performing arts. However, this cultural consumption is not passive. The new middle classes are educated or employed to engage critically with all forms of popular culture. Many work as 'cultural intermediaries' in the service sector, setting trends or educating the public on how to consume specific products (Featherstone 1991b).

The New Middle Classes and Contemporary Football Media

There is strong evidence that the new middle classes have a sizeable stake in the production, mediation and consumption of post-fan football culture. The new supporters' organizations, such as the Football Supporters' Association (FSA) or the Independent Supporters' Associations (ISAs), tend to be filled with white-collar service workers. Fanzine writers are drawn from new middle-class employment, such as sales, middle management or further education (Giulianotti 1997c: 219). Moreover, the fanzine's staple content is riddled with post-fan irony and parody (Curren and Redmond 1991; Haynes 1992).

The new middle classes are at the heart of the production and consumption of mainstream football media, which mushroomed throughout the 1990s. It is relatively strong in disposable income and media literacy, and particularly unsatisfied by schoolboy football magazines, like *Shoot!* and *Goal*. The success of football fanzines, especially *When Saturday Comes*, encouraged mainstream publishing companies to publish their own titles, such as *Four–Four–Two, Total Football* and *90 Minutes*, and copy the fanzines' strategies of flexible accumulation: quick organization, low overheads, flexible production and management arrangements, and easily imposed liquidation (in this case, by head office, on workers employed on short-term contracts). Mainstream publishers have also recruited many journalists from the fanzines and dip into their pages for stories and gossip (see Rowe 1995: 28, 40).[3] UK television stations (satellite and terrestrial) have released a surfeit of football chat shows, most notably *Standing Room Only, The Rock and Goal Years*, and *Fantasy Football*. The latter programme is the television spin-off from the 'Fantasy Football' league that is promoted in all newspapers and played by thousands of readers. Indeed, the newspaper which organizes the 'official' Fantasy Football League, the *Daily Telegraph*, is the leading upmarket daily, has an ageing readership and is regarded as the bastion of conservatism in its coverage of news events (Tunstall 1996: 16). Its use of football reflects not only its populist pursuit of younger readers, but also the rising stock of the game among young middle-class readers. Finally, the game's fashionability has enabled one young entrepreneur to found *Philosophy Football*, selling to more cerebral consumers a host of shirts emblazoned with great football *aperçus* by Baudrillard, Camus, Wittgenstein et al.

The new media thrive upon some fundamental changes in the associative nature of football fandom. The old working-class spectators were raised to discuss football intersubjectively, at work, in the pub, on the street or in the home. They attended matches in groups, either with their family or their peers

(Clarke 1978). Conversely, football is experienced in a more solitary way by the new middle classes. Primary and secondary relationships are less football centred. Football match attendance occurs in smaller groups, especially with female partners. The new football media seek to fill this dialogical hole in a virtual fashion by becoming the source of football chat for new middle-class readers. Female journalists are recruited partly to encourage the 'significant others' of male fans to take an interest in the game.

Some qualifications are necessary in linking post-fandom with the new middle classes. First, critical or ironic fandom is not purely the preserve of this class fraction. The football ground has always harboured a 'post-fan' element, ready to dispense ironic invective and self-effacing insights. Second, 'post-fandom' can be practised by a diversity of fan types. In Scotland, for example, the ambassadorial 'Tartan Army' are highly skilled in manufacturing their reputation abroad. Some hooligans are equally adept at manipulating the police or press through deliberate misinformation (Armstrong and Giulianotti 1998c). Third, football's 'cultural intermediaries' or 'style-setters' do not always hail from the new middle classes. As I argued in chapter 3, other sub-cultures (even hooligan ones) can generate new fan identities that are consolidated by mainstream supporters. Finally, we should beware the tendency of cultural sociologists to exaggerate the social and cultural importance of their specific class strata. Football or other forms of popular culture may now be legitimate topics of conversation at liberal dinner parties, but that does not confirm by itself an epochal shift in the social meaning and structural significance of these practices.

Nevertheless, the long-standing critical and reflexive dimensions of 'post-fandom' are increasingly associated with the new middle classes. This class possesses the intellectual and technological capital to transfer the critical impulse of football crowds, from the Socratic context of the open terraces to the more permanent medium of the fanzine, the web page or the football novel. As mainstream and independent kinds of football media have multiplied, so the intermediary influence of the new middle classes has expanded in tandem.

Class and Geography: North v. South, traditionalists v. arrivistes

A critical point here concerns the fact that, within a football context, the new middle class is not a homogeneous entity. Important internal differences exist along social class and geographical lines. At the local level, particularly in northern England and Scotland, there is a strong traditionalist undercurrent within the fanzines and ISAs which is deeply critical of football's commodification and the marginalization of long-standing fans. The new middle-class fans associated with these movements tend to have a long personal immersion in football. Even among northern actors, musicians and writers who move south, the close bond with the supported club tends to be insoluble (for example,

Sean Bean at Sheffield United, Noel Gallagher at Manchester City or Harry Pearson [1994] at Middlesborough).

While fanzines and ISAs in southern England share such traditionalist impulses, they have been overshadowed by the genesis of a metropolitan cadre of football followers. At the vanguard of this new football class is an oligarchy of metropolitan journalists and Oxbridge graduates which has acquired a literary hegemony over the game. Their personal background in football is usually very limited; their club affiliations are also rather flexible. Dubbed the London *soccerati*, this cadre includes the novelists Martin Amis, Bill Buford (1991), Nick Hornby (1992) and Roddy Doyle (1993); the journalists Simon Kuper (1994, 1997), Emma Lindsey and Anne Coddington (1997); and comedians like David Baddiel (Giulianotti 1997a). The *soccerati* favour the redevelopment of football stadia to the benefit of their class on the assumed grounds that this has eradicated hooliganism and enabled more women and ethnic minorities to attend. The *soccerati* are particularly popular among football *arrivistes*, a strata of London-based white collar workers who 'do football' to flesh out the popular culture dimension of their social curriculum vitae. Through use of the new football media, they may learn the game's lexicon and teach themselves all about the players and playing systems. This knowledge is of the autodidactic type, and not engrained with time, reflection or experience in playing the game.

It is here that a serious conflict begins to emerge over football's cultural politics in a manner not dissimilar to the north–south dispute of one hundred years earlier. In contrast to the protective approach of the northern new middle classes, the southern elite openly attacks working-class fandom. Simon Kuper, for example, lambasts

> this idea that I've been following my team for 30 years and my dad did before me and my grandad did before him, that football is about blood and toil and belonging. This is very dangerous for two reasons. First football is about more than belonging and community, it's about art and great moments: George Best beating three defenders down the wing; a Platini free kick. Second, it makes Asian fans, black fans, women fans feel excluded. How can you come in if you didn't belong before?
>
> (quoted in Coddington 1997: 74–5)

Kuper's seductive opinion crystallizes many of the false assumptions and prejudices about the nature and traditions of working-class fandom. A few of the fallacies may be summarized: that working-class fans don't change teams between generations; that working-class fans are unable to appreciate or practise the aesthetics of the game; that a sense of 'belonging' precludes an appreciation of footballing genius; that working-class fans are the most racist and sexist; that working-class chauvinisms rather than more deep-seated economic and cultural inequalities prevent less powerful social groups from football involvement. Indeed, Kuper is guilty of blaming one less powerful social group (the working classes) for the social exclusion experienced by others (ethnic minorities and women). His analysis simply mirrors the same kind of scapegoat rhetoric that is employed by right-wing groups to support their racism, whereby one weak community (an ethnic minority) is blamed for the troubles of another (the working classes).

Significantly, a counter-hegemonic movement has emerged within the new middle classes to challenge both this elite and the wider commodification of football. The CRASH satirical cultural project (CRASH stands for 'Creating Resistance to Society's Haemorrhoids') has published pamphlets attacking the middle-class 'new laddism' of television's football celebrities (*Independent on Sunday*, 3 August 1997). Resistance emanates from supporter pressure groups, social movements and more critical football commentators, such as Horton (1997) and Conn (1997). The pressure group (Football Fans Against the Criminal Justice Act) (FFACJA) was founded to oppose legislation that extended police powers over supporters. A popular supporters' network called Libero! was formed by those 'who are opposed to the growing regulation of our beautiful game', organizing a number of well-attended, dissenting supporter forums in London. The success of books on hooliganism and football's commodification suggests that the Oxbridge hegemony over 'good writing' on the game can be challenged.

These contemporary conflicts indicate that class issues remain central to the cultural politics of the game. The fact that the most acute conflicts take place within the new middle classes tells us something instructive about post-1990, post-modern UK football, and the marginalization of working-class supporters. However, class is not the only issue, nor always the dominant one, within the cultural politics of football. Two other fundamental conflicts are those relating to issues of gender and issues of ethnicity. It is to an assessment of these questions that I now turn.

Football and Women: the historical context

Within the broad historical and global framework, women's general exclusion from football has been relatively recent and particularly apparent in more 'civilized' societies. Guttmann (1991: 47–8) reports that, from the twelfth century onwards, women took a very prominent role in the 'ludic turbulence' of folk football. On some occasions, teams of women were pitted against each other according to marital status; their play was no less hardy than the men's, and they suffered the same injuries.

Following the establishment of association football, women were gradually squeezed out of attending British matches. Many clubs had admitted women free of charge, but as professionalization struck by the mid-1890s, admission fees were introduced, often at half of the men's price. Mason (1980: 152–3) argues that rising working-class crowds saw women dislocated from the terraces and eased into the stands.[4] By the 1930s, this migration had given rise to the stereo-type, as popular as it was disputed, that female football fans were stoically from the middle classes (Fishwick 1989: 57–8). Though English football's cultural peculiarities are noteworthy, it seems that this process was generally replicated elsewhere. In Brazil, for example, Lever (1983: 40–1) found that football's colonization by the working classes in the 1910s finalized the demise of 'the fashionable ladies in the stands'.[5] Meanwhile, throughout South America, the gender barriers were being broken down outside of football grounds, as young players became heroes in local *barrios*, attracting a steady flow of female admirers especially at dances (Carvallo et al. 1984: 22–3).

In England, there is clear evidence from the inter-war years that the football authorities saw the rise of women's football as a threat to the male game. The famous 'Dick, Kerr Ladies XI' became remarkably successful, embarking on international tours and proving unbeatable at home. In 1921, they played 67 matches in the UK before around 900,000 spectators; one match in Liverpool on Boxing Day of 1920 drew over 53,000 fans (Newsham 1994: 61, 55). Yet within a year, the English FA effectively outlawed major female football matches by instructing clubs not to lease out their grounds. The decree secured men's future domination of commercial football and represents a blow from which English women's football has never truly recovered (Lopez 1997: 6–7).

Women, Fan Violence and Match Attendance

Substantial debate surrounds the relationship of female match attendance to different levels of football hooliganism. English sociologists have argued that female attendance causes men to soften or 'feminize' their behaviour, thereby reducing the frequency and seriousness of violent or disorderly incidents (see Jennifer Hargreaves 1992: 174–5; Taylor 1991a; Williams 1986). One solution to fan hooliganism, it is argued, lies in the promotion of football as a modern, 'family' game (Murphy et al. 1990: 224–5).[6]

Several criticisms may be directed at this viewpoint. First, the football industry is keen to attract women for business rather than pro-feminist reasons. After facing a spectacular decline in attendances from the 1960s to the late 1980s, football's business controllers sought out a 'reserve army of leisure' to fill the spaces vacated by men (Russell 1998). Second, we might question the ethics of using women to solve football hooliganism as the latter phenomenon is purely a male problem (Clarke 1992: 217). Third, the feminization thesis mistakenly assumes that hooligan fans are the most abusively sexist. Many of football's oldest and most sexist chants or epithets emanate from mainstream male supporters and officials. Football hooligans are rarely the most voluble chanteurs of standards like 'Get Your Tits Out For the Lads'. Meanwhile, football coaches and spectators routinely couch their encouragement of players in classically masculine terms, invoking them to stop 'playing like poofters' or 'tackling like women'. Fourth, we need to question the rather essentialized and

Victorian assumption that femininity is ontologically rooted in a family-centred and physically inert role. There is even evidence to suggest that women can participate in or actively support boisterous or violent fan behaviour. In continuation of Mason's (1980: 158–9) records on Victorian women 'behaving badly' at football matches, we can note female participation in hooligan or 'militant' groups through to the current day; for example in Scotland (see Finn 1994b: 123n), Germany and Italy (Roversi 1994: 375–7).[7] If we look to South American evidence, we find that the links between hooliganism and female attendance are just as inconclusive. In Brazil, Lever (1995: 13) suggests that the violence of *torcidas* during the 1980s was highly off-putting to women, whereas other research indicates that falling female attendance reflected a deeper structural decline in the domestic game (Helal 1994). In neighbouring Argentina, hooliganism among fans increased markedly during the 1990s, but so too did the attendance of female supporters (Alabarces 1998).

In the UK, there are serious doubts as to whether female attendance at football has increased significantly. Some research claims to demonstrate that the 'modernization' of English football *has* increased female interest in football: more are attracted to matches (SNCCFR 1995: 14), and more are watching on television (Woodhouse and Williams 1991: 87). During the early 1980s, most surveys of football supporters had shown that women constituted 12–20 per cent of the crowd (Canter et al. 1989: 20; SNCCFR 1983: 124). Subsequent research in Aberdeen suggested females constituted 13 per cent of the crowd (Giulianotti 1992: 13). Annual surveys for the English FA point to similar findings today. Coddington (1997: 1) argues that up to 25 per cent of football's new fans are female, though this may signify only that there is a higher turnover of female fans relative to males. Domestically, more women are watching football on television, but then it is also increasingly prevalent in the schedules. It is also easier for males to watch televised matches if they can socialize females into enjoying the game or if they can 'trade' viewing football at one time for watching their partner's programme on another occasion (see Gantz and Wenner 1995). Recent proponents of football's gender transformation appear to ignore a key finding from the early 1970s, that female spectating is indicative of football's more fundamental transformation into a middle-class sport (Taylor 1971: 149). One protagonist of the 'sexual revolution' has criticized this position, declaring that 'Our alleged class is being used as a convenient mask to attack our gender' (Coddington 1997: 13). But, she does little to sustain this point, since almost all of her interviewees, as a sample of modern female fans, are university graduates and / or employed in white-collar work.[8]

Masculinities and Football: class and analytical issues

When discussing the gender politics of football, male power and the cultures of masculinity within the game are also crucial issues. Initially, the evidence all favours the conclusion that football's 'hegemonic masculinity' is uniformly aggressive and humourlessly chauvinistic. Earlier chapters highlighted the centrality of male domination within football. Male public schools created the rules of association football, while the game's organizational hierarchies continue to be bastions of male power. Professional football sides became all-male representations of the founding community. Until the 1960s, football helped to reproduce the modern sexual division of labour and leisure. Men dominated workplaces and public spaces (such as football grounds); women were relegated to private domains like the home. Football's playing aesthetics preach a traditional masculinity; 'It's a man's game after all . . . players should accept a bit of boot.'[9] The players' occupational sub-culture is dominated by the rapacious pursuit of 'birds' for sexual conquest. The mass media's football coverage caters continuously to the male gaze. The front pages of tabloids 'expose' the sexual secrets of top stars; the back pages mix football stories with adverts for sex chat lines, 'lap dancing' clubs and lingerie; inside, semi-nude female models pose provocatively in football regalia.

Football's modern industrial heartlands might be typified as places of hard toil, where tough masculine norms are reproduced through football. Examples from the major football nations include the shipyard and coalfield towns of Scotland; the heavy industry centres of north England; the steel towns (Lens) and port cities (Marseille, Rotterdam) of France or Holland; the industrial Ruhr area of Germany; the tough, uncompromising style of working-class teams from these localities, or even from South America (such as Boca Juniors in Argentina).

Many supporter cultures celebrate traditional idioms of masculine identity through an uncomplicated public emasculation or feminization of the 'others' (such as opposing players, supporters, match officials). Supporters aim epithets such as 'poofter', 'fanny' and 'nonce' at the allegedly weak masculinity of players and officials. Fans gesticulate to insult opponents as 'wankers' (sexually inactive men) or 'dickheads' (stupid males). Football hooligans often use graphic metaphors of sexual power ('We fucked them', 'We shagged them') to assert their masculine superiority over their opponents. Even the anti-hooligan 'carnival' fans possess a masculine culture that is conventionally intoxicated and avowedly heterosexual.

While these features of football culture demonstrate the strong presence of traditional masculine norms and identities, their pre-eminent status is thrown into serious doubt by the presence of other, more complex constructions of masculinity. We may note, initially, that there are important cultural differences in the masculinity that football dramatizes. Northern and southern European teams show clear differences in the aggression they bring to the game. More subtle differences exist in the songs and chants of various supporters, regarding the metaphors of sexual power they use to disparage 'others'. In the UK, 'realist' and performative locutions are employed to reassert male power over these others.[10] Conventional categories of 'normal' and 'deviant' sexual identity tend to be utilized. The most reflexive fan groups might label themselves with absurdly deviant identities, leaving any further epithets thrown at them by opposing fans looking pathetically weak.[11] Conversely, in southern Europe, a wider and more figurative range of sexual impurities is associated with opponents through song. In Latin America, allegorical images of sexual control (including male rape) serve to feminize the other (particularly opposing fans) (see Guttmann 1996: 67).[12]

Masculine identity is complex and multi-faceted for all groups of supporters. Hooligans are not the eternal prisoners of 'aggressive masculinity' (see Dunning, Murphy and Williams 1988) or a 'yob culture'. Outside football, they adopt other masculine roles as partners, parents, children, workmates and social friends. Among carnival fans, conventional forms of masculinity are also inverted and mocked. Songs and comments about their instrumental sexual prowess are often self-effacing.[13] Moreover, with regard to the aesthetics of playing football, most working-class clubs and supporters have always contained a deep penchant for non-violent or non-aggressive forms of masculinity. The most 'artistic' or technical players are greatly revered, particularly their sophisticated and deceptive skills which outmanoeuvre or ridicule 'tough-tackling' or 'hard' opponents.[14] Many working-class teams traditionally emphasize flowing, entertaining football rather than a 'blood and thunder' style (for example, West Ham, Glasgow Celtic, Newcastle, Napoli). Players noted for their 'aggressive' or 'dirty' style are mocked for their lack of guile, grace and dexterity. *Pace* Williams and Taylor's (1994) simplistic study of changing masculine norms, one cannot reduce the diverse and contradictory meanings of a player like Paul Gascoigne to a 1990s 'lad' or 'yob' culture.

Generally, then, we may observe that football cultures have always enabled the expression and appreciation of different forms of masculinity. One particular aspect of this masculine identity should not be emphasized to the exclusion of others. A specific masculine aesthetic cannot be pinned solely upon a singular class *habitus*, just as one cannot restrict extreme expressions of male dominance (such as beating female partners) to one social class.[15] Given the tendency of some gender sociologists to personalize the debate, I should add that I am in no way seeking to excuse or condone the more sexist forms of masculine identity. My intention here is merely to emphasize that contemporary masculine identities are far from one dimensional, no matter the social class.[16]

The critical investigation of masculinity is making slow progress within sociology. Through the post-feminist turn, a new field emerged in recent years as male academics came to reflect upon the epistemological and critical consequences of feminism for their gender. Unfortunately, rather than forward a detached yet critical analysis of masculinity issues, many enquiries have been too obviously preoccupied with lifestyle politics or plain navel-gazing. The gendered ghosts of the writer's past are exorcized, the narrative slips into a solipsistic and confessional style of prose. Cohen's (1990) excursus on masculinity is inspired and coloured by his experience of divorce. Redhead (1995:

108) rails against the 'male-dominated, and machismo' culture of football, adding paradoxically that the game was a retreat from the 'vicious male bullying at school and in the street' which he suffered as a boy. The American sociologists, Messner and Sabo (1994), produce an exceptionally onanistic enquiry into masculinity and sport.[17] The more sophisticated, critical sociologists sometimes lapse into this auto-narrative.[18] If personal reflection upon the 'inner self' does provide deeper insights on masculinity, then 'sociologists' of this ilk have effectively written themselves out of a job. New Age gurus or psychotherapists are more empowered by contemporary Western culture to locate the phenomenology of the self and map its contours. Professional essayists and novelists possess the Leavisite credentials of 'good writing' to unmask the personal properties of emotional and social experiences. Sociologists analysing male identity have to get back to writing critically and objectively on their subject, rather than advertising their personal worth as 'corrected males'.

Women and Participation in the Football Culture

While academics cavil over the gender politics of their colleagues and themselves, women struggle on in making headway within football. In the West, more women are playing and reporting on the game. The rise in registered female players has been sudden, reaching around 25,000 in England alone, with greater numbers of clubs organized into women's leagues (Lopez 1997: 235–6; see Duke and Crolley 1996). As late as 1978, the English FA had been supported by the Court of Appeal in excluding women from football teams. One judge, Lord Denning, ruled that a dissenting view would be an 'absurdity', rendering the Sex Discrimination Act 1975 'an ass – an idiot' if it were strictly applied to football (McArdle 1996: 157). Today, most schools encourage female pupils to play in PE classes or representative matches.

These advances are unlikely to revolutionize women's relationship to physical culture. They remain far more committed than men to fitness and body shape than to team competitions like football (Buñuel 1991; Markula 1995). Female footballers still experience the same treatment as athletes and tennis players. Both men and women comment on their 'lesbian tendencies' and their physical 'masculinization' through 'overdevelopment' of limbs in the heat of 'unfeminine' competition (see Griffin 1992). Technically, among children, there is often little to separate the sexes. Nelson (1996: 78–9) cites the case of a ten-year-old goal-keeper in Baltimore who performed so well that flabbergasted parents insisted she pull her pants down to prove her gender. In separate cases in Virginia and Ohio, all-girl teams were recognized by soccer coaches as superior to all-boy ones, resulting in the boys' unwillingness to compete in cross-gender tournaments. Nevertheless, in coaching the game, the 'glass ceiling' remains intact in the oldest football nations, as it is in other international sports (see Theberge 1993). In 1997, the Equal Opportunities Commission backed a top English female coach in her sex discrimination case against the national FA (*The Guardian*, 24 September 1997).

Women's professional football leagues continue to endure low economic and social status. Female players in the top leagues (Italy and Scandinavia, for example) earn a mere fraction of the fortunes earned by their male counterparts. Only 2,200 fans turned up in Oslo to watch the 1997 final of the Women's European Championship, between Italy and Germany, although the event was televised in 135 nations. Female international football is given its strongest global media coverage during the Olympics, where public and corporate interest in the male tournament remains relatively low. The mediascape of female football has yet to produce its superstar player, with full access to advertising contracts, major interviews and the enveloping celebrity circuit. The first such superstars will follow other female sports celebrities (such as 'FloJo' in athletics, Gabriella Sabatini in tennis or Manon Rhéuame in ice hockey), in being rewarded commercially for feminine beauty rather than sporting expertise (see Laberge 1995: 142). In this way, the patriarchal gaze retains its power as the price of admission to an exclusive male sporting world.

Further sex barriers are constructed through media presentations and discourses on football. The 'football talk' of sports presenters invents an exclusively masculine 'football world'. Ex-professional commentators employ discourses that are grounded in the male world of public work, rather than the female realm of private intimacy and emotion (Johnson 1994). In the past decade, some women have emerged prominently within the football media. In southern Europe, female reporters regularly interview football personalities or compere television shows. However, their visual attractiveness rather than analytical abilities are at a premium; few women fill the position of resident tactical expert or chief interviewer, deferring instead to older male colleagues. In the UK, journalists like Eleanor Levy (former editor of *90 Minutes* magazine) have established a prominence among football writers. Again, however, this may say more about the relatively low esteem of both football glossies and women within the fourth estate than it does about any equalization of gender roles.

I noted in chapter 2 that football's twentieth-century development was heavily dependent upon the modernization of nations, and the related establishment of class and gender identities. Throughout Europe and Latin America, the game became dominated by the working classes and, more particularly, men. Conversely, we find that the new, post-modern football cultures have become the most accommodating towards women. In Japan, women are in the vanguard of new cultural trends, and have taken to football spectating more readily than men (Horne 1996: 541–2). In the United States, women comprise roughly 40 per cent of all soccer players (Andrews et al. 1997: 265); the game has around 27 million 'involved family participants', and is particularly supported among white suburban mothers, the 'soccer moms', that were explicitly targeted by the 1996 Clinton re-election campaign. Large numbers of women participate in the carnival culture following Ireland, Norway and Denmark, including the stereo-typically 'male' predilections of heavy drinking, earthy language and carousing (Giulianotti 1996a and 1996b; Eichberg 1992).

Elsewhere, strong cultural pressures undermine female involvement. In sub-Saharan Africa, female sports participation is culturally proscribed at the local level; in the most extreme circumstances, such as war or famine, care of the family is prioritized (Richards 1997: 150). In old socialist societies like Poland, the football ground remained the preferred public space for males; the theatre or some other social event was favoured by women (Ciupak 1973: 97). Women of Eastern extraction, such as Muslims or Hindus, experience a stark cultural division between male/public space and female/private space. Even among second and third generation Western immigrants, formidable barriers prevent or dissuade women from taking an interest in football, never mind playing the game (Zaman 1997: 62). However, some reports from the Muslim world suggest that football participation can help women to challenge their traditional gender role. In Zanzibar, the Women Fighters team has been formally recognized by the national FA, although players are forced to wear the traditional Muslim *higab* and some are beaten by 'disgraced' male relatives (*New Internationalist*, December 1997). In Iran, women defied an eighteen-year ban from sports stadia by storming into Tehran's Azadi Stadium to celebrate the national side's qualification for France '98.

Generally, important class and cultural divisions shape women's experience of football. The expertise of young, middle-class women in earning greater freedom within the realms of lifestyle and leisure politics is not mirrored among older, working-class women who have less economic and cultural capital. Further differences tend to be cultural. The new football cultures in the West (admittedly with greater middle class participation) are more accommodating towards female involvement. Conversely, new football nations in the developing world tend to obstruct women's involvement in the game for cultural reasons, although at the national level some women's teams perform with notable success (for example, China, Nigeria). Racism and ethnic intolerance may prove to be a cross-cutting source of inequality, which I examine below in fuller detail.

Football Racism: the scope of the problem

Racism within football appears to be a cultural universal, occurring between and within ethnic groupings. Elementary expressions of racism involve the abuse and discriminatory treatment of non-white players. More complex racism includes prejudicial treatment by the powerful against the relatively powerless within the same ethno-national community, such as the *terroni* insults aimed at southern Italians by northern counterparts, or the former West Germans' maltreatment of the *ossies* of eastern Germany (Merkel 1998).

The ubiquity of football racism is most starkly illustrated in Brazil. Initially, the nation appears as an ethnic 'melting pot': Brazil's national football is ethnically mixed; the word *raça* ('race') has an empowering meaning within football culture, designating vigour and energy rather than a Darwinian 'racial' hierarchy. Nevertheless, Brazil's complex history of slavery, racialized divisions and vast economic inequalities leaves a deep impression on football (Leite Lopes 1997). Contrary to popular belief, football 'offers almost no opportunities for significant upward mobility' (Evanson 1982: 403).[19] Brazil's white elites resisted football's organized dissipation among the black population.[20] Only managerial pragmatism persuaded top clubs to admit black players. Vasco da Gama were the first to field non-white players in 1923 and promptly stormed to the Rio league championship, encouraging other sides to follow suit (Oliver 1992: 615). The national side continued to exclude black players, such as for the 1938 World Cup semi-final against Italy, which Brazil lost 2–1 (Allison 1978: 219–20). Brazil's shock defeat in the 1950 World Cup finals has been commonly blamed on black players, especially the goal-keeper. (Significantly, Brazilian sides still favour white goal-keepers, through their 'racial' characteristics of reliability and rationality). Black players were pivotal to Brazil's successes during the 1960s and 1970s, yet white middle-class hegemony over football's powerful positions was reasserted. Meanwhile, domestic football still highlights Brazil's ethno-regional divisions; affluent south-easteners deride poorer north-east people as *paraibas* due to their large black constituency.

In the West, football racism is particularly acute during periods of political and economic restructuring. In Italy, the *mezzogiorno* tensions see both northern and southern people routinely defining themselves against 'the other', such as Africans and Afro-Caribbeans; hence the routine insults (*'Negro di Merda'*) directed at black players like Abedi Pele and Paul Ince. In the UK, racist abuse was routinely aimed at players such as Paul Elliott, Mark Walters, Ian Wright and, most famously, John Barnes throughout the 1970s and 1980s (Hill 1989). Meanwhile, the Thatcher government was stoking anti-immigration sentiments within the white working class. In Germany, terrace racism is associated with the rise of the far right, particularly in the old East where deep social and economic insecurities prevail (see Lash 1994: 131, 168). Even in traditionally liberal nations such as Sweden and Holland, outbreaks of supporter racism are highly reflective of growing anti-immigrant sentiments within mainstream society (see Bairner 1994: 213).

Anti-Racism Campaigns: strengths and limitations

In the UK, anti-racism campaigns have been initiated, especially through spectator organizations and the professional players themselves. Fan groups following Leeds United, Leicester City, Newcastle United, Hibernian and Hearts were among the first to form anti-racist organizations (Thomas 1995: 98). Many club fanzines were inspired by supporters sickened at the racist abuse meted out to players, and campaigned for fellow fans to intervene against such attacks (Giulianotti 1997c; Holland et al. 1996: 178–83). The Commission for Racial Equality and the Professional Footballers' Association launched a joint campaign in August 1993, entitled 'Let's Kick Racism Out of Football'. The Football Offences Act 1991 criminalized racial chanting or abuse (Armstrong 1998: 127–8). In Germany, public awareness campaigns have countered perceived rises in fan racism at matches. In December 1992, all Bundesliga clubs wore shirts emblazoned with the legend *'Mein Freund ist Ausländer'* ('My Friend is a Foreigner'), while Frankfurt fans carried banners announcing 'Germany without foreigners is like a piano without black keys' (Merkel 1994: 113). The Italian players' association organized *'No al Razzismo'* ('no to racism') pre-match demonstrations and sparked wider debate on racism. The most militant anti-racism comes from specific fan groups. Hamburg's second division club, St Pauli, attracts a leftist core support, which has distributed anti-Nazi fanzines and stickers, and tackled racist fans more physically (Benson 1993: 57). Supporter groups following Manchester United and Celtic have also fought with members of fascist movements.

A recurring weakness of some campaigns is their concentration on the perceived racism of football hooligans (see Fleming and Tomlinson 1996: 83). Typically, this grossly exaggerates the prevalence of racist or neo-Nazi groups within the hooligan networks. Few hooligans are ideologically racist or members of extreme right-wing movements. Indeed, hooligan groups are far more likely to include some black lads, for whom racist rhetoric is anathema. Moreover, most hooligans would undermine their evasion of police attention if they were openly associated with racist or neo-Nazi movements.[21] Rising racism among German supporters is often pinned on hooligan groups, particularly those from the East. But, it would appear that their use of 'Nazi' symbols and slogans reflects a deeper, more generalized alienation towards wealthier Westerners rather than a popular and coherent political ideology. Punks during the 1970s were similarly interested in using swastikas to shock and upset, rather than to signify underlying fascist sentiments (see Hebdige 1979: 116–17).[22]

Pinning the blame on hooligan groups does some violence to the real complexity of fan racism. It nurtures the smug, self-justifying inference that 'ordinary' football people are far removed from such anti-social extremism. Far more insidious is the deep-seated and 'normalized' racism within football's mainstream institutions. First, there is the more routinized racist vernacular of the football crowd, employed stereotypically to explain the game to fellows, and to influence the performance of players. Football players are still blithely discussed in racial idioms ('Pakis', 'darkies', etc) (see Back et al. 1996a; 1996c: 58). Academic and liberal interpretations of fan racism are too keen to condemn rather than understand its cultural properties. For example, when John Barnes became Liverpool's first black player in modern times, fans of all-white neighbours Everton taunted their rivals by chanting 'Nigger-pool, Nigger-pool'. Such abuse might commonly receive condemnation, but it carried a further perlocutionary force. Certainly, it was intended to put Barnes off his game. But it was also intended to affront the vast majority of Liverpool fans since they (as the Everton fans knew) were probably just as 'racist' (Back et al. 1996b).

Secondly, fan racism is less problematic to black players than their maltreatment by more powerful football figures. Football coaches and officials decide when the non-white player can play and in what position. For non-white athletes, experience of racism begins at school. Teachers expect relatively limited academic standards from black pupils, tacitly aware that their job prospects are poor. The curriculum is shuffled to maximize their 'natural' sporting ability. Vince Hilaire, touted during the 1970s as the future first black England international, reports his schooling experience: 'I was pushed into certain sports at school, like athletics. The teachers naturally thought, because you're black, you must have some sort of athletic ability in you; but I didn't even want to do athletics, at all' (quoted in Cashmore 1982: 98). Conversely, teachers possess the equally racial assumption that Asians are not 'natural' athletes, and so discourage them from competitive sports (Dimeo and Finn 1998). The positive responses of black pupils to such treatment seems, on the surface, to support stereotypes about their ethnicity. However, high unemployment and a dearth of successful role models within mainstream society underline sport's greater potential for enabling rapid social mobility.

Playing the White Man: racism within football's institutions

Once ensconced within football, young black players are less likely to share in the banter and camaraderie of white team-mates. Racial stereo-types about black athleticism and low intelligence continue through team selection. Like other team sports such as rugby union, American football and baseball, soccer players are stacked into 'central' or 'non-central' / 'peripheral' positions. Central players form the team spine of goal-keeper, sweeper, midfield play-maker, centre-forward. They represent its 'intelligent centre', shaping the pattern of play according to the team's ability and the demands of each match. Peripheral players, such as full-backs and wingers, are valued intellectually, although their athleticism and individualism are vital in exploiting width, especially in attack. Black players tend to be 'stacked' into these peripheral positions due to their coaches' racial beliefs, that they cannot match the decision-making skills or consistency of white players, although their speed and unpredictable style are essential on the wings (Maguire 1988; 1991: 102–13). Thus, football coaches and the media tend to assume that black players possess erratic qualities ('natural ability'), while white players have more controllable capabilities ('hard work' or 'dedication') (see Murrell and Curtis 1994). African players are seen as 'magical' and 'irrational' in the West (Hoberman 1997: 70, 117); European clubs import them to provide something 'unpredictable', a touch of the 'exotic', to help break down scientifically organized, Western defences. In further contrast, Asian players that advance to the youth leagues or to trials with professional clubs, find that they are played consistently out of position by white coaches who still expect little from them (Holland et al. 1996: 166).

One problem in elucidating player stacking is that football coaches and players have long associated particular nationalities with specific playing qualities. Even in cosmopolitan France, clubs have practised what may appear to be crude stereo-typing in their acquisition of foreign talent: in goal, we have Yugoslavs; on the wing, Africans and South Americans; in attack, the South American or the Yugoslav; in midfield, Austro-Hungarians or the Dutch; in defence, Germans or Danes (Lanfranchi 1994: 69–72). Future research into positional segregation and racism would do well to recognize the complexity of this issue.

The dominant discourses within the professional game reproduce racist assumptions. In the 1970s, top English manager Ron Atkinson 'joked' about the three 'sambos' in his West Bromwich Albion side (see Redhead 1986b: 28). When commentating for television on the England–Cameroon match in 1990, Atkinson described the Africans as lacking in professional nous, attributing this to their recent descent from the trees. The Welsh manager, Bobby Gould, was accused of racism by one of his players, Noel Blake, who then withdrew from the national side while Gould retained his position (Back et al. 1998). The Nigeria coach, the Dutchman Clemens Westerhof, placed his players under virtual house arrest at the 1994 World Cup finals, claiming that they were 'immature and easily diverted' (Hoberman 1997: 120–1).[23] In the upper echelons of football officialdom, the UEFA President, Lennart Johannson, made unguarded, racist jokes about 'darkies' in South Africa to a Swedish newspaper (Sugden and Tomlinson 1998). In the UK, before the mid-1970s, such racism meant that very few black players broke into the top leagues, particularly in Scotland (Holland 1995: 571; Horne 1995: 38–9). Successful players tended to be air-brushed from football's official histories, even though the lineage of black players goes back to Arthur Wharton in 1889 (Cosgrove 1991; Vasili 1995). Even latterly, researchers from Middlesex University found that top British clubs remained reluctant to participate in anti-racism campaigns (*Independent on Sunday*, 7 September 1997).

Young black players do employ certain strategies of empowerment. Some nurture their ethnicity by forming all-black or all-Asian clubs or leagues (see Williams 1993, 1994). Top players like Ruud Gullit and Brendan Batson use their professional kudos and intellect to campaign publicly against racism (see Orakwue 1998). The UK government has announced its intention to criminalize racism at all levels of the game. Yet racism, prejudice and social intolerance may be expressed in particularly insidious ways that are difficult to establish beyond reasonable doubt. If a coach claims that the poorer players in his playing system 'just happen' to be Pakistani, how do you 'prove' legally his racism? We may assume that non-white players will continue to be discriminated against in team selection; remain underpaid relative to their merits; and stay under-rewarded through secondary income, such as in public relations work or merchandising deals. In that sense, anti-racism strategies continue to fail when they seek 'technical' solutions (such as a penal code on racism) rather than a full moral and intersubjective debate involving all football people on the social principles of the game.

Beyond the millennium: the new cultural politics of class

Clearly, football cultures throughout the world have much work to do to establish social equality. Traditionally, women and ethnic minorities have been the most marginal social groups, particularly as men re-established their hegemony over football during the inter-war years. Latterly, some figures suggest that female attendance at matches has increased, although the evidence remains stretched. Instead, the sudden surfeit of female sports writers and journalists reflects the growing football interests of young, new middle-class women. Traditional male prejudices and stereo-types continue to be directed at female participants, but the new 'post-national' football cultures of Japan, USA and Ireland highlight the potential of women's involvement.

Ethnic minorities and non-whites struggle with prejudicial treatment inside the game. In the West, structural inequalities and cultural antagonisms underlie both manifest and latent forms of racism. Even in Brazil, where non-whites have used football for social and economic advancement, white elites predominate. In the UK, political legislation and anti-racism campaigns have been introduced. Yet, so long as these measures fail to confront the routinized racism within mainstream football, fans and coaches will continue to racialize the players.

While 'race' and gender remain important in their own right, each is heavily influenced by the vicissitudes of social class relationships. For the majority of Afro-Caribbean and Asian youths, the 'racial' aspects of their disadvantage are superseded by class dynamics. Many inhabit a post-modern urban 'underclass' that is unable to join the small, upwardly mobile, middle-class stratum of Afro-Caribbean or Asian descent which football's marketeers are drawing into the stands (see Wilson 1987).[24]

A similar point may be made about the millions of women in the UK who find themselves trapped in an underclass conundrum of low pay, part-time work, childcare expenses and meagre state benefits. Football's institutions may claim that these men and women receive a 'non-discriminatory' opportunity to participate in the contemporary game. However, a reasonable disposable income is essential to purchase the kit or pay the pitch fees to play football, or to afford the match ticket or monthly television subscription to watch the matches. The football clubs and the authorities are not, of course, responsible for the sub-standard schooling and housing, or the abysmal employment prospects that characterize the 'life chances' (*sic*) of this underclass. But they do reproduce these deep inequalities by opening football to an unfettered market system, disadvantaging people along the lines of their class (and relatedly, of their 'race' or their gender). We may note here that 'liberal' critiques of football's 'traditional masculinity' also benefit the game's commodification, since they contain thinly veiled assaults on its working-class male culture.

The concept of the 'post-fan' crystallizes these class conflicts in two particular ways. First, it highlights the fact that football's working-class 'traditions' are not unidimensional. They may include strong elements of sexism and racism (as one finds throughout society at large). But they also include irony, wit, humour and a critical perspective on the club, the football authorities and the state of the game in general. These post-fan characteristics figured among football supporters long before the new middle classes discovered the sport.

Secondly, more significantly, post-fandom points to divisions within football's new middle classes. There are 'traditionalist' new middle-class fans, seeking to protect the interests of their fellow supporters by publishing critical fanzines and forming ISAs. Alternatively, a metropolitan elite of football *arrivistes* ignores the 'post-fan' impulses within working-class fandom, exaggerating instead the latter's reactionary aspects. This class seeks to assume a monopoly on 'good football writing' or critical insights into the contemporary game. The future of football culture in the UK and other Western societies is heavily dependent upon the relative influence of this new class.

Afterword

To conclude, I intend to limit this discussion to three particular topics. First, I seek to draw together some of the key strands of previous chapters to provide a genealogy of football culture. In doing so, I employ the periodizations that were first discussed in the foreword and then utilized throughout – namely, football's 'traditional', 'modern' and 'post-modern' phases. The second of these periods (modernity) is broken into three shorter stages: 'early modernity', 'intermediate modernity' and 'late modernity'. After that, I turn to outline some specific research issues that academics may address towards and beyond the millennium. The final section organizes some of the key themes of football research according to the strategic logic of the game itself. Metaphorically, I imagine the general research exercise as a football match; hence, the key themes must be located into football positions if the sociological study is to proceed.

A Concise Genealogy of Football Culture

In constructing a genealogy of football, we may state that the traditional period lasts until after the First World War. It is marked by the establishment of the game's rules, their international diffusion and the formation of national associations to administer the sport, under the aegis of ruling elites. In Britain, former public schoolboys and the upper middle classes preserve their political influence. National 'playing styles' are formulated; international fixtures remain irregular except for those between neighbouring nations. The Home Nation's cultural hegemony is accepted overseas; British teams represent the benchmark test for overseas sides, while British input helps to legitimize FIFA's global purchase. English lingers in Latin America as the official language for football affairs. Football becomes hugely popular among the new urban working classes, but the structural consequences are resisted by the game's governing elites in each nation. Major grounds are erected, segregating the social classes while increasing match revenues. The Home Nations legalize professionalism, but resent the practice and blame it for the game's troubles. In Latin America, professionalism remains officially barred; leading clubs ban the signing of black or mulatto players. The manager's position remains under-developed, as does football's tactical dimension; the emphasis remains on attack, although significant cultural differences do exist (for example, Scottish passing or the English 'kick and rush'). Culturally, the players have the position of 'local heroes'; leading internationalists may earn contracts to endorse commercial products that are normally associated with health and fitness.

'Early modernity' lasts from the early 1920s to the end of the Second World War. The Olympic Games and the World Cup cement football's global status and showcase the rise of Latin American and south European nations. The game becomes heavily associated with nationalism. International fixtures unify individual nations and symbolize the rivalries and conflicts between them. Vast major stadia are built throughout the world, often with public money, highlighting civic and national pride in the representative football team. Radio transports the football event to all corners of the nation. The UK struggles to sustain its on-field hegemony, while southern Europe (especially Italy) ex-ploits Latin American nations by hiring the finest talents and 'naturalizing' them as *oriundi*. The cultural symbolism of top players continues to rise as they become national figures, filmed and interviewed for cinema or radio news programmes. They enjoy higher than average wages but lack long-term secu-rity or industrial freedom. Managers become far more established; Herbert Chapman (Arsenal) and Vittorio Pozzo (Italy) symbolize their efficacy in maximizing the team's 'productivity'. The new offside rule inspires tactical innovations (for example, 'WM', switching the centre-half into defence); the team's division of labour becomes more complex and Fordist. Throughout this period, football becomes the major national sport in Europe and Latin America, surrounded by a male, working-class popular culture. Economic decline, un-employment and military conflict attest to the difficult social circumstances of football's supporters. Yet they remain strikingly non-violent and passive in their 'supporter' identity at matches, and show only limited involvement in radical left politics outside the game. Intellectuals begin to muse on football's ideological effect, in distracting the masses from their abject conditions, or enabling elites and fascists to exploit the public through the sports event *qua* mass nationalist rally.

Many of these aspects of early modernity continue throughout the post-war period of 1945 to the early 1960s which constitutes the 'intermediate modernity' of football. Further modern developments include the establish-ment of continental tiers of football government, such as the Asian Football Confederation (AFC) and the Confédération Africaine de Football (CAF); and the creation of Europe-centred competitions. The Home Nations enter the

World Cup finals with increasing commitment. The traumatic defeats of England and Scotland by Central European and Latin American nations mark a watershed in the UK's football status. Television becomes more prevalent in family homes. The skills of the world's top sides (Hungary, Brazil, Real Madrid) are globally recognized. International players like Puskás, Di Stéfano, Garrincha and Pelé become global heroes, whose public identity is still heavily tied to their on-field masterstrokes rather than their off-field lifestyles. The great World Cup-winning Brazilian sides represent the link between the modern and 'late modern' period; their early 4–2–4 formation and vibrant playing style constitute football's 'high modernity'.

Football's late modernity runs from the early 1960s to the late 1980s. Consumer culture and youth culture come to have an intense impact upon the game. Players become 'celebrities' and 'superstars'; financially, they become more secure as their legal emancipation in Europe gradually increases. Football clubs and tournaments become more and more commodified. Chief executives appear to oversee and co-ordinate the football 'business'. Revenues from trackside advertising, shirt sponsorship and club merchandising begin to overtake the income from gate-money. The wealthier football nations lose many working-class fans to other leisure industries. Global competitions are recognized as the supreme test of football status. Tactical 'fashions' change every few years: 4–3–3 (England), *catenaccio* (Italy), 3–4–3 (Holland), 4–4–2 (English clubs). Fear of defeat and defensive sterility predominate. Administrative power over football switches to the New World; the developing world secures a greater prominence at the World Cup through the machinations of Havelange. Ground modernization emphasizes safety, solidity and the functional, although cultural variations do exist: Latin America builds mass theatres; the UK and North Europe prefer rectangular stages; southern Europe and some major cities favour multi-purpose stadia with running tracks. The Hillsborough disaster attests to the failure of UK football authorities to modernize grounds, just as the Home Nations had failed to upgrade other aspects of the game. As in other forms of cultural life, football experiences its first signs of post-modernization through architecture, the Munich 'Olympiastadion' being a prominent example. Yet perhaps the most prominent emblems of late modernity are to be found in the new fan cultures. In the UK, football hooligan sub-cultures emerge with a strong attachment to youth cultural styles. In Italy and throughout southern Europe, the *ultràs* establish their hegemony in the *curvas*. In Latin America, fan sub-cultures like the *barras bravas* and the Raça provide a forum for militant fandom that turns increasingly violent. Latterly, 'carnival' supporters emerge across northern Europe. The fanzine movement in the UK reflects an increasingly reflexive and critical fan culture keen to shake off the political passivity of previous supporters.

Football's 'post-modern' epoch reflects greater middle-class hegemony over its culture; heightened commodification of this cultural activity; and the further influence of television companies in controlling clubs, organizing tournaments and financing the game. Football becomes highly fashionable. In the East, it symbolizes advanced modernity and entry to European culture; in the West, it is *de rigueur* leisure among the new middle classes. The 'post-fans' of the 1990s and beyond represent a new and critical kind of football spectator keen to produce and consume a variety of football media. Television revenues and market capitalization multiply the revenues at the top clubs. In Latin America clubs will also become private business enterprises to be bought and sold by the richest supporters. Major football tournaments become huge business expositions. Television deals and ticket distribution policies maximize income but damage the interests and rights of the most dedicated supporters. FIFA establish a niche for the game in multi-cultural 'post-national' societies such as the United States. Rule changes speed up the game and maximize its spectacular features for new audiences. Tactically, coaches turn to explore playing positions that may break down the fixed, 'modern' patterns of opponents or the stalemate in matches. The elite players enjoy the financial and industrial benefits of the Bosman ruling that collapsed European borders and increased the circulation of professional labour. Latin American and African players look increasingly to the lucrative European transfer market. However, sharpening economic and social inequalities leave a deep impression on contemporary football. Access to the heart of football culture is increasingly the preserve of the middle classes, who come to dominate the stands and the pitch just as they have always controlled the game's corridors of power.

Research into Football: some academic issues

As football enters the new millennium, future research might turn to address a number of key problematics.

1   During the 1990s, several collections explored the heterogeneity of football cultures throughout the world.[1] This research should continue for nomothetic, ideographic and critical reasons. First, it enables theories about football's social properties to be tested more rigorously than would be the case if these hypotheses were analysed within one society or several similar societies. Second, it enhances our understanding of the richness of football's social practice and cultural meanings; it also prepares a unique vantage-point for looking into the culture and identity of the particular peoples who practise the game. Third, comparative studies of football cultures also encourage us to look critically at the social relations of these societies, paying particular attention to the inequalities and conflicts that arise within and between them.

2   UK researchers are particularly guilty of paying relatively little attention to the playing styles and general aesthetics of football. This perhaps says something about their lack of long-term personal involvement in the game, as players or spectators. Hence, they would do well to expand upon the work of

European and Latin American scholars in bringing about a fuller social, cultural and historical understanding of football techniques and playing styles.

3   Researchers should explore the cultural hybridity of football relative to other sports. In what way is football culturally influenced by basketball, cricket, rugby and other sports? In the UK, there are signs that an inter-penetration exists between football and cricket's 'carnival' supporters, while playing tactics and training regimens are influenced by basketball's geometry.

4   Researchers should continue to look critically at how football reflects wider social inequalities, specifically those of age, ethnicity, gender and class. Fieldwork has concentrated disproportionately upon those at the sharp end of social stratification; more critical research needs to be undertaken with football's privileged groups (Andrews and Zwick 1998). In the US, this means doing critical ethnography with white, middle-class suburban football teams. In the UK, critical research is needed with powerful groups within football's key institutions, such as the clubs, the football authorities, the players' unions and the game's various think-tanks. It also needs to be undertaken with football's new middle-class fans, however uncomfortable this may prove for academics who find themselves researching their friends and neighbours (or even themselves).

5   There has also been a very noticeable lack of fieldwork undertaken into the day-to-day running of football clubs. In the UK, BBC TV has produced two lengthy television series about English football clubs (Sheffield United and Sunderland) as well as numerous shorter studies of British clubs. Journalists like Hunter Davies (1972) have undertaken extended studies of their own. Social researchers need to demonstrate the value of their various disciplines through detailed studies of football clubs from the inside.

6   The methods employed by social researchers must be scrutinized critically. Too often, social researchers on football leave themselves open to the accusation of 'armchair theorizing'. They draw upon newspaper reports or other poor secondary sources rather than assemble data through empirical research (see MacAloon 1992: 110). 'Easy options' or 'shortcuts' must be avoided during fieldwork. For example, if the researcher wants to publish articles about football hooligans, then he or she must go out and meet self-identifying, core 'football hooligans'.

7   Future generations of UK researchers should adopt a far more critical and theoretically sophisticated approach in studying football culture. Currently, conservative young sociologists tend to tailor or otherwise replicate the writings of their supervisors, thus producing work that is unworthy of citation. In Gramsci's terms, 'traditional' writers who have little to say are coming to outnumber the more critical, 'organic' intellectuals. This state of affairs becomes explicable when we look at the 'field' of football sociology, or sports sociology more generally. According to Bourdieu (1991b: 229–30), a 'field' is structured by power relations and conflicts over various kinds of capital: economic, cultural, symbolic and social. Among UK football academics, the struggle

for personal 'symbolic' capital (such as prestige and status) is all too evident in research and written work. Senior academics 'lift' the ideas of junior researchers without acknowledgement. Journal referees protect their status by demanding that submitted articles must cite their work. Research grants are awarded by funding bodies when applicants include fawning respect towards possible referees. Doctoral candidates recapitulate the thinking of their supervisors, who reciprocate by helping to get the completed work accepted for publication. This client-oriented system of knowledge production is worthy of a research project in itself.

Towards a Team of the Future: sociological research as football formation

One way forward for researchers is to imagine football-related research within a match situation. In this scenario, the researcher becomes a manager who must organize his methodological and analytical interests into a team formation. To win, the researcher must be able to defend the value of academic research from attack by its opponents. He or she must also 'score' by capturing the essence of the game. In this way, the researcher constructs a compelling 'team' of analytical positions through which the social aspects of football may be researched and explained.

Personally, I would organize these research strategies into a 4–2–4 system, created by the Paraguayans and copied to devastating effect by the Brazilians. The deployment of this playing formation here will also suggest to the observant reader where my epistemological loyalties lie relative to debates about modern/post-modern sociology.

My four 'defenders' of the sociological approach are the classic topics for sociologists, specifically *age*, *class*, *gender* and *ethnicity*. It is impossible to do modern sociology without recognizing their ontological centrality to social life. Age, class, ethnicity and gender can effectively function as 'stoppers', in preventing social actors from gaining full or even partial access to the economic and social resources within the society. They help to explain the reproduction of social inequalities. When those hostile to social science begin to question its relevance to football, sociologists and other academics can always turn to these four social 'facts of life' to validate their enquiries. Yet, in an attacking sense, these four categories do have some real weaknesses. They do not explain by themselves how people who belong to different social categories have a genuine passion for football, nor do they unpack the positive, aesthetic or cultural aspects of football.

To get into the heart of football culture itself, we have to move upfield and enter the 'engine-room' of midfield. This is where the shape and texture of the match are decided, whether it becomes fast or slow, intricate or direct. In intellectual terms, the middle of the park is hermeneutic territory, where the identity of arguments is worked out, in terms of what can and cannot be postulated. The midfielders themselves must be able to accomplish defensive duties and perform the attacking functions that I discuss later. For the researcher, the midfield must involve an enquiry into identity formation. The two midfielders in my playing formation represent the twin dimensions of identity-formation. One is the *semantic* side of identity: the expressive, the creative and the playful face of football, which becomes possible so long as the social actors have the basic resources in their possession. To express themselves, midfield 'play-makers' need the most basic of resources (including the ball). Likewise, expressive forms of football identity are only possible when social actors have other fundamental resources at their disposal (such as knowing the rules, having a 'feel' for the game, as well as experience in playing or watching). Conversely, there is the *syntactic* side of identity: the combative, competitive side of football, in which actors gain a sense of themselves only by defining themselves against their opponents (who perhaps begin with more resources). Syntax and semantics cannot be divorced but must always go together. Great visionaries need ball-winners and protectors on the park; people always need to mark themselves off from others, no matter how self-confident they may be about their own identity. Syntax and semantics therefore make up the midfield 'identity' of the research.

In attack, we must fill four positions. On the wings, we find aspects of the exceptional and unconventional within football culture, which may still on occasion shake the game to its foundations. On the left flank we might find the *deviance* within football: the hooligan sub-cultures among the fans, the unreconstructed individualists and entertainers among the players, the 'giant-killing' clubs who survive and prosper by challenging the omnipotent. Without these deviant features, football would become colourless and predictable. Culturally, football still celebrates its maverick players and surprise moments, just as every society gives a special meaning and status to those who are not quite 'normal'. On the right flank we find the *epic* features of football: the definitive moments in the history of a specific football culture. The *epic* aspects do not necessarily need to centre on success, glory and victory. Indeed most football nations tend to refer to epic defeats that say much about the contemporary condition of their football culture.[2] The hermeneutics of these *epics* underpin the historiography of the football culture. They provide an important link between the midfield of identity and the aesthetic aspects of attack.

In the middle of attack, we have the deep-lying forward and the out-and-out striker. The former position has been made famous by the likes of Puskás, Pelé, Maradona, Hagi and Baggio. Players such as these reveal the cultural beauty of the game. It is here that sociologists must turn to enquire into the *aesthetics* of football, to try to capture what it means to appreciate particular playing styles, technical skills or kinds of fandom within a specific football culture. By unravelling the meaning of the football aesthetic, and relating it to other cultural practices and beliefs, we begin to unmask the more complex aspects of the society that produces this interpretation of the global game.

Finally, in the shape of the striker, we find football's culturally *sublime* qualities. We explore those moments when the profane, mundane and every-day aspects of existence are transcended, when the senses are numbed or overpowered by sights on the field or experiences off it that are barely comprehensible or explicable. Any game within any culture must be capable of producing subliminal, ecstatic moments. An astonishing manoeuvre, a breath-taking save, or the winning goal to crown a match of extraordinary drama may be central to football's ecstatic moments. They may include the experience of deep immersion and *communitas* within the general body of supporters; the ecstasy of sharing in a 'walk on' display of flags and scarves for one's club; or the 'buzz' of seeing and charging opponents in hooligan confrontations. The subliminal aspects of football are created and transmitted to social actors through the popular culture of the game. The hope of experiencing these ecstatic moments is what keeps people going to matches, to participate on the pitch or in the stands.

Football players and supporters know very well when these subliminal aspects of football are artificially manufactured. Television adverts may speak incessantly of the 'joy' of football. But they cannot simulate and bottle these pleasures into a ubiquitous 30-second advert for Coca-Cola or Nike sportswear. The ecstatic moments of the game will be weakened rather than enhanced by, for example, widening the goals to increase the number of goals, or sanitizing the ground to reduce spontaneous behaviour. These measures belong to the realm of what Brazilians call *decepcionado* (the 'disenchanted'), for those who no longer or never will engage with the football aesthetic, the goal of the game (Helal 1994: 5). In framing their research agendas, football academics would do well to remember this point. Without its deep subliminal features, the game falls into stalemate, the spectacle can no longer deliver, the match cannot be won. True football ends.

Notes

Chapter 1   The Essence of Football

1   The rules of these games were rather more specialized and different from those of folk football. Moreover, the small ball used for *harpastum* was nearer the size for golf than football.

2   For example, two teams consisting of twelve players each kicked a ball around; goals were scored by kicking the ball into a designated space. Match officials oversaw proceedings. My thanks to Jianhua Lu for this information.

3   The goals might have been the space between two sticks stuck in the ground; or a symbolic landmark such as the local parish church.

4   *Soule* was performed on *le jour de mardi gras*, surviving well into the nineteenth century. Guttmann (1991: 47) speculates that it formed part of a fertility rite, celebrating the 'vernal equinox', 'to mark and celebrate the rebirth of vegetation after winter's death'.

5   For example, Corinthians beat three-time cup-winners Blackburn Rovers on each occasion in the 1880s, and then thrashed Bury 10–3 in 1904.

6   Within thirty years, the attendance for the FA Cup final had shot up from 2,000 (1872) to 110,802 (1901) (McIntosh 1987: 73).

7   For example, the 1910 Corinthians tour of Brazil caught the local imagination, as did the 1904 Glasgow Rangers tour of Austria (Meisl 1955: 57, 68).

8   My thanks to Pablo Alabarces for this insight.

9   The conflict lasted 100 hours, produced 6,000 dead, 12,000 wounded, 50,000 homeless, and no observable change in either nation's borders (Kapuscinski 1992: 157ff).

10   The Red Army team were CDKA (later known as CSKA); Moscow Dinamo were sponsored by the KGB; Lokomotiv were backed by the Ministry of Railways; Torpedo were supported by the largest autoworks company.

11   For example, Dinamo Berlin, Dukla Prague, Honved Budapest, Legia Warsaw, Steaua Bucharest and CSKA Sofia.

12   My thanks to Jianhua Lu for this insight.

13   Research from the North American basketball league, the National Basketball Association (NBA), found home advantage to be at its optimum when the stadium was small, compact and centrally located. The team should also have a long tradition, and

represent a city with a strong sense of local pride that is not expressed through any other cultural medium (Mazruchi 1985).

14 For a short critique of Sebreli, in Spanish, see Alabarces (1997).

15 To some extent, Mason is arguing against a false target as Lever's (1983: 159) change of position is noteworthy: 'Few are fooled by the government's manipulation of sport for its nationalistic goals . . . Brazilians want to share both the wealth of a modern nation and the excitement offered by winning soccer teams. If one can promote the other, so much the better.'

16 In a peculiar betrayal of leftist elitism, we may note here that Keir Hardie, a legendary figure in Labour Party history and the first socialist parliamentarian, took a dim view of sport, describing it as 'degrading' and dismissing football as an 'abomination' (Smith & Williams 1980: 121).

17 Morgan (1988) has counter-argued that Adorno's hostility to sport has been exaggerated. Yet there is no disguising the haughty, privileged epistemology and cultural conservatism which the Frankfurt School claim for themselves in diagnosing sport's ideological role.

18 My thanks to John Sugden for this observation.

19 See Corry (1994: 102); Mason (1989a: 173); Sugden & Bairner (1993: 82–3).

20 My thanks to Mark Nuttall for this fascinating piece of information.

21 Durkheim (1965) notes that totemism produces a particular veneration of ancestors, who come to be treated as 'gods' and thus are accorded the status of tribal founders. People who attend the funerals of top football players and managers show such respect. The prevailing sentiment is that, without the deceased, the football club (as a tribe, including the supporters) would not have enjoyed its glorious successes. Examples here include the funerals of Matt Busby (Manchester United), Jock Stein (Glasgow Celtic) and Billy Bremner (Leeds United).

Chapter 2   The Twentieth-century Sport

1 Vidacs (1997) notes that in Cameroon, Zambia and other African nations, radio stations broadcast live coverage of matches involving the national team, enabling the call for national unity to be made.

2 The complexity and hybridity of this 'soccerscape' is neatly exemplified by the Australia–Saudi Arabia fixture played in Sydney in 1988. The match was part of a tournament celebrating the Australian bicentenary, although football in Australia is renowned for its ethnic (rather than majority) support. The Saudi team had been invited to participate primarily for economic reasons (the sale of television rights overseas). The Saudis hired most of the trackside advertising boards, covering them in Arabic script slogans that promoted strictly Western consumer goods such as Mars bars (Rowe et al. 1994: 671–2).

3 This process has been documented in exceptional detail elsewhere, and I do not propose to rehearse that analysis. See Tomlinson (1986, 1994), Sugden & Tomlinson (1997, 1998), and Sugden, Tomlinson & Darby (1998).

4 The founders were Belgium, Denmark, France, The Netherlands, Spain, Sweden and Switzerland (Tomlinson 1994: 13).

5 Up to 250,000 attended the 1923 Cup final, known as the 'White Horse Final' for the police horse that helped to push spectators off the pitch (Dunning et al. 1988: 91; Signy 1969: 48). In Scotland 150,000 attended the Scotland–England fixture at Hampden Park, Glasgow in 1937; a week later, over 165,000 fans attended the Scottish Cup final between Celtic and Aberdeen (Webster 1990: 87).

6 As a reflection of the UK's continuing influence on football's development overseas, Signy (1969: 51) reports that this Austrian side had been tutored by Jimmy Hogan, 'the English coach with the Scottish methods'.

7 Dinamo drew 3–3 with Chelsea, beat Cardiff City 10–1 then Arsenal 4–3, and finally drew with Glasgow Rangers 2–2. Around 260,000 fans watched the four games.

8 FIFA's omnipotence is reflected in the priority given to its major football tournament, the World Cup, over all other events, including the Olympic Games. Qualifying matches for the World Cup finals are given international priority over every other fixture.

9 CONCACAF's Spanish title reflected Central American political influences and successes on the park, but its headquarters' location in New York indicated where economic and cultural growth was expected to appear.

10 The International Board is empowered to oversee and amend the laws of football. It has eight seats: four controlled by FIFA, and one controlled by each of the four British Home Nations. A minimum of six votes is required for a motion on the laws to be passed by the board.

11 Appadurai (1995) makes a similar point when discussing cricket matches between India and Pakistan. He argues that these matches are not simply 'a release valve for popular hostility between the two nations', but are instead a 'complex arena' for dramatizing the animosity and fraternity that exist between the two nations.

12 Research exercises in American positivism still continue to advance the view that organized, non-competitive sport is a strong preventive device from a life of delinquency among the young (see Agnew & Petersen 1989).

13 See, for example, the Woolfenden Committee on *Sport and the Community* (1960); the Albemarle report on the *Youth Service* (1960); the Crowther Report *15–18* (1960); the Newsom report, *Half Our Future* (1963).

14 Personal research in Scotland found that hooligan groups in Aberdeen and Edinburgh founded their own football clubs, which in no way reduced their players' violent activities when spectating at matches.

15 The major exponents of the historical relationship between British football and the urban working class were the leftist sociologists of the 1970s, most notably Ian Taylor (1970, 1971, 1982a, 1982b, 1987, 1991a, 1991b), Phil Cohen (1972), Chas Critcher (1971, 1979) and John Clarke (1978).

16 In 1909, a team of Italian immigrants from New York drew with the Olympic champions of Great Britain. At the 1950 World Cup finals in Brazil, England were humiliated by a 1–0 loss to the USA side.

17 Japan's new soccer league has encountered similar problems: a history of failure in forming professional leagues; falling attendances in the new J-League.

18 For example, the Belgian club Mouscron has sought to play its home games inside a larger stadium in France; the British clubs of Wimbledon and Clydebank have actively considered moving to Dublin, where a young and unfulfilled football market is thought to exist.

Chapter 3   Spectator Cultures

1 See *Sociological Review* 1991; Giulianotti, Bonney & Hepworth 1994; Redhead 1993; Armstrong & Giulianotti 1997, 1998a; Brown 1998; Giulianotti & Williams 1994; Williams & Wagg 1991.

2 Clare narrated a notorious BBC TV *Panorama* documentary on young Millwall fans in

1978, in which he identified sub-divisions and hierarchies structured on the basis of age and fighting prowess.

3 Perhaps a little pedantically, Dunning (1994) and Redhead (1991b: 480) suggest that this schism means the term 'Leicester School' is no longer applicable. Nevertheless, their work still retains a deep epistemological commitment to Elias, even without any later contribution from Williams.

4 The exchange attracted an unpublished reply (Harris 1992) and an extraordinary statement by the journal editors (*Sociological Review* 1992).

5 A female journalist found herself watching the most famous sociologists on television while she was travelling with England fans to a match in Ireland. She reports: 'Most of the fans' derision was reserved for various football professors, who got two-fingered gestures. "Oh, here we go . . . All to do with fucking society and all that"' (*Scotland on Sunday*, 19 February 1995). Interestingly, the report portrays the fans as deeply offensive, but the journalist does not mention any abuse being hurled at her on the basis of her gender or employment position with a Scottish newspaper.

6 See, for example, Armstrong (1994, 1998); Finn & Giulianotti (1998); Giulianotti (1998); Hobbs & Robins (1991).

7 For example, German hooligans have a penchant for Chevignon gear, while their Serbian counterparts at Red Star Belgrade (the *Dieselistas*) favour the Diesel designer label.

8 See also the fictional work of Irvine Welsh (1993, 1994, 1995), John King (1996, 1998) and Gavin Anderson (1996).

9 For example, the hooligan documentaries on Millwall (*Panorama*, BBCTV 1978), West Ham (*Hooligan*, ITV 1985), Millwall & West Ham (*Inside Story*, BBCTV 1994) and the European Championships (*Inside Story*, BBCTV 1996) are often to be found in the video-libraries of football hooligans, and reviewed at regular intervals.

10 For example, Fiorentina and Torino *ultràs* were friendly with one another at the same time as they were divided on either axis of the Sampdoria–Genoa rivalry. The overtures of Fiorentina *ultràs* towards Sampdoria, that the latter should ameliorate their position towards Torino *ultràs*, received short shrift in Genoa, to the extent that the Fiorentina–Sampdoria alliance was subsequently inverted into a rivalry.

11 In Peru during the 1920s, the emergence of the *barras* coincided with the most pyrotechnic of fan displays and violent of confrontations. Matches between Atlético Chalaco and Alianza Lima were highly volatile affairs. Many Chalaco supporters were fishermen and would occasionally throw lighted dynamite sticks onto the pitch during games (Stein *et al.* 1986: 70).

12 Charanga Rubro Negra translates as 'Red Black Band', the colours being those of Flamengo, and celebrating the musical 'band' that the fans contained.

13 Comparisons may also be drawn with the carnival behaviour of the 'Barmy Army' that follows the England cricket team abroad (MacQuillan 1996).

14 In the case of Irish fans, for example, important dynamics include those discussed in the last chapter: the rise of football culture generally in Ireland, the emergence of a southern Irish nationalism, and the growing political and social influence of women (especially among the new middle classes).

Chapter 4   Football Grounds

1 See Bale (1980, 1982, 1989a, 1989b, 1990, 1991b, 1992, 1993a, 1993b, 1994; Bale & Moen 1995).

2 Conversely, while undertaking research with colleagues Greg Lloyd and Stuart Black at the local Aberdeen ground, we found that many residents there felt the 'negative externalities' of disorderly fan behaviour and traffic congestion were outweighed by 'positive externalities', such as their enjoyment of watching crowds moving through the locality, and catching the atmosphere of the occasion.

3 Following this disaster, FIFA paid out £4,000 to relatives of each of the 81 victims.

4 This perhaps makes Young's contribution less culpable, given that he lives and works in North America. By contrast, Taylor and Williams both have personal relationships to Hillsborough: Taylor is a Sheffield Wednesday fan, while Williams is a Liverpool fan who witnessed the disaster from an adjoining stand.

5 Ironically, research suggests that a failed bid for a major tournament is a more cost-effective exercise. It publicizes the city to boost tourism and investment, and avoids the expense of actually hosting the event (Roche 1992: 587).

6 The biggest impact of ground redevelopment had been experienced in the pre-Taylor modernization of Ibrox, which fell from about 100,000 in 1977 to the final figure of 45,000 in 1981; an extension to one stand has raised this to 52,000.

7 Prior to the 1998 World Cup finals in France, one FIFA-recognized ticket agent was reported to be making a profit of £10 million by selling over-priced 'football packages' (including match tickets) for the tournament.

8 While the 'gaze' within the modern stadium emphasizes visibility, Eichberg (1995: 339) notes how the reverse may occur. The ground becomes a *demi-monde* of non-visibility, a symbol of deep topophobia, employed to secrete the excesses of those that control it. In Chile, Pinochet used stadiums to help 'disappear' political militants and imagined opponents. The military government of Indonesia used the Senayan national stadium as a political detention centre from 1965 to 1970 (Colombijn 1998).

9 Fiske (1993: 84–5) describes modern sports stadia as reversed or 'inverted panopticons'. Instead of the few in the centre surveying the powerless masses on the periphery, sports stadia are arranged so that those in the middle have their every move scrutinized by the masses. Meanwhile, most up-to-date facilities provide fans with numerous television monitors, slow motion replays and immediate data outputs (such as the speed of the ball). However, unbeknown to Fiske, the original panopticon metaphor still applies in football stadia. Fans are constantly surveilled and filmed, and have limited access to the information within the ground that is held by the police and football officials.

10 Eichberg (1986: 110–11) argues that the 'green Olympics' of Munich 1972 were housed in one of the earliest post-modern stadia. The architecture celebrated the 'greenification' of sports, through verdant spaces where people can 'get back into the open'. To support the theme, the stadium's industrial metallic structures were painted green or camouflaged by shrub transplantation.

11 For example, during pitch invasions by streakers or hooligans, televised sport markedly refuses to transmit the on-field action, focusing instead on the watching crowd.

Chapter 5 The Price of Victory

1 The playing side mirrored this rudimentary boardroom division of labour. The manager controlled all team affairs, including recruitment and transfers, team selection, player discipline, and even fitness tests. At bigger clubs, the manager might appoint several underlings to control the reserve and youth teams, and scouting. No separation existed between coaching the team and managing its affairs, as had become standard practice on the continent since the war.

2   Due to this corporate structure, Argentinian clubs have struggled to compete in the transfer market with the purchasing power and salary pull of top European clubs. In 1997, Boca Juniors introduced a scheme to attract private capital without compromising the influence of its *socios*. A public investment fund was introduced, whereby the fund would buy players aged under twenty-six and loan them to the club; profits from player sales would be divided equally between club and fund. The fund's organizers hoped that investors would be genuine Boca fans willing to forgo any quick profiteering through the sale of top players. The immediate objective was to raise some £12 million for Boca's manager to enter the transfer market.

3   The 1997 BSkyB deal with English football stipulates that half of the income is divided equally among member clubs; one-quarter is allocated according to final league position; the final quarter is divided according to television appearances.

4   For example, in Italy, if the total number of all television viewers is 30 million at the time a match is screened live on PPV, and its audience share is 2% (or 600,000 viewers), then setting the viewing fee at 28,000 lire (approximately £10) will still net the highly profitable sum of 16.8 billion lire (or £6 million).

5   At the time of writing, there are four South American tournaments for the continent's big clubs. All receive substantial television coverage.

6   The nations involved in the bid were Denmark, Finland, Norway, Iceland, Sweden and the Faroe Islands.

7   In American football, the 'reverse draft' system enables the poorest performing teams to receive first pick of the players who emerge from college. In the case of a player transfer, the selling club receives recompense for its player at a level that it ultimately decides.

8   Further examples of this are found in England, with Caspian's acquisition of Leeds United; in France, with Canal Plus buying into Paris St Germain; in Germany, with Bertelsmann's involvement in Hertha Berlin; in Spain, with Antenne 3 buying into Real Madrid; in Turkey, with the ownership of Star TV by Istanbulspor president Cem Uzan; the Dutch electronics giant Philips owning PSV Eindhoven; and, most successfully, Silvio Berlusconi's Fininvest acquiring AC Milan.

9   To counter the rise of private television, Spain's right-wing government allowed the state broadcaster, Telefonica, to acquire the rights to Spanish league fixtures, *after* these had been sold to private enterprise. The contractual dispute led to intervention by the European Union. Whichever broadcaster succeeds in the long term, it is doubtful if top Spanish clubs will be seriously affected. Even before digital television, Barcelona were pulling in £23 million of television money for the 1996–7 season, dwarfing the £9 million guaranteed annually to English clubs by BSkyB.

10 In Scotland, there is the 'myth' that referees are often members of Protestant Masonic lodges, and thus likely to favour Glasgow Rangers over any other team. Some seductive evidence is lent to this conspiracy theory through the famous admission by one long-serving referee, made at a Masonic dinner, that he had never allowed Rangers to lose a match in which he had officiated.

11 The football pools first appeared in the UK in 1923 and in the inter-war years became a popular method of gambling, a pleasure that was otherwise heavily circumscribed. The pools companies spent heavily on 'recruitment', advertising in the press, and hiring celebrities to dish out large wins, thereby adding to their 'fantastic' potential in delivering people from poverty at times of massive unemployment. By the mid-1930s, £30 million was being spent annually on the pools (Jones 1992: 52). While middle-class Protestants and staid left-wingers criticized its corrupting aspects, working-class cultural assertiveness established the pools as a popular amusement (Fishwick 1989:

132–3). By 1949, the pools were continuing through the summer months by listing matches in the Australian league. They were fully institutionalized in 1959 when the football authorities established a share of the profits.

12   Some fans have boycotted products that are advertised by rival clubs. Sunderland fans boycotted breakfast cereal advertised by Newcastle players; Parmalat products were boycotted by fans throughout Portugal due to a shirt sponsorship deal with Benfica; McEwan's lager was boycotted throughout Scotland due to its investment in Glasgow Rangers. These direct actions are relatively rare and usually have a limited effect upon national or international consumption patterns.

Chapter 6   Football's Players

1   Totalitarian regimes may transfer unsatisfactory or 'anti-social' players to more sinister total institutions. Many skilful Soviet players found themselves transferred to Stalin's gulags. In Iraq, two rounds of prison torture were inflicted on national team players after their failure to qualify for the 1998 World Cup finals (*The Observer*, 20 July 1997)

2   See, for example, Dunphy (1976) and Nelson (1995).

3   The rebel league lasted four years and included a startling array of international talent, such as England internationalists (Mason 1994). The financial wealth behind this enterprise was such that it was dubbed El Dorado, though Colombia's non-affiliation with FIFA saw the league's players incur international bans (Del Burgo 1995: 59–60).

4   Wagg (1984: 192) notes that this common bond exists to some extent among football managers, although it is universally recognized that a win for one can mean unemployment for the other.

5   Some alarming parallels exist here between football and academe. Career and research pressures typically mean that academics too display clear signs of low-status crystallization. Family life can be limited, leisure and recreation tend to be built around research interests, conferences become holidays, while academics make little or no contribution to local political and cultural associations.

6   Similarly, Sorlin (1994: 130) notes that 'Stardom is a crucial aspect of the relationship between the media and the society in which they develop. The very existence of stars is vital for the media.'

7   For example, the Italy v Germany World Cup final of 1982 was 'replayed' thirteen years later, in June 1995, and televised live in Italy.

8   Case C-415/93 *Union Royale Belge des Sociétés de Football Association ASBL and Others v. Jean-Marc Bosman and Others* [1995] ECR I-4921, [1996] 1 CMLR 645, [1996] 1 CEC 38, hereafter referred to as *Bosman*.

9   The court did consider whether pressing reasons of public interest might justify the regulations. One counter-argument had been that transfer fees functioned to safeguard the competitive and financial balance between clubs, and the recruitment and training of talented young players. But in a rather critical statement on European football's infrastructure, the court applauded these ideals while dismissing the transfer system as unable to achieve them in fact.

10   The '3+2 rule' permitted European clubs to field no more than three 'foreign' and two 'assimilated' players during matches. 'Assimilated' players were foreigners who had been played for an uninterrupted period of five years, including three as a junior, in the relevant nation (Greenfield & Osborn 1998: 16, 22).

11   Prior to *Bosman*, French and Spanish club football had established a 'free transfer'

system for all players who had completed long contracts (Thomas 1996: 24; Campbell & Sloane 1997: 3).

12   For example, in the 1997–8 season, the top earners annually in Germany were on £2 million, the lowest on £25,000; in France, the top wage was £1.9 million, the lowest £15,000; in Italy, the top wage was £3.5 million, the lowest £13,000 (*World Soccer*, March 1998).

13   Real Madrid immobilized Clarence Seerdorf by imposing a buyout clause of some £91 million. Real Betis's world-record acquisition of the Brazilian Denilson for $35 million, on an 11–year deal, contains within it a guarantee of £260 million to be paid to the club by anyone buying out his contract.

14   In Bilbao at least, the young stars may find the commercial appeal of *Bosman* to be counterpoised by more engrained social norms: the ideological attraction of playing for the local club which is the institutional embodiment of Basque nationalism (MacClancy 1996a).

Chapter 7   The Goal of Winning?

1   Anthropologists have made the fullest interpretation of football aesthetics thus far. Archetti (1996) and Hognestad (1997) argue that football enables individuals to express deep sentiments like joy, laughter and sorrow, and to explore existential and moral themes, such as fortune, mortality and gender identity.

2   My thanks to Gerry Finn for this historical point.

3   In an early instance of brand marketing through a public medium, Chapman pressurized London Underground to change the name of the tube station nearest to Highbury from 'Gillespie Road' to 'Arsenal'.

4   Grozio (1990) argues that a mixture of rigid defence and swift counter-attack (*contropiede*) was central to Italian football culture from the 1920s to the 1980s.

5   In the Soviet Union, young players were subjected to basic psychological testing before they were recruited to youth teams.

6   Quoted by Brian Glanville in *World Soccer*, November 1997.

7   The international sports media had been particularly critical of the process that allowed a physical Argentinian team to reach the World Cup final. FIFA moved to counteract many of the Argentinians' perceived tactics, such as feigning injuries, diving in the box and persistent fouling.

8   My thanks to Rafael Bayce for recounting his memory of this goal from his seat in the Maracanã.

9   A third Brazilian innovation might seem to be Pelé's famous 'bicycle kick'. However, the technique was invented in Chile by Ramón Unzaga and exported to Spain during the 1920s by David Arellano, where it became known as *la chilena* (Galeano 1997: 48).

10   For example, Clarke & Clarke (1982) criticize the mass media for using stereotypes about the 'inscrutable Chinese', the 'fiery Welsh', the 'sly and unstable Latins', the 'devil-may-care casualness of Brazilians' and so on. Yet, over a decade later, Sugden & Tomlinson (1994) employ similarly racialized metaphors to speak innocently about 'the aggression of the Argentinians, the free spirit of the Cameroons, . . . the endeavour of the Scandinavians, the volatility of the Italians'.

11   One problem here concerns the racial self-labelling of particular peoples. For example, the pre-war French explained their footballing fortunes according to their 'racial' characteristics. French players were seen as launching frenzied attacks on more disciplined and

organized opponents, who soaked up these impulsive energies and struck decisively near the end. French football and identity were therefore symbiotically related to the Celtic nations of Scotland, Wales and Ireland, full of inspiration and courage, rather than the teutonic mechanics of Germany or the dispassionate strength of England.

12 My thanks to my Brazilian friends, José Sergio Leite Lopes and colleagues for this information.

13 For example, Mendoza is renowned for its cyclists, Córdoba and Bahía Blanca for basketball, Tucumán for rugby and San Juan for roller-hockey.

Chapter 8   The Cultural Politics of Play

1 See the work of Jean-Marie Brohm, Chas Critcher, John Hargreaves, Ian Taylor and Gerhard Vinnai.

2 The term 'post-fan' has itself acquired some academic permanence. I first introduced the term in a working paper that formed part of a series for Manchester Metropolitan University's Institute for Popular Culture (Giulianotti 1993). The notion of 'post-fandom' was then lifted, without acknowledgement to me, by one of the series editors, Steve Redhead, and appeared in the title of one of his short texts on football. I am reclaiming the term here.

3 There are strong parallels here with the music industry. During the late 1970s and early 1980s, many 'independent' labels sprung up in opposition to the major labels. However, the latter used their financial power to recruit the top 'independent' bands and copied the new labels' managerial style by creating small production units and devolving day-to-day power.

4 Tranter (1998: 79) makes the related point that, up until the First World War, middle- rather than working-class women played football matches far more frequently.

5 South American clubs still charge the concessionary half-price figure for women.

6 In a televised interview, one figurational sociologist recommended that clubs should promote female involvement at all levels of football. These measures would, he argued, help to transform the atmosphere among football crowds (Patrick Murphy, 'Send for the Sisters', *World in Action*, ITV, January 1990).

7 While conducting research in Germany, I came across a female fan at the centre of violence between rival club supporters. In Italy, leading women in the Sampdoria *ultràs* are just as supportive of violent behaviour as their male counterparts.

8 Elsewhere, Coddington betrays a southern, metropolitan bias when arguing that football should not be about 'cloth-capped men trudging to the game straight from a hard morning's work at the factory' (1997: 18).

9 Derek Dooley, star striker during the late 1940s and early 1950s, is quoted in Hopcraft (1988: 63–4). Dooley's comment is given particular poignancy by the fact that his playing career was tragically cut short at the age of twenty-two; a serious injury led to his right leg being amputated from the middle of the thigh.

10 For example, opponents are insulted through public accusations of falling outside the realm of male heterosexual relations: 'He's gay, he's bent, his arse is up for rent, Ian Durrant' (Aberdeen fans towards a controversial Rangers player).

11 For example, Aberdeen fans often sing, 'We fuck sheep, we fuck sheep.' Hartlepool fans produce the absurdist song: 'We've got a nasty reputation for soliciting little boys / For raping old age pensioners and nicking kiddies toys / We're the perverts of the nation, the worst you've ever seen / We're a pack of foul mouthed bastards / And they call us Hartlepool!' (Merrills 1997: 145).

12 For example, Boca fans chant against their rivals: 'Huracan, Huracan / They'll give you it up the arse; Fandom, fandom, there is only one / That's Boca's fans / That will break the arse of the lot of them; Cordoban, Cordoban / Wipe your bottom well / 'Cos we're coming to screw you' (Archetti 1992). Argentinian fans imagined the 1982 Falklands War and the 1986 World Cup 'revenge' over England as a sexual battle between the two nations' respective leaders. Hence, a popular chant was: 'Thatcher, Thatcher, Thatcher / Where is she? / Maradona's looking for her / To screw her' (1992).

13 For example, at the 1992 European Championships in Sweden, the bedraggled Scottish Tartan Army often sang, in true absurdist style, 'We're too sexy for the Swedes.'

14 Illustrations here include Davie Cooper, Jimmy Johnstone in Scotland; George Best, Tony Currie, Denis Law in north England; Chris Waddle, Dejan Stojkovic at Marseille; Gullit at Feyenoord; Maradona and Caniggia at Boca Juniors.

15 Indeed, it is worth noting here that football fans direct mocking chants at players who are publicly accused of 'wife-beating'.

16 In a journal article, one sociologist made an oblique reference to the relatively low interest that I have in gender issues. However, he later explained to me that he did not really support that criticism, but that he felt under strong pressure to make it from a journal referee. If he had not done so, he believed the entire article may have been jeopardized. Needless to say, the assertive referee enjoyed anonymity. In reply to that opponent, I would point out that no sociological text on football contains more than a few pages on women and the game. Anyone who criticizes a fellow researcher on these grounds should look to the balance of his or her own work. For my own part, I have endeavoured to promote the work of female researchers through my earlier football collections. Indeed, the sole exception is the collection *Game Without Frontiers*, co-edited with John Williams, which has an all-male cast of researchers.

17 Each chapter begins with an episode of 'masculinity in action' involving one of the authors. Perhaps the most cringe-inducing involves Don Sabo arm-wrestling with the black inmates of a local 'joint' ('as I like to call it'). Sabo (1994: 161–2) 'enjoys the physical connection with other men', the contest 'allows me to climb outside the bourgeois husk of my life'; 'the manly juices start flowing again, though . . . I want to learn that it is OK to be vulnerable to defeat'.

18 Tony Jefferson (1998), for example, begins a superb critique of sociological studies of the masculine body by relating two stories about the pain of his liberal impulses while teaching physical education as a young man.

19 Research in the Caribbean found that poverty did enable black players to find the time, space and supportive culture for learning football skills, but it also undermined the organizational continuity of lower-class teams (who often failed to become regularized 'clubs') and pushed players into joining middle-class clubs for payment (Austin 1990).

20 In Peru, the brilliant Alianza Lima side of the 1920s experienced similar prejudice as many of its players and supporters were black (Stein et al. 1986: 75–7).

21 Back, Crabbe and Solomos (1998) make this point, confirming earlier work that highlighted the fragile links between football hooligans and organized racism (Armstrong 1998; Giulianotti 1996c).

22 The case of FC Berlin may be instructive. Formerly known as Dinamo Berlin, the club had been the sports vehicle of East Germany's police and security forces, notably the hated *stasi* (secret police) and its chief, Erich Mielke. The loss of fans after German reunification left Dinamo with a hooligan rump of supporters, particularly at away matches. These supporters acquired a reputation for chanting a bizarre

repertoire of Nazi and Communist songs, reflecting through hyperbole the deep-seated alienation of old East Germans towards their new, Western predicament (Kuper 1994: 17–8).

23 Westerhof claimed that there are two kinds of Nigerian: 'the ones who play soccer, and the others who deal drugs all over the world' (Hoberman 1997: 120–1).

24 Solomos and Back (1996: 70–1) note that the discovery of a racialized underclass occurred first in the United States. They argue that in both the UK and the US there has been 'a hardening of racial and ethnic cleavages among lower class groups', adding that 'the situation in Britain's "inner cities" may be moving closer to the one that is prevalent in the United States' (1996).

Afterword

1 In tandem with various colleagues, I have sought to contribute to this end through several on-going edited collections (see Giulianotti et al. 1994; & Williams 1994; Armstrong & Giulianotti 1997, 1998a). The work of the Brighton-based researchers is valuable in this regard (see Tomlinson & Whannel 1986; Sugden & Tomlinson 1994; Sugden & Bairner 1998). See also Brown (1998).

2 For example, Scotland's 1978 World Cup campaign, England's loss to Hungary in 1953, Argentina's 6–1 loss to the Czechs in 1958, Brazil's 1950 loss to Uruguay.

References

Adorno, T. (1967) *Prisms*, London: Spearman.

Adorno, T. (1991) *The Culture Industry*, London: Routledge.

Agnew, R. and D.M. Petersen (1989) 'Leisure and Delinquency', *Social Problems*, 36 (4): 332–350.

Agozino, B. (1996) 'Football and the Civilizing Process', *International Journal of the Sociology of Law*, 24 (2): 163–88.

Alabarces, P. (1997) 'De la heteronomía a la continuidad? Las culturas populares en el espectáculo futbolístico', *Punto de Vista*, 57.

Alabarces, P. (1998) 'Post-modern Times: identities and violence in Argentine football', in G. Armstrong and R. Giulianotti (eds) (1998a).

Alabarces, P. and M. Rodrigues (1999) 'Football and Fatherland: the crisis of national representation in Argentinian football', *Culture, Sport, Society* 2 (3): in press.

Allan, J. (1989) *Bloody Casuals: diary of a football hooligan*, Glasgow: Famedram.

Allison, L. (1978) 'Association Football and the Urban Ethos', in J.D. Wirth and R.L. Jones (eds) *Manchester and São Paulo: problems of rapid urban growth*, Stanford: Stanford University Press.

Alt, J. (1983) 'Sport and Cultural Reification: from ritual to mass consumption', *Theory, Culture & Society*, 1 (3): 93–107.

Anderson, B. (1983) *Imagined Communities*, London: Verso.

Anderson, G. (1996) *Casual*, Dunoon: Low Life.

Andersson, T. and A. Radmann (1998) '"The Swedish Model": football and social development in Sweden', in G. Armstrong and R. Giulianotti (eds) (1998a).

Andrews, D. and Z. Mazur (1995) 'Jordanki: global localization and the intertextual dialectic of mediated popular culture', paper to the second Theory, Culture & Society Conference: Culture and Identity: City, Nation, World, Berlin, 10–14 August.

Andrews, D., R. Pitter, D. Zwick and D. Ambrose (1997) 'Soccer's Racial Frontier: sport and the suburbanization of contemporary America', in G. Armstrong and R. Giulianotti (eds) (1997).

Andrews, D. and D. Zwick (1998) 'The Suburban Soccer Field: sport and America's culture of privilege', in G. Armstrong and R. Giulianotti (eds) (1998a).

Appadurai, A. (1990) 'Disjuncture and Difference in the Global Cultural Economy', *Theory, Culture & Society*, 7 (2–3): 295–310.

Appadurai, A. (1995) 'Playing with Modernity: the decolonisation of Indian cricket', in C.A. Breckenridge (ed.) *Consuming Modernity: public culture in a south Asian world*, Minneapolis: University of Minnesota Press.

Arbena, J. (1989) 'Dimensions of International Talent Migration in Latin American Sports', in J. Bale and J. Maguire (eds) *The Global Sports Arena*, London: Frank Cass.

Arbena, J. (1990) 'Generals and *Goles*: assessing the connection between the military and soccer in Argentina', *International Journal of the History of Sport*, 7 (1): 120–30.

Arbena, J.L. (1998) 'Dimensions of Latin American Soccer On and Off the Field', *Studies in Latin American Popular Culture*, 17: in press.

Archer, R. (1987) 'An Exceptional Case: politics and sport in South Africa's townships', in W.J. Baker and J.A. Mangan (eds) (1987).

Archetti, E. (1992) 'Argentinian Football: a ritual of violence?', *International Journal of the History of Sport*, 9 (2): 209–35.

Archetti, E. (1993) 'Idioms and Rituals of Manhood: the worlds of tango and football in Argentina', unpublished paper.

Archetti, E. (1994) 'Models of Masculinity in the Poetics of the Argentinian Tango', in E.P. Archetti (ed.) *Exploring the Written: anthropology and the multiplicity of writing*, Oslo: Scandinavia University Press.

Archetti, E. (1996) 'In Search of National Identity: Argentinian football and Europe', in J.A. Mangan (ed.) *Tribal Identities: nationalism, Europe, sport*, London: Frank Cass.

Archetti, E. (1997a) ' "And Give Joy to My Heart": ideology and emotions in the Argentinian cult of Maradona', in G. Armstrong and R. Giulianotti (eds) (1997).

Archetti, E. (1997b) *Guinea-Pigs: food, symbol and conflict of knowledge in Ecuador*, Oxford: Berg.

Archetti, E. and A. Romero (1994) 'Death and Violence in Argentinian Football', in R. Giulianotti et al. (eds) (1994).

Ariès, P. (1983) *The Hour of Our Death*, New York: Arnold Knopf.

Armstrong, G. (1993) 'Like that Desmond Morris?', in D. Hobbs and T. May (eds) *Interpreting the Field*, Oxford: Oxford University Press.

Armstrong, G. (1994) 'False Leeds: the construction of hooligan confrontations', in R. Giulianotti and J. Williams (eds) (1994).

Armstrong, G. (1998) *Football Hooligans: knowing the score*, Oxford: Berg.

Armstrong, G. and R. Giulianotti (1995) 'Avenues of Contestation: football hooligans running and ruling urban spaces', paper to the British Sociological Association (BSA) Annual Conference, University of Leicester, 10–13 April.

Armstrong, G. and R. Giulianotti (eds) (1997) *Entering the Field: new perspectives on world football*, Oxford: Berg.

Armstrong, G. and R. Giulianotti (eds) (1998a) *Football, Cultures, Identities*, Basingstoke: Macmillan.

Armstrong, G. and R. Giulianotti (1998b) 'From Another Angle: surveillance and football hooligans', in C. Norris, G. Armstrong and J. Moran (eds) *Surveillance, CCTV and Social Control*, Aldershot: Avebury / Gower.

Armstrong, G. and R. Giulianotti (1998c) 'Comportamenti Scorretti: gli hooligan, i media e la construzione della notorietà', in R. De Biasi (ed.) *You'll Never Walk Alone: il mito del tifo inglese*, Milano: SHAKE.

Armstrong, G. and R. Harris (1991) 'Football Hooligans: theory and evidence', *Sociological Review*, 39 (3): 427–58.

Armstrong, G. and D. Hobbs (1994) 'Tackled from Behind', in R. Giulianotti et al. (eds) (1994).

Armstrong, G. and M. Young (1997) 'Legislators and Interpreters: the law and "football hooligans"', in G. Armstrong and R. Giulianotti (eds) (1997).

Austin, R.L. (1990) 'A Parkboy Remembers Colts: products of a subculture of sport', *Arena Review*, 14 (1): 75–85.

Back, L., T. Crabbe and J. Solomos (1996a) 'Campaign Trail', *When Saturday Comes*, December.

Back, L., T. Crabbe and J. Solomos (1996b) 'The Culture of Racism in Football', paper to Fanatics! Football and Popular Culture in Europe: an International Conference, Institute for Popular Culture, Manchester Metropolitan University, 11–13 June.

Back, L., T. Crabbe and J. Solomos (1996c) *Alive and Still Kicking: a report by the advisory group against racism and intimidation*, London: Commission for Racial Equality.

Back, L., T. Crabbe and J. Solomos (1998) 'Racism in Football: patterns of continuity and change', in A. Brown (ed.) (1998).

Bairner, A. (1994) 'Sweden and the World Cup: soccer and Swedishness', in J. Sugden and A. Tomlinson (eds) (1994).

Bairner, A. and P. Shirlow (1997) 'The Territorial Politics of Soccer in Northern Ireland', paper to the North American Society for the Sociology of Sport (NASSS) Annual Conference: Crossing Borders, University of Toronto, Canada, 5–8 November.

Baker, W.J. (1987) 'Political Games: the meaning of international sport for independent Africa', in W.J. Baker and J.A. Mangan (eds) (1987).

Baker, W.J. (1988) *Sports in the Western World*, revised edition, Urbana: University of Illinois Press.

Baker, W.J. and J.A. Mangan (eds) (1987) *Sport in Africa: essays in social history*, New York: Holmes & Meier.

Bakhtin, M. (1968) *Rabelais and His World*, Cambridge: MIT Press.

Bale, J. (1980) 'Football Clubs as Neighbours', *Town & Country Planning*, 49 (3): 93–4.

Bale, J. (1982) *Sport and Place*, London: Hurst.

Bale, J. (1989a) *Sports Geography*, London: Spon.

Bale, J. (1989b) 'Football and Topophilia: the public and the stadium', paper to the symposium Le Football et ses Publics, 19–21 October, EUI Colloquium Papers, 232 / 89 (col. 36).

Bale, J. (1990) 'In the Shadow of the Stadium: football grounds as urban nuisances', *Geography*, 75 (4): 325–34.

Bale, J. (1991a) *The Brawn Drain*, Urbana: University of Illinois Press.

Bale, J. (1991b) 'Playing at Home: British football and a sense of place', in J. Williams and S. Wagg (eds) (1991).

Bale, J. (1992) *Sport, Space and Society*, London: Routledge.

Bale, J. (1993a) 'The Spatial Development of the Modern Stadium', *International Review for the Sociology of Sport*, 28 (2 / 3): 121–34.

Bale, J. (1993b) 'Territoriality and the Environment of British Football', in S. Glyptis (ed.) *Leisure and the Environment: essays in honour of Professor J.A. Patmore*, London: Belhaven Press.

Bale, J. (1994) *Landscapes of Modern Sport*, Leicester: Leicester University Press.

Bale, J. and O. Moen (eds) (1995) *The Stadium and the City*, Keele: Keele University Press.

Banck, G.A. (1995) 'Fragments of Cosmopolis in the Tropical Heat: anthropological reflections on aestheticization of the city-squatters, politicians and middle-class flaneurs in Vitória, Brazil', paper to the second Theory, Culture & Society Conference: Culture and Identity: City, Nation, World, Berlin, 10–14 August.

Bateson, G. (1972) *Steps to an Ecology of Mind*, New York: Ballantine.

Batty, E. (1980) *Soccer Coaching: the European Way*, London: Souvenir.

Baudrillard, J. (1983) *In the Shadow of the Silent Majorities*, New York: Semiotext (e).

Baudrillard, J. (1990) *Seduction*, Basingstoke: Macmillan.

Baudrillard, J. (1993a) *The Transparency of Evil*, London: Verso.

Baudrillard, J. (1993b) *Symbolic Exchange and Death*, London: Sage.

Baudrillard, J. (1996) *The System of Objects*, London: Verso.

Bazzano, C. (1994) 'The Italian–American Sporting Experience', in G. Eisen and D.K Wiggins (eds) *Ethnicity and Sport in North American History and Culture*, Westport, CT: Praeger.

Beck, U. (1994) 'The Reinvention of Politics: towards a theory of reflexive modernization', in U. Beck, A. Giddens and S. Lash (1994) *Reflexive Modernization*, Cambridge: Polity.

Benjamin, W. (1975) 'The Work of Art in the Age of Mechanical Production', in *Illuminations*, London: Fontana.

Benjamin, W. (1979) 'A Small History of Photography', in *One Way Street and Other Writings*, London: NLB.

Benson, R. (1993) 'Football v Racism', *The Face*, March.

Betz, H.-G. (1992) 'Postmodernism and the New Middle Class', *Theory, Culture & Society*, 9: 93–114.

Birley, D. (1993) *Sport and the Making of Britain*, Manchester: Manchester University Press.

Birley, D. (1995a) *Land of Sport and Glory: sport and British society, 1887–1910*, Manchester: Manchester University Press.

Birley, D. (1995b) *Playing the Game: sport and British society, 1910–45*, Manchester: Manchester University Press.

Black, J.S. and M.G. Lloyd (1992) 'Home or Away? Stadia redevelopment and relocation in Scotland', *Scottish Geographical Magazine*, 108 (1): 45–9.

Black, J.S. and M.G. Lloyd (1993) 'Stadia Refurbishment and Relocation in England and Wales: development options and planning issues', *Research Paper*, 6, Department of Land Economy, University of Aberdeen.

Black, J.S. and M.G. Lloyd (1994) 'Football Stadia Developments: land use policy and planning controls', *Town Planning Review*, 65 (1): 1–18.

Blain, N., R. Boyle and H. O'Donnell (1993) *Sport and National Identity in the European Media*, Leicester: Leicester University Press.

Blake, A. (1996) *The Body Language*, London: Lawrence & Wishart.

Bourdieu, P. (1984) *Distinction*, London: Routledge.

Bourdieu, P. (1991a) 'Sport and Social Class', in C. Mukerji and M. Schudson (eds) *Rethinking Popular Culture*, Oxford: University of California Press.

Bourdieu, P. (1991b) *Language and Symbolic Power*, Cambridge: Polity.

Bourgeois, N. (1995) 'Sports Journalists and their Source of Information: a conflict of interests and its resolution', *Sociology of Sport Journal*, 12 (2): 195–203.

Bowden, M. (1995) 'Soccer', in K.B. Raitz (ed.) *The Theater of Sport*, Baltimore: Johns Hopkins University Press.

Boyne, R. (1991) 'The Art of the Body in the Discourse of Postmodernity', in M. Featherstone, M. Hepworth and B.S. Turner (eds) (1991) *The Body: social process and cultural theory*, London: Sage.

Brailsford, D. (1991) *Sport, Time and Society*, London: Routledge.

Braverman, H. (1974) *Labor and Monopoly Capital*, New York: Monthly Review Press.

Brick, C. (1997) 'We're Not Singing Anymore', *90 Minutes*, 26 April.

Brimson, E. and D. (1995) *Everywhere We Go*, London: Headline.

Brimson, E. and D. (1996) *England, My England*, London: Headline.
Brimson, E. and D. (1997) *Capital Punishment*, London: Headline
Brimson, E. and D. (1998) *Derby Days*, London: Headline.
Brisaboa, J. (1996) *De Rosario y de Central*, Rosario: Homo Sapiens Ediciones.
Broere, M. and R. van der Drift (1997) *Football Africa!*, Amsterdam: KIT.
Brohm, J.-M. (1978) *Sport: a prison of measured time*, London: Pluto.
Bromberger, C. (1992) 'Lo Spettacolo delle Partite di Calcio: alcune indicazioni di analisi etnologica', in P. Lanfranchi (ed.) *Il Calcio e Il Suo Pubblico*, Roma: Edizioni Scientifiche Italiane.
Bromberger, C. (1993) ' "Allez l'OM, Forza Juve": the passion for football in Marseille and Turin', in S. Redhead (ed.) (1993).
Bromberger, C. (1995a) 'Football as World-View and as Ritual', *French Cultural Studies*, 6: 293–311.
Bromberger, C. (1995b) *Le Match de Football*, Paris: Editions de la Maison des sciences de l'homme.
Broussard, P. (1991) 'Les Mauvaises Passes du Foot', *Quel Corps? Anthropophagie du sport*, 41: 121–4.
Brown, A. (ed.) (1998) *Fanatics! Power, race, nationality and fandom in European football*, London: Routledge.
Brug, H.H. van den (1994) 'Football Hooliganism in the Netherlands', in R. Giulianotti et al. (eds) (1994).
Buford, B. (1991) *Among the Thugs*, London: Secker & Warburg.
Buñuel, A. (1991) 'The Recreational Physical Activities of Spanish Women: a sociological study of exercising for fitness', *International Review for the Sociology of Sport*, 26 (3): 203–15.
Burns, J. (1996) *Hand of God: the life of Diego Maradona*, London: Bloomsbury.
Buzzetti, J.L. (1969) 'La nacionalización del fútbol', in (various editors) *El Fútbol (antología)*, Montevideo: CEDAL.
Cameron, S. (1997) 'The Regulation of the Broadcasting of Sporting Events', *Economic Affairs*, 17 (3): 37–41.
Campbell, A. and P.J. Sloane (1997) 'The Implications of the Bosman Case for Professional Football', *Discussion Paper*, 97–02, Department of Economics, University of Aberdeen.
Canter, D., M. Comber and D. Uzzell (1989) *Football in its Place*, London: Routledge.
Carmeli, Y. and I. Bar (1998) 'Team Selection and the Chosen People in Israel: the case of Hapoel Taibeh', in G. Armstrong and R. Giulianotti (eds) (1998a).
Carvallo, J.D., S. Stein and S.C. Stokes (1984) 'Soccer and Social Change in Early Twentieth Century Peru', *Studies in Latin American Popular Culture*, 3: 17–27.
Cashmore, E.E. (1982) *Black Sportsmen*, London: Routledge & Kegan Paul.
Chambers, I. (1986) *Popular Culture: the metropolitan experience*, London: Routledge.
Chaney, D. (1993) *Fictions of Collective Life*, London: Routledge.
Ciupak, Z. (1973) 'Sports Spectators: an attempt at a sociological analysis', *International Review for the Sociology of Sport*, 8 (2): 89–102.
Clarke, A. (1992) 'Figuring a Brighter Future', in E. Dunning and C. Rojek (eds) (1992).
Clarke, A. and J. Clarke (1982) 'Highlights and Action Replays: ideology, sport and the media', in J. Hargreaves (ed.) (1982).
Clarke, G. and B. Humberstone (eds) (1997) *Researching Women and Sport*, Basingstoke: Macmillan.
Clarke, J. (1978) 'Football and Working Class Fans: tradition and change', in R. Ingham (ed.) (1978).
Clayton, A. (1987) 'Sport and African Soldiers', in W.J. Baker and J.A. Mangan (eds) (1987).

Clignet, R. and M. Stark (1974) 'Modernisation and Football in Cameroun', *Journal of Modern African Studies*, 12 (3): 409–421.

Coddington, A. (1997) *One of the Lads: women who follow football*, London: HarperCollins.

Cohen, A. (1993) *Masquerade Politics*, Oxford: Berg.

Cohen, D. (1990) *Being A Man*, London: Routledge.

Cohen, P. (1972) 'Sub-cultural conflict and working class community', *Working Papers in Cultural Studies*, 2, Birmingham: Centre for Contemporary Cultural Studies (CCCS).

Cohen, P. and D. Robins (1978) *Knuckle Sandwich*, Harmondsworth: Penguin.

Colombijn, F. (1998) 'View from the Periphery: football in Indonesia', in G. Armstrong and R. Giulianotti (eds) (1998a).

Conn, D. (1997) *The Football Business*, Edinburgh: Mainstream.

Corry, E. (1994) *Going to America*, Dublin: Torc.

Cosgrove, S. (1991) *Hampden Babylon*, Edinburgh: Canongate.

Crampsey, R. (1990) *The First 100 Years*, Glasgow: Scottish Football League.

Cresswell, P. and S. Evans (1997) *European Football: a fans' handbook*, London: Rough Guides.

Crisell, A. (1997) *An Introductory History of British Broadcasting*, London: Routledge.

Critcher, C. (1971) 'Football and Cultural Values', *Working Papers in Cultural Studies*, 1, Birmingham: CCCS.

Critcher, C. (1979) 'Football since the War', in J. Clarke, C. Critcher and R. Johnson (eds) *Working Class Culture: studies in history and theory*, London: Hutchinson.

Critcher, C. (1994) 'England and the World Cup: world cup willies, English football and the myth of 1966', in J. Sugden and A. Tomlinson (eds) (1994).

Csikszentmihalyi, M. (1975) *Beyond Boredom and Anxiety*, San Francisco: Jossey-Bass.

Curren, M. and L. Redmond (1991) 'We'll Support You Evermore? Football club allegiance: a survey of *When Saturday Comes* readers', University of Leicester, Sir Norman Chester Centre for Football Research (SNCCFR).

Dabscheck, B. (1979) '"Defensive Manchester": a history of the Professional Footballers Association', in R. Cashman and M. McKernan (eds) *Sport in History*, Brisbane, Queensland University Press.

Dal Lago, A. (1990) *Descrizione di una battaglia*, Bologna: Il Mulino.

Dal Lago, A. and R. De Biasi (1992) 'Italian Football Fans', paper to the International Conference: Soccer, Culture and Identity, University of Aberdeen, 1–4 April.

Dal Lago, A. and R. De Biasi (1994) 'The Social Identity of Football Fans in Italy', in R. Giulianotti et al. (eds) (1994).

Daly, J.A. (1988) 'A New Britannia in the Antipodes: sport, class and community in south Australia', in J.A. Mangan (ed.) (1988).

Davies, D. (1992) 'Chapman's Arsenal', in I. Hamilton (ed.) *The Faber Book of Soccer*, London: Faber & Faber.

Davies, H. (1972) *The Glory Game*, London: Weidenfeld & Nicolson.

De Biasi, R. (1996) '*Ultra*-political: football culture in Italy', in V. Duke & L. Crolley (1996).

De Biasi, R. and P. Lanfranchi (1997) 'The Importance of Difference: football identities in Italy', in G. Armstrong and R. Giulianotti (eds) (1997).

Del Burgo, M.B. (1995) 'Don't Stop the Carnival: football in the societies of Latin America', in S. Wagg (ed.) (1995b).

Deleuze, G. (1995) *Negotiations*, New York: Columbia University Press.

Di Giano, R. (1995) 'Effects of Modernity on Football Styles: tradition and change in the way of playing football', *La Marea*, 3 (2).

Dimeo, P. and G. Finn (1998) 'Scottish Racism, Scottish Identities: the case of Partick Thistle', in A. Brown (ed.) (1998).

Doyle, R. (1993) 'Republic is a Beautiful Word', in N. Hornby (ed.) (1993).

Duke, V. (1994) 'The Drive to Modernisation and the Supermarket Imperative: who needs a new football stadium', in R. Giulianotti and J. Williams (eds) (1994).

Duke, V. (1995) 'Going to Market: football in the societies of Eastern Europe', in S. Wagg (ed.) (1995b).

Duke, V. and L. Crolley (1996) *Football, Nationality and the State*, London: Longman.

Dunning, E. (ed.) (1970) *The Sociology of Sport*, London: Frank Cass.

Dunning, E. (1989) 'The Figurational Approach to Leisure and Sport', in C. Rojek (ed.) *Leisure for Leisure*, Basingstoke: Macmillan.

Dunning, E. (1993) 'Sport in the Civilizing Process: aspects of the development of modern sport', in E. Dunning et al. (eds) (1993).

Dunning, E. (1994) 'The Social Roots of Football Hooliganism: a reply to critics of the "Leicester School"', in R. Giulianotti et al. (eds) (1994).

Dunning, E., J. Maguire and R. Pearton (eds) (1993) *The Sports Process: a comparative and developmental approach*, Champaign, IL: Human Kinetics.

Dunning, E., P. Murphy and I. Waddington (1991) 'Anthropological versus Sociological Approaches to the Study of Soccer Hooliganism: some critical notes', *Sociological Review*, 39 (3): 459–78.

Dunning, E., P. Murphy and J. Williams (1988) *The Roots of Football Hooliganism*, London: Routledge.

Dunning, E. and C. Rojek (eds) (1992) *Sport and Leisure in the Civilizing Process*, Toronto: University of Toronto Press.

Dunning, E. and K. Sheard (1979) *Barbarians, Gentlemen and Players*, Oxford: Martin Robinson.

Dunphy, E. (1976) *Only a Game? The diary of a professional footballer*, London: Kestrel.

Durkheim, E. (1893) *The Division of Labour*, Glencoe, IL: Free Press.

Durkheim, E. (1965) *The Elementary Forms of the Religious Life*, Glencoe, IL: Free Press.

Eagleton, T. (1990) *The Ideology of the Aesthetic*, Oxford: Blackwell.

Eco, U. (1984) 'The Frames of Comic Freedom', in T.A. Sebeok (ed.) *Carnival!*, New York: Mouton.

Eco, U. (1986) *Travels in Hyperreality*, London: Picador.

Edelman, R. (1993) *Serious Fun: a history of spectator sports in the USSR*, Oxford: Oxford University Press.

Ehrenberg, A. (1991) *Le Cult de la Performance*, Paris: Calmann-Lévy.

Eichberg, H. (1986) 'The Enclosure of the Body: on the historical relativity of "health", "nature" and the environment of sport', *Journal of Contemporary History*, 21: 99–121.

Eichberg, H. (1992) 'Crisis and Grace: soccer in Denmark', *Scandinavian Journal of Medicine and Science in Sport*, 2 (3): 119–28.

Eichberg, H. (1995) 'Stadium, Pyramid, Labyrinth: eye and body on the move', in J. Bale and O. Moen (eds) (1995).

Eisenberg, C. (1989) 'The Beginnings of Football in Germany, 1890–1914', paper to the symposium Le Football et ses Publics, 19–21 October, EUI Colloquium Papers, 233 / 89 (col. 37).

Eitzen, D.S. (1988) 'Conflict Theory and Deviance in Sport', *International Review for the Sociology of Sport*, 23 (3): 193–203.

Elias, N. (1978a) *What is Sociology?*, London: Hutchinson.

Elias, N. (1978b) *The Civilizing Process: the history of manners*, Oxford: Blackwell.

Elias, N. (1982) *The Civilizing Process: state formation and civilization*, Oxford: Blackwell.

Elias, N. (1985) *The Loneliness of the Dying*, Oxford: Basil Blackwell.

Elias, N. (1997) 'Towards a Theory of Social Processes: a translation', *British Journal of Sociology*, 48 (3): 355–83.

Elias, N. and E. Dunning (1970) 'Folk Football in Medieval and Early Modern Britain', in E. Dunning (ed.) (1970).

Elias, N. and E. Dunning (1986) *Quest for Excitement*, Oxford: Blackwell.

Escobar, G. (1969) 'The Role of Sports in the Penetration of Urban Culture to the Rural Areas of Peru', *Kroeber Anthropological Society Papers*, 40: 72–81.

Euchner, C.C. (1993) *Playing the Field: why sports teams move and cities fight to keep them*, Baltimore: Johns Hopkins University Press.

Evans, A. (1986) 'Freedom to Trade under the Common Law and European Community Law: the case of the football bans', *Law Quarterly Review*, 102 (October): 510–48.

Evans, A. (1989) 'Football Law in the United Kingdom', paper to the symposium Le Football et ses Publics, 19–21 October, EUI Colloquium Papers, 253 / 89 (col. 45).

Evanson, P. (1982) 'Understanding the People: *futebol*, film, theater and politics in present-day Brazil', *South Atlantic Quarterly*, 81 (4): 399–412.

Fates, Y. (1990) 'Jeunesse: sport et politique', *Peuples Méditerranéens*, 52–3: 57–72.

Featherstone, M. (1991a) 'The Body in Consumer Culture', in M. Featherstone, M. Hepworth and B.S. Turner (eds) *The Body*, London: Sage.

Featherstone, M. (1991b) *Consumer Culture & Postmodernism*, London: Sage.

Featherstone, M. (1995) *Undoing Culture*, London: Sage.

Finn, G.P.T. (1991a) 'Racism, Religion and Social Prejudice: Irish Catholic Clubs, Soccer and Scottish society. I – The historical roots of prejudice', *International Journal of the History of Sport*, 8: 70–93.

Finn, G.P.T. (1991b) 'Racism, Religion and Social Prejudice: Irish Catholic Clubs, Soccer and Scottish Society. II – Social identities and conspiracy theories', *International Journal of the History of Sport*, 8: 370–97.

Finn, G.P.T. (1994a) 'Sporting Symbols, Sporting Identities: soccer and intergroup conflict in Scotland and Northern Ireland', in I.S. Wood (ed.) *Scotland and Ulster*, Edinburgh: Mercat Press.

Finn, G.P.T. (1994b) 'Faith, Hope and Bigotry: case-studies of anti-Catholic prejudice in Scottish soccer and society', in G. Jarvie and G. Walker (eds) *Sport in the Making of the Nation: ninety minute patriots?*, Leicester: Leicester University Press.

Finn, G.P.T. (1994c) 'Football Violence: a societal psychological perspective', in R. Giulianotti et al. (eds) (1994).

Finn, G.P.T. (1997) 'Scotland, Soccer, Society: global perspectives, parochial myopia', paper to the NASSS Annual Conference: Crossing Borders, University of Toronto, Canada, 5–8 November.

Finn, G.P.T. and R. Giulianotti (1998) 'Scottish Fans, Not English Hooligans! Scots, Scottishness and Scottish football', in A. Brown (ed.) (1998).

Fishwick, N. (1989) *English Football and Society, 1910–1950*, Manchester: Manchester University Press.

Fiske, J. (1992) 'Cultural Studies and the Culture of Everyday Life', in L. Grossberg, C. Nelson and P. Treichler (eds) *Cultural Studies*, London: Routledge.

Fiske, J. (1993) *Power Plays, Power Works*, London: Verso.

Fleming, S. and A. Tomlinson (1996) 'Football, Racism and Xenophobia in England (I): Europe and the Old England', in U. Merkel and W. Tokarski (eds) *Racism and Xenophobia in European Football*, Aachen: Meyer & Meyer.

Forsyth, R. (1990) *The Only Game: the Scots and world football*, Edinburgh: Mainstream.

Foucault, M. (1975) *The Birth of the Clinic*, New York: Vintage.

Foucault, M. (1977) *Discipline and Punish*, London: Peregrine.

Foucault, M. (1981) *History of Sexuality*, vol. 1, London: Allen Lane.

Foulds, S. and P. Harris (1979) *America's Soccer Heritage: a history of the game*, Manhattan Beach, CA: Soccer For Americans.

Francis, M. (1997) *Guvnors*, Guernsey: Milo.

Fynn, A. and L. Guest (1994) *Out of Time: why football isn't working*, London: Simon & Schuster.

Gadamer, H.-G. (1975) *Truth and Method*, London: Sheed & Ward.

Galeano, E. (1995) *El Futbol: a sol y sombra*, Buenos Aires: Catálogos.

Galeano, E. (1997) *Football: in sun and shadow*, London: Fourth Estate.

Gantz, W. and L.A. Wenner (1995) 'Fanship and the Television Sports Viewing Experience', *Sociology of Sport Journal*, 12 (1): 56–74.

Gearing, M. (1997) 'More Than A Game: the experience of being a professional footballer in Britain', *Oral History*, spring: 63–70.

Gehrmann, S. (1994) 'Football and Identity in the Ruhr: the case of Schalke 04', in R. Giulianotti and J. Williams (eds) (1994).

Gellner, E. (1983) *Nations and Nationalism*, Oxford: Blackwell.

Giddens, A. (1984) *The Constitution of Society*, Cambridge: Polity.

Giddens, A. (1990) *The Consequences of Modernity*, Cambridge: Polity.

Giddens, A. (1991) *Modernity and Self-Identity*, Cambridge: Polity.

Giulianotti, R. (1989a) 'A Critical Overview of British Sociological Investigations into Soccer Hooliganism in Scotland and Britain', *Working Papers on Football Violence*, 1, Department of Sociology, University of Aberdeen.

Giulianotti, R. (1989b) 'A Participant Observation Study of Aberdeen Football Fans at Home and Away', *Working Papers on Football Violence*, 2, Department of Sociology, University of Aberdeen.

Giulianotti, R. (1991) 'Scotland's Tartan Army in Italy: the case for the carnivalesque', *Sociological Review*, 39 (3): 503–27.

Giulianotti, R. (1992) 'Putting the Dons on the Spot: the Aberdeen soccer fan questionnaire', unpublished M. Litt. dissertation.

Giulianotti, R. (1993) 'Soccer Casuals as Cultural Intermediaries: the politics of Scottish style', in S. Redhead (ed.) (1993).

Giulianotti, R. (1994a) 'Scoring Away from Home: a statistical study of Scotland football fans at international matches in Romania and Sweden', *International Review for the Sociology of Sport*, 29 (2): 171–200.

Giulianotti, R. (1994b) 'Social Identity and Public Order: political and academic discourses on football violence', in R. Giulianotti et al. (eds) (1994).

Giulianotti, R. (1994c) 'Taking liberties: Hibs casuals and Scottish law', in R. Giulianotti, N. Bonney and M. Hepworth (eds) (1994).

Giulianotti, R. (1994d) 'Calcio e Violenza in Europa: le differenze tra Nord e Sud', *Il Discobolo*, November–December.

Giulianotti, R. (1995a) 'Football and the Politics of Carnival: an ethnographic study of Scottish fans in Sweden', *International Review for the Sociology of Sport*, 30 (2): 191–224.

Giulianotti, R. (1995b) 'Participant Observation and Research into Football Hooliganism: reflections on the problems of entrée and everyday risks', *Sociology of Sport Journal*, 12 (1): 1–20.

Giulianotti, R. (1996a) 'Back to the Future: an ethnography of Ireland's football fans at the 1994 World Cup Finals in the USA', *International Review for the Sociology of Sport*, 31 (3): 323–48.

Giulianotti, R. (1996b) ' "All the Olympians: A Thing Never Known Again?", Reflections on Irish football culture and the 1994 World Cup finals', *Irish Journal of Sociology*, 6: 101–26.
Giulianotti, R. (1996c) 'A Sociology of Scottish Football Fan Behaviour and Related Youth Subcultures', End-of-Award Report to the UK Economic and Social Research Council (ESRC).
Giulianotti, R. (1996d) 'A Sociology of Scottish Football Fan Culture', unpublished Ph.D. thesis, Department of Sociology, University of Aberdeen.
Giulianotti, R. (1997a) 'Football Media: a cultural studies perspective', *Lecturas: Educación Física y Deportes*, electronic journal of the Faculty of Social Sciences, University of Buenos Aires, Argentina (www.sirc.ca / revista / efdxtes.htm).
Giulianotti, R. (1997b) 'Guaraní and Maté: football culture and national identity in the small South American nations of Uruguay and Paraguay', paper to the NASSS Annual Conference: Crossing Borders, University of Toronto, Canada, 5–8 November.
Giulianotti, R. (1997c) 'Enlightening the North: Aberdeen fanzines and local football identity', in G. Armstrong and R. Giulianotti (eds) (1997).
Giulianotti, R. (1998) 'Hooligans and Carnival Fans: Scottish football supporter identities', in G. Armstrong and R. Giulianotti (eds) (1998a).
Giulianotti, R. (1999) 'Built by the Two Valeras: football culture and national identity in Uruguay', *Culture, Sport, Society*, 2 (3): in press.
Giulianotti, R. and G. Armstrong (1997) 'Reclaiming the Game: an introduction to the anthropology of football', in G. Armstrong and R. Giulianotti (eds) (1997).
Giulianotti, R., N. Bonney and M. Hepworth (1994) (eds) *Football, Violence and Social Identity*, London: Routledge.
Giulianotti, R. and J. Williams (eds) (1994) *Game without Frontiers: football, identity and modernity*, Aldershot: Arena.
Glanville, B. (1976) *The Dying of the Light*, London: Secker & Warburg.
Glanville, B. (1997) *The Story of the World Cup*, London: Faber & Faber.
Goddard, V.A., J.R. Llobera and C. Shore (eds) (1995) *The Anthropology of Europe*, Oxford: Berg.
Goffman, E. (1961) *Asylums*, Harmondsworth: Penguin.
Goksøyr, M. and H. Hognestad (1998) 'No Longer Worlds Apart? British influences upon the creation of a Norwegian football tradition', in G. Armstrong and R. Giulianotti (eds) (1998a).
Goodwin, R. (1997) *The Pride of North London*, London: Polar.
Gorn, E.J. and W. Goldstein (1993) *A Brief History of American Sports*, New York: Hill & Wang.
Gouldner, A. (1970) *The Coming Crisis of Western Sociology*, New York: Basic Books.
Greenfield, S. and G. Osborn (1998) 'From Feudal Serf to Big Spender: the influence of legal intervention on the status of English professional footballers', *Culture, Sport, Society*, 1 (1): 1–23.
Griffin, P. (1992) 'Changing the Game: homophobia, sexism and lesbians in sport', *Quest*, 44: 251–65.
Grozio (ed.) (1990) *Catenaccio e Contropiede: materliali e immaginari del football italiano*, Rome: Antonio Pellicani.
Gruneau, R. and D. Whitson (1993) *Hockey Night in Canada*, Toronto: Garamond Press.
Gruneau, R., D. Whitson and H. Cantelon (1988) 'Methods and Media: studying the sports / television debate', *Loisir et Société*, 11 (2): 265–81.
Guest, L. and P. Law (1997) 'The Revolution will be Televised', *World Soccer*, January.

Guttmann, A. (1991) *Women's Sports: a history*, New York: Columbia University Press.
Guttmann, A. (1994) *Games and Empires: modern sports and cultural imperialism*, New York: Columbia University Press.
Guttmann, A. (1996) *The Erotic in Sports*, New York: Columbia University Press.
Habermas, J. (1970) *Toward a Rational Society*, Boston: Beacon Press.
Habermas, J. (1987a) *The Philosophical Discourses of Modernity*, Cambridge, MA: MIT Press.
Habermas, J. (1987b) *The Theory of Communicative Action*, vol. 2: *The Critique of Functionalist Reason*, London: Heinemann.
Hall, S. (1978) 'The Treatment of Football Hooliganism in the Press', in R. Ingham (ed.) (1978).
Hammond, D. (1993) *Foul Play: a class analysis of sport*, London: Ubique.
Hannerz, U. (1990) 'Cosmopolitans and Locals in World Culture', *Theory, Culture & Society*, 7: 237–52.
Hannigan, J.A. (1995) 'The Postmodern City: a new urbanization?', *Current Sociology*, 43 (1): 151–217.
Hargreaves, Jennifer (ed.) (1982) *Sport, Culture and Ideology*, London: Routledge & Kegan Paul.
Hargreaves, Jennifer (1992) 'Sex, Gender and the Body in Sport and Leisure: has there been a civilizing process?', in E. Dunning and C. Rojek (eds) (1992).
Hargreaves, Jennifer (1994) *Sporting Females: critical issues in the history and sociology of women's sports*, London: Routledge.
Hargreaves, John (1986) *Sport, Power and Culture*, Cambridge: Polity.
Hargreaves, John (1992) 'Sport and Socialism in Britain', *Sociology of Sport Journal*, 9: 131–53.
Harrington, J.A. (1968) *Soccer Hooliganism*, Bristol: John Wright.
Harris, R. (1992) 'On Taking the Rough with the Smooth' (unpublished paper).
Harvey, D. (1989) *The Condition of Postmodernity: an inquiry into the origins of cultural change*, Oxford: Blackwell.
Hay, R. (1998) 'Soccer at the Crossroads', *Geelong Advertiser*, 15 September.
Haynes, R. (1992) *The Football Imagination*, Aldershot: Arena.
Hebdige, D. (1979) *Subculture: the meaning of style*, London: Routledge.
Heinilä, K. (1966) 'Notes on the Inter-Group Conflicts in International Sport', *International Review of Sport Sociology*, 1: 31–40.
Helal, R.G. (1994) 'The Brazilian Soccer Crisis as a Sociological Problem', unpublished Ph.D. thesis, Department of Sociology, New York University.
Hibbins, G.M. (1992) 'The Cambridge Connection: the English origins of Australian Rules Football', in J.A. Mangan (ed.) (1992).
Hill, D. (1989) *Out Of His Skin: the John Barnes phenomenon*, London: Faber & Faber.
Hobbs, D. (1993) 'Obituary: Bobby Moore', *Independent*, 26 February 1993.
Hobbs, D. and D. Robins (1991) 'The Boy Done Good: football violence, changes and continuities', *Sociological Review*, 39 (3): 551–79.
Hoberman, J. (1997) *Darwin's Athletes*, Boston: Houghton Mifflin.
Hobsbawm, E.J. (1969) *Industry and Empire*, Harmondsworth: Penguin.
Hobsbawm, E. and T. Ranger (eds) (1983) *The Invention of Tradition*, Cambridge: Cambridge University Press.
Hoch, P. (1973) *Rip Off the Big Game*, Garden City, New York: Anchor Books.
Hognestad, H. (1997) 'The Jambo Experience: an anthropological study of Hearts fans', in G. Armstrong and R. Giulianotti (eds) (1997).
Holland, B. (1995) '"Kicking Racism out of Football": an assessment of racial harassment in and around football grounds', *New Community*, 21 (4): 567–86.

Holland, B., L. Jackson, G. Jarvie and M. Smith (1996) 'Sport and Racism in Yorkshire: a case study', in J. Hill and J. Williams (eds) *Sport and Identity in the North of England*, Keele: Keele University Press.

Holmes, M. (1994) 'Symbols of National Identity and Sport: the case of the Irish football team', *Irish Political Studies*, 9: 81–98.

Holt, R. (1981) *Sport and Society in Modern France*, Basingstoke: Macmillan.

Holt, R. (1989) *Sport and the British: a modern history*, Oxford: Oxford University Press.

Holt, R. (1996) 'Contrasting Nationalisms: sport, militarism and the unitary state in Britain and France before 1914', in J.A. Mangan (ed.) *Tribal Identities*, London: Frank Cass.

Hopcraft, A. (1988) *The Football Man*, London: Simon & Schuster.

Horak, R. (1991) 'Things Change: trends in Austrian football hooliganism from 1977–1990', *Sociological Review*, 39 (3): 531–48.

Horak, R. (1992) 'Viennese Football Culture: some remarks on its history and sociology', *Innovation*, 5 (4): 89–94.

Horak, R. (1995) 'Gender, Football and Cinema: the formation of popular culture in 1920s Vienna' (unpublished paper).

Horak, R. and W. Maderthaner (1996) 'A Culture of Urban Cosmopolitanism: Uridil and Sindelar as Viennese coffee-house heroes', *International Journal of the History of Sport*, 13 (1): 139–55.

Hornby, N. (1992) *Fever Pitch*, London: Victor Gollancz.

Hornby, N. (ed.) (1993) *My Favourite Year: a collection of new football writing*, London: Witherby / When Saturday Comes.

Horne, J. (1995) 'Racism, Sectarianism and Football in Scotland,' *Scottish Affairs*, 12 (summer): 27–51.

Horne, J. (1996) ' "Saka" in Japan', *Media, Culture & Society*, 18: 527–47.

Horne, J. and D. Jary (1987) 'The Figurational Sociology of Sport and Leisure of Elias and Dunning: an exposition and a critique', in J. Horne et al. (eds) (1987).

Horne, J., D. Jary, and A. Tomlinson (eds) (1987) *Sport, Leisure and Social Relations*, Sociological Review Monograph 33, London: Routledge & Kegan Paul.

Horowitz, I. (1974) 'Sports Broadcasting', in R.G. Noll (ed.) (1974).

Horton, E. (1997) *Moving the Goalposts*, Edinburgh: Mainstream.

Houlihan, B. (1991) *The Government and Politics of Sport*, London: Routledge.

Hoy, M. (1994) 'Joyful Mayhem: Bakhtin, football songs, and the carnivalesque', *Text & Performance Quarterly*, 14: 289–304.

Hughson, J. (1992) 'Australian Soccer: "ethnic" or "Aussie" – the search for an image', *Current Affairs Bulletin*, 68 (10): 12–17.

Hughson, J. (1996) 'A Feel for the Game: an ethnographic study of soccer support and social identity', University of New South Wales, School of Sociology, unpublished Ph.D.

Hughson, J. (1997a) 'The Bad Blue Boys and the "Magical Recovery" of John Clarke', in G. Armstrong and R. Giulianotti (eds) (1997).

Hughson, J. (1997b) 'Football, Folk Dancing and Fascism: diversity and difference in multicultural Australia', *Australian and New Zealand Journal of Sociology*, 33 (2): 167–86.

Hughson J. (1998) 'Among the Thugs: the "New Ethnographies" of sporting subcultures', *International Review for the Society of Sport*, 33 (1): 43–57.

Huizinga, J. (1950) *Homo Ludens*, Boston: Beacon Press.

Humphreys, D.C., C.M. Mason and S.P. Pinch (1983) 'The Externality Fields of Football Grounds: a case study of the Dell, Southampton', *Geoforum*, 14 (4): 401–11.

Hunt, M. (1989) *There We Were: Germany '88*, Kilkenny: Sparrow Press.

Hutchinson, J. (1982) *The Football Industry*, Glasgow: Richard Drew.

Igbinovia, P. (1985) 'Soccer Hooliganism in Black Africa', *International Journal of Offender Therapy and Comparative Criminology*, 29: 135–46.

Ingham, R. (ed.) (1978) *Football Hooliganism: the wider context*, London: Inter-Action Imprint.

Inglis, F. (1977) *The Name of the Game*, London: Heinemann.

Inglis, F. (1995) *Raymond Williams*, London: Routledge.

Inglis, S. (1987) *The Football Grounds of Great Britain*, London: Willow.

Inglis, S. (1990) *The Football Grounds of Europe*, London: Collins Willow.

Ivanov, V.V. (1984) 'The Semiotic Theory of Carnival as the Inversion of Bipolar Opposites', in T.A. Sebeok (ed.) *Carnival!*, New York: Mouton.

Jameson, F. (1991) *Postmodernism, Or, the Cultural Logic of Late Capitalism*, London: Verso.

Jarvie, G. and G. Walker (1994) *Ninety Minute Patriots: Scottish sport in the making of a nation*, Leicester: Leicester University Press.

Jary, D., J. Horne and T. Bucke (1991) 'Football Fanzines and Football Culture: a successful case of cultural contestation', *Sociological Review*, 39 (3): 581–98.

Jefferson, T. (1998) 'Muscle, "Hard Men" and "Iron" Mike Tyson: reflections on desire, anxiety and the embodiment of masculinity', *Body & Society*, 4 (1): 77–98.

Jeffrey, I. (1992) 'Street Rivalry and Patron-Managers: football in Sharpeville 1943–1985', *African Studies*, 51 (1): 69–94.

Jenkins, R. (1992) 'Salvation for the Fittest? A West African sportsman in the age of the new imperialism', in J.A. Mangan (ed.) (1992).

Johnson, S. (1994) 'A Game of Two Halves: on men, football and gossip', *Journal of Gender Studies*, 3 (2): 145–54.

Jones, S. (1992) *Sport, Politics and the Working Class*, Manchester: Manchester University Press.

Jose, C. and W.F. Rannie (1982) *The Story of Soccer in Canada*, Lincoln, Ontario: W.F. Rannie.

Jun, T. and S. Kazue (1993) 'Scoring Big with Soccer', *Japan Quarterly*, 40 (4): 418–25.

Kahn, L.M. (1992) 'The Effects of Race on Professional Football Players' Compensation', *Industrial and Labor Relations Review*, 45 (2): 295–310.

Kapuscinski, R. (1992) *The Soccer War*, New York: Vintage International.

Katz, D. (1994) *Just Do It: the Nike spirit in the corporate world*, Holbrook, MA: Adams.

Kerr, C., J.T. Dunlop, F.H. Harbison and C.A. Myers (1973) *Industrialism and Industrial Man*, Harmondsworth: Penguin.

Kidd, B. (1988) 'The Campaign Against Sport in South Africa', *International Journal*, 43 (autumn): 643–64.

King, J. (1996) *The Football Factory*, London: Jonathan Cape.

King, J. (1998) *England Away*, London: Jonathan Cape.

King, J. and J. Kelly (1997) 'Introduction. The Cult of the Manager: do they *really* make a difference?', in J. King and J. Kelly (eds) *The Cult of the Manager*, London: Virgin.

Kirk, D. (1994) 'Physical Education and Regimes of the Body', *Australian and New Zealand Journal of Sociology*, 30 (2): 165–77.

Klein, A. (1991) 'Sport and Culture as Contested Terrain', *Sociology of Sport Journal*, 8: 79–85.

Korr, C. (1986) *West Ham United: the making of a football club*, London: Duckworth.

Kreckel, R. (1997) 'Social Integration, National Identity and German Unification', public lecture at the University of Aberdeen, King's College, 5 June.

Krotee, M.L. (1979) 'The Rise and Demise of Sport: a reflection of Uruguayan society', *American Academy of Political and Social Science Annals*, 445: 141–54.

Kuhn, T. (1962) *The Structure of Scientific Revolutions*, Chicago: Chicago University Press.

Kuhn, W. (1996) 'Franz Beckenbauer: a symbol of German soccer?', *ISHPES Studies*, 4: *Sport as Symbol, Symbols in Sport*, Berlin: Academia.

Kuper, L. (1965) *An African Bourgeoisie: race, class and politics in South Africa*, New Haven: Yale University Press.

Kuper, S. (1994) *Football against the Enemy*, London: Orion.

Kuper, S. (ed.) (1997) *Perfect Pitch: home ground*, London: Headline.

Laberge, S. (1995) 'Toward an Integration of Gender into Bourdieu's Concept of Cultural Capital', *Sociology of Sport Journal*, 12 (2): 132–46.

Lalic, D. (1993) *Torcida: pogled iznutra*, Zagreb: AGM.

Lalic, D. and S. Vrcan (1998) 'From Ends to Trenches and Back: football in the former Yugoslavia', in G. Armstrong and R. Giulianotti (eds) (1998a).

Lambourne, L. (1996) *The Aesthetic Movement*, London: Phaidon.

Lanfranchi, P. (1994) 'Exporting Football: notes on the development of football in Europe', in R. Giulianotti and J. Williams (eds) (1994).

Lanfranchi, P. (1995) 'Cathedrals in Concrete: football in southern European society', in S. Wagg (ed.) (1995b).

Lanfranchi, P. and A. Wahl (1996) 'The Immigrant as Hero: Kopka, Mekloufi and French football', *International Journal of the History of Sport*, 13 (1): 114–27.

Lash, S. (1990) *Sociology of Postmodernism*, London: Routledge.

Lash, S. (1994) 'Reflexivity and its Doubles: structure, aesthetics, community', in U. Beck, A. Giddens and S. Lash (1994), *Reflexive Modernization*, Cambridge: Polity.

Laughlin, C.D. (1993) 'Revealing the Hidden: the epiphanic dimension of games and sport', *Journal of Ritual Studies*, 7 (1): 85–104.

Leach, E. (1986) 'Violence', *London Review of Books*, 23 October.

Leifer, E.M. (1990) 'Inequality among Equals: embedding market and authority in league sports', *American Journal of Sociology*, 96 (3): 655–83.

Leifer, E.M. (1995) 'Perverse Effects of Social Support: publics and performance in major league sports', *Social Forces*, 74 (1): 81–118.

Leite Lopes, J.S. (1997) 'Successes and Contradictions in "Multiracial" Brazilian football', in G. Armstrong and R. Giulianotti (eds) (1997).

Leite Lopes, J.S. and S. Maresca (1987) 'La disparition de la joie du peuple: notes sur la mort d'un joueur de football', *Actes de la Recherche en Sciences Sociales*, 79: 21–36.

Leseth, A. (1997) 'The Use of *Juju* in Football: sport and witchcraft in Tanzania', in G. Armstrong and R. Giulianotti (eds) (1997).

Lever, J. (1972) 'Soccer: opium of the Brazilian people', *Trans-Action*, 7 (2): 36–43.

Lever, J. (1983) *Soccer Madness*, Chicago: University of Chicago Press.

Lever, J. (1995) 'Preface to Reissue', *Soccer Madness*, Chicago: University of Chicago Press.

Levi-Strauss, C. (1966) *The Savage Mind*, London: Weidenfeld & Nicolson.

Levine, P. and P. Vinten-Johansen (1981) 'The Historical Perspective: violence and sport', *Arena Review*, 5 (1): 22–30.

Levinsky, S. (1995) *El Negocio del Fútbol*, Buenos Aires: Ediciones Corregidor.

Lewis, J.M. (1982a) 'Crowd Control at English Football Matches', *Sociological Focus*, 15: 417–27.

Lewis, J.M. (1982b) 'Fan Violence: an American social problem', *Research in Social Problems and Public Policy*, 2: 175–206.

Lewis, J.M. (1989) 'A Value-Added Analysis of the Heysel Stadium Soccer Riot',

Current Psychology, 8: 15–29.

Lewis, R.W. (1996) 'Football Hooliganism in England before 1914: a critique of the Dunning thesis', *International Journal of the History of Sport*, 13 (3): 310–39.

Lightbown, C. (1992) *Millwall in the Community*, London: Millwall FC.

Lopez, S. (1997) *Women on the Ball: a guide to women's football*, London: Scarlet Press.

Lowerson, J. (1993) *Sport and the English Middle Classes: 1870–1914*, Manchester: Manchester University Press.

Loy, J.W., D.L. Andrews and R.E. Rinehart (1993) 'The Body in Culture and Sport', *Sport Science Review*, 2 (1): 69–91.

Lüschen, G. (1984) 'Status Crystallization, Social Class, Integration and Sport', *International Review for the Sociology of Sport*, 19 (3): 283–94.

Lüschen, G. and A. Rütten (1991) 'The Specificity of Status Crystallization and its Meaning in Sport', *International Review for the Sociology of Sport*, 26 (3): 217–31.

Lusted, D. (1991) 'The Glut of the Personality', in C. Gledhill (ed.) *Stardom: industry of desire*, London: Routledge.

Lynch, R. (1992) 'A Symbolic Patch of Grass: crowd disorder and regulation on the Sydney Cricket Ground Hill', *ASSH Studies in Sports History*, 7: 10–48.

Lyng, S. (1990) 'Edgework: a social psychological analysis of voluntary risk taking', *American Journal of Sociology*, 95 (4): 851–86.

Lyotard, J.-F. (1984) *The Postmodern Condition*, Minnesota: Minneapolis University Press.

MacAloon, J.J. (1992) 'The Ethnographic Imperative in Comparative Olympic Research', *Sociology of Sport Journal*, 9: 104–30.

MacClancy, J. (1996a) 'Nationalism at Play: the Basques of Vizcaya and Athletic Bilbao', in J. MacClancy (ed.) (1996b).

MacClancy, J. (ed.) (1996b) *Sport, Identity and Ethnicity*, Oxford: Berg.

Macdonald, R. and E. Batty (1971) *Scientific Soccer in the 1970s*, London: Pelham.

MacQuillan, I. (1996) 'Who's Afraid of the Barmy Army', in A. McLellan (ed.) *Nothing Sacred: the new cricket culture*, London: Two Heads.

Maffesoli, M. (1996) *The Time of the Tribes*, London: Sage.

Magoun, F.P. Jr. (1938) *History of Football: from the beginnings to 1871*, Bochum-Langendreer: Verlag Heinrich Pöppinghaus.

Maguire, J. (1988) 'Race and Positional Segregation in English Soccer: a preliminary analysis of ethnicity and sport in Britain', *Sociology of Sport Journal*, 5: 257–69.

Maguire, J. (1991) 'Sport, Racism and British Society: a sociological study of England's elite male Afro-Caribbean soccer and rugby union players', in G. Jarvie (ed.) *Sport, Racism and Ethnicity*, London: Falmer Press.

Mangan, J.A. (ed.) (1988) *Pleasure, Profit, Proselytism: British culture and sport at home and abroad 1700–1914*, London: Frank Cass.

Mangan, J.A. (ed.) (1992) *The Cultural Bond: sport, Empire, society*, London: Frank Cass.

Markula, P. (1995) 'Firm but Shapely, Fit but Sexy, Strong but Thin: the postmodern aerobicizing female bodies', *Sociology of Sport Journal*, 12 (4): 424–53.

Marples, M. (1953) *A History of Football*, London: Secker & Warburg.

Marqusee, M. (1995) *Anyone But England*, London: Verso.

Marschik, M. (1994) 'Foreign Players in Football: celebrated stars, tolerated workers', paper to the International Committee for the Sociology of Sport Conference: Contested Boundaries and Shifting Solidarities, Bielefeld, 18–23 July.

Marsh, P. (1978a) 'Life and Careers on the Soccer Terraces', in R. Ingham (ed.) (1978).

Marsh, P. (1978b) *Aggro: the illusion of violence*, London: Dent.

Marsh, P., E. Rosser and R. Harré (1978) *The Rules of Disorder*, London: Routledge &

Kegan Paul.

Martin, P.M. (1991) 'Colonialism, Youth and Football in French Equatorial Africa', *International Journal of the History of Sport*, 8 (1): 35–57.

Marx, K. (1963) *Selected Writings in Sociology and Social Philosophy*, ed. T. Bottomore and M. Rubel, London: Penguin.

Mason, C. and A. Moncrieff (1993) 'The Effect of Relocation on the Externality Fields of Football Stadia: the case of St Johnstone FC', *Scottish Geographical Magazine*, 109 (2): 96–105.

Mason, C. and R. Roberts (1991) 'The Spatial Externality Fields of Football Stadiums: the effects of football and non-football uses at Kenilworth Road, Luton', *Applied Geography*, 11: 251–66.

Mason, T. (1980) *Association Football and English Society 1863–1915*, Brighton: Harvester.

Mason, T. (1986) 'Some Englishmen and Scotsmen Abroad: the spread of world football', in A. Tomlinson and G. Whannel (eds) (1986) *Off the Ball*, London: Pluto.

Mason, T. (1989a) 'Football', in T. Mason (ed.) *Sport in Britain: a social history*, Cambridge: Cambridge University Press.

Mason, T. (1989b) 'Stanley Matthews', paper to the symposium Le Football et ses Publics, 19–21 October, EUI Colloquium Papers, 239 / 89 (col. 43).

Mason, T. (1992) 'Football on the Maidan: cultural imperialism in India', in J.A. Mangan (ed.) *The Cultural Bond: sport, empire, society*, London: Frank Cass.

Mason, T. (1994) 'The Bogotá Affair', in J. Bale and J. Maguire (eds) *The Global Sports Arena*, London: Frank Cass.

Mason, T. (1995a) *Passion of the People? Football in South America*, London: Verso.

Mason, T. (1995b) 'Futbol and Politics in Latin America', *Race & Class*, 36 (4): 71–86.

Mason, T. (1996) '"Our Stephen and Our Harold": Edwardian footballers as local heroes', *International Journal of the History of Sport*, 13 (1): 71–85.

Mazruchi, M.S. (1985) 'Local Sports Teams and Celebration of Community: a comparative analysis of the home advantage', *Sociological Quarterly*, 26 (4): 507–18.

Mazrui, A.A. (1987) 'Reflections on the Gender Gap', in W.J. Baker and J.A. Mangan (eds) (1987).

McArdle, D. (1996) 'Brothers in Arms: sport, the law and the construction of gender identity', *International Journal of the Sociology of Law*, 24: 145–62.

McGuire, E.J., K.S. Courneya, W.N. Widmeyer and A.V. Carron (1992) 'Aggression as a Potential Mediator of the Home Advantage in Professional Ice Hockey', *Journal of Sport and Exercise Psychology*, 14: 148–58.

McIlvanney, W. (1991) *Surviving the Shipwreck*, Edinburgh: Mainstream.

McInman, A.D. and J.R. Grove (1991) 'Peak Moments in Sport: a literature review', *Quest*, 43: 333–51.

McIntosh, P. (1987) *Sport in Society*, London: West London Press.

McKay, J., G. Lawrence, T. Miller and D. Rowe (1993) 'Globalization, Postmodernism and Australian Sport', *Sport Science Review*, 2 (1): 10–28.

McMaster, B. (1997) 'The Market for Corporate Control in Professional Football: is there an agency problem', *Economic Affairs*, 17 (3): 25–9.

Meisl, W. (1955) *Soccer Revolution*, London: Pheonix.

Melnick, M.J. (1986) 'The Mythology of Football Hooliganism: a closer look at the British experience', *International Review for the Sociology of Sport*, 21 (1): 1–21.

Melucci, A. (1988) 'Social Movements and the Democratization of Everyday Life', in J. Keane (ed.) *Civil Society and the State: new European perspectives*, London: Verso.

Mennell, S. (1989) *Norbert Elias: an introduction*, Oxford: Blackwell.

Merkel, U. (1994) 'Germany and the World Cup: solid, reliable, often undramatic – but successful', in J. Sugden and A. Tomlinson (eds) (1994).

Merkel, U. (1998) 'Football Identity and Youth Culture in Germany', in G. Armstrong and R. Giulianotti (eds) (1998a).

Merrills, R. (1997) *Dicks Out 2: you're not singing anymore?*, London: Red Card.

Messner, M. (1990) 'When Bodies are Weapons: masculinity and violence in sport', *International Review for the Sociology of Sport*, 25 (3): 203–20.

Messner, M.A. and D.F. Sabo (1994) *Sex, Violence & Power in Sports: rethinking masculinity*, Freedom, CA: The Crossing Press.

Mestrovic, S.G. (1993) *The Barbarian Temperament: toward a postmodern critical theory*, London: Routledge.

Métoudi, M. (1987) 'Les Leçons de la Publicité', *Esprit*, 4: 73–8.

Mignon, P. (1994) 'New Supporter Cultures and Identity in France: the case of Paris Saint-Germain', in R. Giulianotti and J. Williams (eds) (1994).

Mignon, P. (1996) 'Football Fan Culture in Paris: from one club to two', paper to the international conference Fanatics! Football and Popular Culture in Europe, Institute for Popular Culture, Manchester Metropolitan University, 11–13 June.

Miller, D.M. and K.R.E. Russell (1971) *Sport: a contemporary view*, Philadelphia: Lea & Febiger.

Mills, C.W. (1956) *The Power Elite*, Oxford: Oxford University Press.

Mills, C.W. (1959) *The Sociological Imagination*, Harmondsworth: Penguin.

Morgan, W. (1996) 'The Scottish Professional Footballers' Association: a comparative study of employment conditions in Scotland and England', unpublished MA thesis, Faculty of Arts, De Montfort University, Leicester.

Morgan, W.J. (1988) 'Adorno on Sport: the case of the fractured dialectic', *Theory and Society*, 17: 813–38.

Mormino, G.R. (1982) 'The Playing Fields of St Louis: Italian immigrants and sport, 1925–1941', *Journal of Sport History*, 9 (summer): 5–16.

Morris, D. (1981) *The Soccer Tribe*, London: Jonathan Cape.

Morrow, S.H. (1992) 'Putting People on the Balance Sheet: human resource accounting applied to professional football clubs', *Royal Bank of Scotland Review*, 174 (June): 10–19.

Mosely, P. (1994) 'Balkan Politics in Australian Soccer', in *ASSH Studies in Sports History, no. 10: Ethnicity and Soccer in Australia*, ASSH / University of Western Sydney: Macarthur.

Murphy, P., J. Williams and E. Dunning (1990) *Football on Trial*, London: Routledge.

Murray, W. (1984) *The Old Firm: sectarianism, sport and society in Scotland*, Edinburgh: John Donald.

Murray, W. (1994) *Football: a history of the world game*, Aldershot: Scolar Press.

Murrell, A.J. and E.M. Curtis (1994) 'Causal Attributions of Performance for Black and White Quarterbacks in the NFL: a look at the sports pages', *Journal of Sport and Social Issues*, 18 (3): 224–33.

Nairn, T. (1981) *The Break-Up of Britain*, second edition, London: NLB.

Nauright, J. (1998) 'Bhola Lethu: football in urban South Africa', in G. Armstrong and R. Giulianotti (eds) (1998a).

Nelson, G. (1995) *Left Foot Forward: a year in the life of a journeyman footballer*, London: Headline.

Nelson, M.B. (1996) *The Stronger Women Get, the More Men Love Football*, London: Women's Press.

Newsham, G.J. (1994) *In a League of their own! Dick, Kerr Ladies Football Club 1917–1965*, Chorley: Pride of Place Publishing.

Noll, R.G. (ed.) (1974) *Government and the Sports Business*, Washington, DC: Brookings

Institute.

O'Donnell, H. (1994) 'Mapping the Mythical: a geopolitics of national sporting stere-otypes', *Discourse & Society*, 5 (3): 345–80.

O'Kelly, D. and S. Blair (eds) (1992) *What's the Story? True confessions of Republic of Ireland soccer supporters*, Dublin: ELO.

O'Toole, F. (1994) *Black Hole, Green Card*, Dublin: New Island.

Oliver, G. (1992) *The Guinness Record of World Soccer*, Enfield: Guinness Publishing.

Orakwue, S. (1998) *Pitch Invaders: the modern black football revolution*, London: Victor Gollancz.

Orozco, J.Y. (1994) *Política y Mafias del Futbol: una combinación ganadora...¿para quién?*, México, DF: Editorial Planeta.

Overman, S.J. (1997) *The Influence of the Protestant Ethic on Sport and Recreation*, Aldershot: Avebury.

Paterson, L. (1994) *The Autonomy of Scotland*, Edinburgh: Edinburgh University Press.

Pearson, H. (1994) *The Far Corner*, London: Warner.

Peitersen, B. (1991) 'If Only Denmark had been there: Danish football spectators at the World Cup Finals in Italy', *Report to the Council of Europe*.

Penny, T. (1992) 'Football and Community', paper to the International Conference: Soccer, Culture and Identity, University of Aberdeen, 1–4 April.

Perkin, H. (1992) 'Teaching the Nations How to Play: sport and society in the British Empire and Commonwealth', in J.A. Mangan (ed.) (1992).

Perryman, M. (1997) 'Football United: New Labour, the Task Force and the future of the game', Fabian Society Pamphlet, 11 Dartmouth Street, London, September.

Peterson, T. (1994) 'Split Visions: the introduction of the Svenglish model in Swedish football', paper to the International Committee for the Sociology of Sport Confer-ence: Contested Boundaries and Shifting Solidarities, Bielefeld, 18–23 July.

Pickering, D. (1994) *The Cassell Soccer Companion*, London: Cassell.

Pilz, G.A. (1996) 'Social Factors Influencing Sport and Violence: on the "problem" of football hooliganism in Germany', *International Review for the Sociology of Sport*, 31 (1): 49–66.

Pitt-Rivers, J.A. (1984) 'El Sacrificio del Toro', *Revista de Occidente*, 36: 27–47.

Podaliri, C. and C. Balestri (1998) 'The *Ultràs*, Racism and Football Culture in Italy', in A. Brown (ed.) (1998).

Polley, M. (1998) *Moving the Goalposts: a history of sport and society since 1945*, London: Routledge.

Pooley, J.C. (1976) 'Ethnic Soccer Clubs in Milwaukee: a study in assimilation', in M. Hart (ed.)

Portelli, A. (1993) 'The Rich and the Poor in the Culture of Football', in S. Redhead (ed.) (1993).

Rachum, I. (1978) 'Futebol: the growth of a Brazilian national institution', *New Scholar*, 7: 183–200.

Radnedge, K. (1997) 'Foreword', in J. King and J. Kelly (eds) *The Cult of the Man-ager*, London: Virgin.

Raitz, K. (1987) 'Place, Space and Environment in America's Leisure Landscapes', *Journal of Cultural Geography*, 8 (1): 49–62.

Raspaud, M. (1989) 'La Violence de L'Exclusion', paper to the symposium Le Foot-ball et ses Publics, 19–21 October, EUI Colloquium Papers, 226 / 89 (col 30).

Raspaud, M. (1994) 'From Saint-Etienne to Marseilles: tradition and modernity in French soccer and society', in R. Giulianotti and J. Williams (eds) (1994).

Redhead, S. (1986a) 'Policing the Field', *Warwick Law Working Papers*, School of Law, University of Warwick, 7 (1).

Redhead, S. (1986b) *Sing When You're Winning*, London: Pluto.

Redhead, S. (1991a) 'An Era of the End, or the End of an Era: football and youth culture in Britain', in J. Williams and S. Wagg (eds) (1991).

Redhead, S. (1991b) 'Some Reflections on Discourses on Football Hooliganism', *Sociological Review*, 39 (3): 479–87.

Redhead, S. (ed.) (1993) *The Passion and the Fashion*, Aldershot: Avebury.

Redhead, S. (1995) *Unpopular Cultures: the birth of law and popular culture*, Manchester: Manchester University Press.

Reefe, T.Q. (1987) 'The Biggest Game of All: gambling in traditional Africa', in W.J. Baker and J.A. Mangan (eds) (1987).

Reisch, M. (1991) 'Alternativas', in (various editors) ¿*Nunca más campeón mundial?*, Montevideo: LOGOS.

Reiss, S.A. (1991) *City Games: the evolution of American urban society and the rise of sports*, Urbana: University of Illinois Press.

Richards, P. (1997) 'Soccer and Violence in War-Torn Africa: soccer and social rehabilitation in Sierra Leone', in G. Armstrong and R. Giulianotti (eds) (1997).

Ricoeur, P. (1970) *Freud and Philosophy*, New Haven: Yale University Press.

Rigauer, B. (1987) *Sport and Work*, New York: Columbia University Press.

Robins, D. (1984) *We Hate Humans*, Harmondsworth: Penguin.

Robins, D. (1992) *Sport as Prevention: the role of sport in crime prevention programmes aimed at young people*, University of Oxford: Centre for Criminological Research.

Robinson, R.J. (1987) 'The Civilizing Process: some remarks on Elias's social history', *Sociology*, 21 (1): 1–17.

Robson, G. (1996) 'No One Likes Us, We Don't Care: Millwall, identity and community', paper to the international conference Fanatics! Football and Popular Culture in Europe, Institute for Popular Culture, Manchester Metropolitan University, 11–13 June.

Roche, M. (1992) 'Mega Events and Micro-Modernisation: on the sociology of the new urban tourism', *British Journal of Sociology*, 43 (4): 563–600.

Rojek, C. (1985) *Capitalism and Leisure Theory*, London: Tavistock.

Rojek, C. (1995) *Decentring Leisure*, London: Sage.

Roversi, A. (1992) *Calcio, Tifo e Violenza*, Bologna: Il Mulino.

Roversi, A. (1994) 'Football Hooliganism in Italy', in R. Giulianotti and J. Williams (eds) (1994).

Rowe, D. (1995) *Popular Cultures: rock music, sport and the politics of pleasure*, London: Sage.

Rowe, D., G. Lawrence, T. Miller and J. McKay (1994) 'Global Sport? Core concern and peripheral vision', *Media, Culture & Society*, 16 (4): 661–75.

Russell, D. (1998) 'Associating with Football', in G. Armstrong and R. Giulianotti (eds) (1998a).

Sabo, D.F. (1994) 'Doing Time, Doing Masculinity: sports and prison', in M.A. Messner and D.F. Sabo (eds) (1994).

Scher, A. (1996) *La Patria Deportista*, Buenos Aires: Planeta.

Schmitt, R.L. and W.M. Leonard II (1986) 'Immortalizing the Self through Sport', *American Journal of Sociology*, 91 (5): 1088–111.

Scotch, N.A. (1951) 'Magic, Sorcery and Football among the Zulus: a case of reinterpretation under acculturation', *Journal of Conflict Resolution*, 5: 70–6.

Scraton, P., A. Jemphrey and S. Coleman (1995) *No Last Rights: the denial of justice and the promotion of myth in the aftermath of the Hillsborough disaster*, Liverpool: Liverpool City Council.

Scully, G.W. (1995) *The Market Structure of Sports*, Chicago: University of Chicago Press.

Sebreli, J.J. (1981) *Fútbol y Masas*, Buenos Aires: Galerna.

Semino, E. and M. Masci (1996) 'Politics is Football: metaphor in the discourse of Silvio Berlusconi in Italy', *Discourse and Society*, 7 (2): 243–69.

Shaw, D. (1985) 'Football under Franco', *History Today*, August.

Signy, D. (1969) *A Pictorial History of Soccer*, London: Hamlyn.

Sik, G. (1996) *I Think I'll Manage*, London: Headline.

Simmons, R. (1997) 'Implications of the Bosman Ruling for Football Transfer Markets', *Economic Affairs*, 17 (3): 13–18.

Slack, T. and D. Whitson (1988) 'The Place of Sport in Cuba's Foreign Relations', *International Journal*, 43 (autumn): 596–617.

Sloane, P.J. (1997) 'The Economics of Sport: an overview', *Economic Affairs*, 17 (3): 2–6.

Smith, D. and G. Williams (1980) *Fields of Praise*, Cardiff: University of Wales Press.

SNCCFR (1983) *All Sit Down: a report on the Coventry City all-seated stadium 1982 / 3*, Leicester: SNCCFR.

SNCCFR (1995) *FA Premier League Fan Surveys: sample report*, Leicester: SNCCFR.

Sociological Review (1991) *The Cultural Aspects of Football*, 39 (3).

Sociological Review (1992) 'Statement by the Editors', *Sociological Review*, 40 (1): 36–7.

Solomos, J. and L. Back (1996) *Racism and Society*, Harmondsworth: Macmillan.

Sorlin, P. (1994) *Mass Media*, London: Routledge.

Stein, S., J.D. Carvallo and S.C. Stokes (1986) 'Soccer and Social Change in Early 20th Century Peru', *Studies in Latin American Popular Culture*, 5: 68–77.

Strinati, D. (1995) *An Introduction to Theories of Popular Culture*, London: Routledge.

Strutt, J. (1969) *The Sports and Pastimes of the People of England*, Bath.

Stuart, O. (1995) 'The Lions Stir: football in African society', in S. Wagg (ed.) (1995b).

Sugden, J. (1994) 'USA and the World Cup: American nativism and the rejection of the people's game', in J. Sugden and A. Tomlinson (eds) (1994).

Sugden, J. and A. Bairner (1993) *Sport, Sectarianism and Society in a Divided Ireland*, Leicester: Leicester University Press.

Sugden, J. and A. Bairner (1998) (ed.) *Sport in Divided Societies*, Aachen: Meyer & Meyer.

Sugden, J. and A. Tomlinson (eds) (1994) *Hosts and Champions*, Aldershot: Arena.

Sugden, J. and A. Tomlinson (1997) 'Global Power Struggles in World Football: FIFA and UEFA, 1954–74, and their legacy', *International Journal of the History of Sport*, 14 (2): 1–25.

Sugden, J. and A. Tomlinson (1998) *Who Rules the People's Game? FIFA and the contest for world football*, Cambridge: Polity Press.

Sugden, J., A. Tomlinson and P. Darby (1998) 'FIFA versus UEFA in the Struggle for the Control of World Football', in A. Brown (ed.) (1998).

Suttles, G. (1968) *The Social Order of the Slum*, Chicago: Chicago University Press.

Suttles, G. (1972) *The Social Construction of Communities*, Chicago: Chicago University Press.

Sweet, W.E. (1987) *Sport and Recreation in Ancient Greece*, Oxford: Oxford University Press.

Szymanski, S. and R. Smith (1997) 'The English Football Industry: profit, performance and industrial structure', *International Review of Applied Economics*, 11 (1): 135–53.

Tampke, J. (1979) 'Politics Only? Sport in the German Democratic Republic', in R. Cashman and M. McKernan (eds) *Sport in History*, Brisbane: Queensland University Press.

Taylor, I. (1969) 'Hooligans: soccer's resistance movement', *New Society*, 7 August.

Taylor, I. (1970) 'Football Mad: a speculative sociology of soccer hooliganism', in E. Dunning (ed.) (1970).

Taylor, I. (1971) 'Soccer Consciousness and Soccer Hooliganism', in S. Cohen (ed.) *Images of Deviance*, Harmondsworth: Penguin.

Taylor, I. (1982a) 'On the Sports–Violence Question: soccer hooliganism revisited', in Jennifer Hargreaves (ed.) (1982).

Taylor, I. (1982b) 'Class, Violence and Sport: the case of soccer hooliganism', in H. Cantelon and R. Gruneau (eds) *Sport, Culture and the Modern State*, Toronto: Toronto University Press.

Taylor, I. (1987) 'Putting the Boot into a Working Class Sport: British soccer after Bradford and Brussels', *Sociology of Sport Journal*, 4: 171–91.

Taylor, I. (1989) 'Hillsborough: 15 April 1989. Some personal contemplations', *New Left Review*, 177: 89–110.

Taylor, I. (1991a) 'English Football in the 1990s: taking Hillsborough seriously?', in J. Williams and S. Wagg (eds) (1991).

Taylor, I. (1991b) 'From Aggravation to Celebration', *Independent on Sunday*, 21 April.

Taylor, P. Lord Justice (Chairman) (1990) *Inquiry into the Hillsborough Stadium Disaster: final report*, London: HMSO.

Taylor, R. and A. Ward (1995) *Kicking and Screaming: an oral history of football in England*, London: Robson Books.

Taylor, R. (1992) *Football and Its Fans*, Leicester: Leicester University Press.

Taylor, R. (1996) 'Hungary and the Making of Modern Football', paper to the international conference Fanatics! Football and Popular Culture in Europe, Institute for Popular Culture, Manchester Metropolitan University, 11–13 June.

Taylor, T. (1988) 'Sport and World Politics: functionalism and the state system', *International Journal*, 43 (autumn): 531–53.

Theberge, N. (1993) 'The Construction of Gender in Sport: women, coaching, and the naturalization of difference', *Social Problems*, 40 (3): 301–13.

Thomas, D. (1996) 'Recent Developments in Sporting Labour Markets: free agency and new slavery?', *Review of Policy Issues*, 2 (2): 19–28.

Thomas, P. (1995) 'Kicking Racism out of Football: a supporter's view', *Race & Class*, 36 (4): 95–101.

Tilly, C. (1985) 'War Making and State Making as Organised Crime', in P. Evans, D. Rueschmeyer and T. Skopcol (eds) *Bringing the State Back In*, Cambridge: Cambridge University Press.

Tolleneer, J. (1986) 'The Sports Scene and the Pop Scene: a comparative structural-functional analysis', *International Review for the Sociology of Sport*, 21 (2 / 3): 229–37.

Tomlinson, A. (1986) 'Going Global: the FIFA story', in A. Tomlinson and G. Whannel (eds) (1986).

Tomlinson, A. (1994) 'FIFA and the World Cup: the expanding football family', in J. Sugden and A. Tomlinson (eds) (1994).

Tomlinson, A. and G. Whannel (eds) (1986) *Off the Ball*, London: Pluto.

Tranter, N. (1995) 'The Cappielow Riot and the Composition and Behaviour of Soccer Crowds in Late Victorian Scotland', *International Journal of the History of Sport*, 12 (3): 125–40.

Tranter, N. (1998) *Sport, Economy and Society in Britain 1750–1914*, Cambridge: Cambridge University Press.

Trivizas, E. (1980) 'Offences and offenders in football crowd disorders', *British Journal of Criminology*, 20 (3): 276–88.

Tuan, Y.-F. (1974) *Topophilia*, Englewood Cliffs: Prentice-Hall.

Tuan, Y.-F. (1979) *Landscapes of Fear*, Oxford: Blackwell.

Tunstall, J. (1996) *Newspaper Power: the new national press in Britain*, Oxford: Clarendon Press.

Urry, J. (1990) *The Tourist Gaze*, London: Routledge.

Vamplew, W. (1988) *Pay Up and Play the Game: professional sport in Britain 1875–1914*, Cambridge: Cambridge University Press.

Vamplew, W. (1994a) ' "Wogball": ethnicity and violence in Australian soccer', in R. Giulianotti and J. Williams (eds) (1994).

Vamplew, W. (1994b) 'Violence in Australian Soccer: the ethnic contribution', in *ASSH Studies in Sports History*, no. 10: *Ethnicity and Soccer in Australia*, ASSH / University of Western Sydney: Macarthur.

Vasili, P. (1995) 'Colonialism and Football: the first Nigerian tour to Britain', *Race & Class*, 36 (4): 55–70.

Veblen, T. (1925) *The Theory of the Leisure Class*, London: Allen and Unwin.

Vélez, F. A. (1995) *Pena Máxima: juicio al fútbol colombiano*, Bogotá: Editorial Planeta.

Venables, T. (1996) *The Best Game in the World*, London: Century.

Vidacs, B. (1997) 'The Expansion and Contraction of Identity within Cameroonian Football', paper to the NASSS Annual Conference: Crossing Borders, University of Toronto, Canada, 5–8 November.

Vinnai, G. (1973) *Football Mania*, London: Ocean.

Virilio, P. (1994) *The Vision Machine*, Bloomington: Indiana University Press.

Vrcan, S. (1992) 'Dal Tifo Aggressivo alla Crisi del Pubblico Calcistico: il caso jugoslavia', *Rassegna Italiana di Sociologia*, 33 (1): 131–44.

Wacquant, L. (1995) 'Pugs at Work: bodily capital and bodily labour among professional boxers', *Body & Society*, 1 (1): 65–93.

Wagg, S. (1984) *The Football World*, Brighton: Harvester.

Wagg, S. (1995a) 'The Missionary Position: football in the societies of Britain and Ireland', in S. Wagg (ed.) (1995b).

Wagg, S. (ed.) (1995b) *Giving the Game Away*, Leicester: Leicester University Press.

Wagner, E.A. (1990) 'Sport in Asia and Africa: Americanization or mundialization', *Sociology of Sport Journal*, 7: 399–402.

Walker, G. (1990) 'There's not a team like the Glasgow Rangers: football and religious identity in Scotland', in G. Walker and T. Gallagher (eds) *Sermons and Battle Hymns*, Edinburgh: Edinburgh University Press.

Walter, T. (1991) 'The Mourning After Hillsborough', *Sociological Review*, 39 (3): 599–626.

Walter, T.O., B. Brown and E. Grabb (1991) 'Ethnic Identity and Sports Participation: a comparative analysis of West Indian and Italian soccer clubs in metropolitan Toronto', *Canadian Ethnic Studies*, 23 (1): 85–96.

Walvin, J. (1975) *The People's Game*, London: Allen Lane.

Walvin, J. (1986) *Football and the Decline of Britain*, Basingstoke: Macmillan.

Walvin, J. (1994) *The People's Game*, revised edition, Edinburgh: Mainstream.

Ward, C. (1989) *Steaming In*, London: Sportspages / Simon & Schuster.

Weber, M. (1978) *Selections in Translation*, (edited by W.G. Runciman), Cambridge: Cambridge University Press.

Webster, J. (1990) *The Dons: the history of Aberdeen football club*, London: Stanley Paul.

Welsh, I. (1993) *Trainspotting*, London: Secker & Warburg.

Welsh, I. (1994) *The Acid House*, London: Jonathan Cape.

Welsh, I. (1995) *Marabou Stork Nightmares*, London: Jonathan Cape.

Whannel, G. (1992) *Fields in Vision*, London: Routledge.

White, J. (1997) 'My Life After Eric', in S. Kuper (ed.) (1997).

Wickham, G. (1992) 'Sports, Manners, Persons, Government: sport, Elias, Mauss, Foucault', *Cultural Studies*, 6 (2): 219–31.

References

Widmeyer, W.N. and J.S. Birch (1984) 'Aggression in Professio strategy for success or a reaction to failure?', *Journal of Psych*

Wilkinson, W.H.G. (1988) *Soccer Tactics: top team strategies exp* Crowood Press.

Williams, J. (1986) 'White Riots: the English football fan abroad', in A. Tom G. Whannel (eds) (1986).

Williams, J. (1991) 'Having an Away Day: English football spectators and the hooligan debate', in J. Williams and S. Wagg (eds) (1991).

Williams, J. (1993) *Highfield Rangers: an oral history*, Leicester: SNCCFR, University of Leicester.

Williams, J. (1994) '"Rangers is a Black Club": "race", identity and local football in England', in R. Giulianotti and J. Williams (eds) (1994).

Williams, J. (1995) 'English Football Stadiums after Hillsborough', in J. Bale and O. Moen (eds) (1995).

Williams, J., E. Dunning and P. Murphy (1984) *Hooligans Abroad*, London: Routledge.

Williams, J. and R. Taylor (1994) 'Boys Keep Swinging', in E. Stanko (ed.) *Just Boys Doing Business*, London: Routledge.

Williams, J. and S. Wagg (eds) (1991) *British Football and Social Change*, Leicester: University of Leicester Press.

Williams, R. (1979) *Politics and Letters*, London: New Left Books.

Willis, P. (1990) *Common Culture*, Milton Keynes: Open University Press.

Wilson, W.J. (1987) *The Truly Disadvantaged: the inner city, the underclass and public policy*, Chicago: University of Chicago Press.

Wolstenholme, K. (1992) 'Armando Picchi', in S.F. Kelly (ed.) *A Game of Two Halves*, London: Mandarin.

Woodhouse, J. and J. Williams (1991) 'Can Play, Will Play? Women and football in Britain', in J. Williams and S. Wagg (eds) (1991).

Wren-Lewis, J. and A. Clarke (1983) 'The World Cup: a political football', *Theory, Culture & Society*, 1 (3): 123–32.

Yaffé, M. (1974) 'The Psychology of Soccer', *New Society*, 14 February.

Young, K., P. White and W. McTeer (1994) 'Body Talk: male athletes reflect on sport, injury and pain', *Sociology of Sport Journal*, 11: 175–94.

Zaman, H. (1997) 'Islam, Well-Being and Physical Activity: perceptions of Muslim young women', in G. Clarke and B. Humberstone (eds) (1997).

Zani, B. and E. Kirchler (1991) 'When Violence Overshadows the Spirit of Sporting Competition: Italian football fans and their clubs', *Journal of Community and Applied Social Psychology*, 1: 5–21.

Zurcher, L.A. and A. Meadow (1967) 'On Bullfights and Baseball: an example of interaction of social institutions', *International Journal of Comparative Sociology*, 8: 99–117.

Index

Aberdeen 21, 44, 46, 48, 68, 154
AC Milan 35, 86, 100, 123
access to football 78–80, 96, 106, 145, 164–5
action: social and structure 127–8; strategic and communicative 97
administration, football: modernization 26–8
advertisements 89, 104, 117
aesthetics 105, 127–9, 169–70, 172–3: analytical problems 136–8; of hooliganism 53; and the other 138–42; post-modernity 142–5; of virtual 84
Africa: diffusion of football 7–8; female sports participation 159; players 162–3; witchcraft 19–20
Africa, North 17: politics 16
Africa, West: player sales 91; religion 18
African players 162–3
Afro-Caribbeans 164
age 170, 171: hooligans 52
agentry, free 122
agents, player 103
aggravation ('aggro') 42–3
aggression 43, 136, 155–6
Ajax 52, 83, 133: youth recruitment 114–15
Amateur FA 5

amateurism 31, 107
America, Central: football prehistory 1; see also specific countries
America, North: football prehistory 1; see also specific countries
America, South: class 147; women 153; see also Latin America; specific countries
Americanization 142–3
anti-hooligan measures 49–50, 83
anti-racism campaigns 146, 160–2, 164
Argentina 142: barras bravas 58–9, 64; class 11, 35; corruption 102; diffusion of football 8; industrial conflict 113; influence of television on match results 96; masculinities 155; national identity 30, 31, 32; nationalist rivalry 13; players 140; privatization of football clubs 88; tactics 141; two-club rivalry 10–11; women 154
Argentinian Football Association (AFA) 113
arrivistes 151, 165
Arsenal 10, 12, 89, 130–1
Asia, East 14
Asian Football Confederation (AFC) 27, 167
Asian players 163
Asians 164

assets, players as 122
Association Football Players'
  Union 107
associations, formation of 26–8, 166
associative nature, football 149–50
Atkinson, Ron 163
atmosphere, football grounds 69
attendance, supporter 150: impact of
  free agentry 122; women 150, 154,
  164
attitude, player 136
audience share, televised football 93
audiences: players and 117–20; *see also*
  supporters
aura, football matches 144–5
Australia 36: diffusion of football 7;
  national identity 37–8
Australian Soccer Federation 38
Austria 8, 25

Baggio, Roberto 17, 135, 172
Bale, John 69
banana kick 138
Barcelona FC 86, 89
Barnes, John 160, 161–2
barras bravas 58–9, 63, 64, 168
basketball, influence of 143, 170
Baudrillard, J. 16, 69, 84, 109, 149
Bayern Munich 12, 30, 35, 86
Belgium 18: Bosman case 121;
  corruption 101; league sharing with
  Holland 94
bench, team 68
Bentham, Jeremy 81
Best, George 116, 117, 118, 120, 140
black players 162–4: in South Africa
  7–8
Blatter, Sepp 28
Bohemia 8
bookings, player 109–10
Bosman case 108, 113, 121–2, 124
Bosnia–Hercegovina 27
boundaries, national: deconstruction
  of 94; threat to 104
Bourdieu, Pierre 108
Brazil 13, 17, 26, 125: class-based
  rivalry 11; corruption 102; diffusion
  of football 8; hooliganism 58, 154;

Maracanã stadium 20, 68;
  merchandising 90–1; *passe*
  system 113; player–club
  relationship 124; players 140–1;
  politics 16; privatization of football
  clubs 88; Raça 59, 64; racism 160,
  164; tactics 132, 133, 137; women
  spectators 153
bread and circuses thesis 15–16
bricoleurs, managers as 136
Britain *see* UK
British League 94
Bulgaria 13

Cameroon 7, 19–20
Canada, diffusion of football 7
Carlos, Roberto 134, 138
carnival fans 63–4, 168, 170: Brazil 59;
  and hooliganism 60; masculinities
  155, 156; Northern European
  59–61; women 158–9
carnivalesque, folk football 3
casuals 46, 63–4: emergence of 50–1;
  organization 51
catenaccio system 132, 135
CCTV 50, 75, 81–2
celebrity status: players 118–20, 124,
  125–6, 168; women 158
Chapman, Herbert 130–1, 167
Charles, John 117, 140
child labour, football merchandise 90
children: football 66; gender of
  players 157
Chile 28: diffusion of football 9;
  football prehistory 1
China 14, 28, 159: folk football 2;
  football prehistory 1
civilizing process, Elias 44–7
class 107, 166–7, 170, 171: and
  football 147–52; in football
  grounds 67; and geography 150–2;
  Germany 29–30; hooligans 46–7; and
  national identity 32–5; new cultural
  politics of 146, 164–5; and
  professionalism 4–5, 6; rivalry
  11–12; spectators 144–5; television
  and merchandising 105; ticketing
  policies 79; *see also* middle class, new

clubs, football: deviant 172; in equity
market 97–100; merchandise 88–91;
names of 33–4; player-club
relationship 104, 107–10, 123–4;
relationship with local community
70–1; research 170; resources 136;
rivalry 10–12; television fees 95–6;
traditional framework 87–8; transfer
system 122
coaches, football 130, 135, 169:
diffusion of football 9; racism 162;
women 157–8
coaching practices 124
collective, individual and 127–8
Colombia 113: corruption 102
commercial interests *see* merchandise
Commission for Racial Equality 161
commodification 40–1, 79, 84, 86,
104–5, 168: *see also* merchandise
commodity fetishism 108
communitarian strategies, need for 97
community, imaginary 23: of
supporters 70
community projects 63
companies: football clubs as 5; sports
clubs as 87
comparative analysis, hooligans 48
computer technology, simulation 84,
144
Confederación Norte-Centro-americana
y del Caribe de Fútbol
(CONCACAF) 27
Confederación Sudamericana de Fútbol
(CONMEBOL) 27
Confédération Africaine de Football
(CAF) 27, 167
confederations, formation of 27
conflict: industrial, of players 112–13,
124; at internationals 139
consciousness, practical and
discursive 120
contracts: buyout clauses 123; freedom
of contract principle 108, 112; long-
term 122–3
control, social: in football grounds
80–2, 83
Corinthians FC 4, 5, 58
corruption 100–3, 104

Creating Resistance to Society's
Haemorrhoids (CRASH) 152
creativity, player 137
cricket 170: India 7
crime, football as alternative to 34
Cruyff, Johan 68, 133, 143
cultural capital, hooligans 51–2
cultural complexity 23
cultural politics 146–65
culture: British influence 9; death 21–2;
genealogy of 166–9; global diffusion
of fan 63–5; spectator 39–65;
ultràs 54–6; women's participation
157–9; *see also* sub-cultures
currency, special: in football grounds 83
Cyprus, nationalist rivalry 13

Daily Telegraph, fantasy football 149
dance 141
death: cultural differences 21–2; of
players 118, 125
decivilizing spurts, Elias 45, 46
democracy: football as participatory 40,
42; football clubs 87
Denmark: capitalization 100; carnival
fans 60, 61, 159; diffusion of
football 8; fan projects 63;
players 123
derby matches 10–12
developing world: football ground
disasters 72–3; manufacture of
football merchandise 90
deviance 172: hooligans 42;
players 111, 120; sexual
identity 155–6
Di Stéfano, Alfredo 113, 117, 168
dictatorships, football grounds 67
Didì 138
direct football 133, 135
directors, club 87, 104, 107–8, 130
disasters: air 118; football ground 72–8
discourse analysis 139: and gender 158
disorder, rules of 42
Donald, Dick 21
dribbling game 4, 129
drugs 110
dugouts 68
Dunning, Eric 44

Durkheim, Emile and Durkheimian
 tradition: folk football 3; religion 17;
 social solidarity 14–16

economic capital, hooligans 51–2
economic inequality, rivalry and 12
edgework 53
education: holistic, for players 115–16,
 124; racism 162
Egypt 17–18
El Salvador 13
Elias, Norbert 127; civilizing
 process 44–7; folk football 2;
 rationalization 3
emotions, and football space 69–72,
 80–1, 147
ends 49, 67: family 81
England: advertisements 89;
 casuals 50; class 146, 147; club
 finance 99; defence 130; fanzines
 62; folk football 2; football ground
 disasters 73–4; football grounds
 66–7, 70–1; Hillsborough disaster
 21–2, 73, 75–8, 168; hooliganism
 39, 64–5; industrial conflict 112;
 masculinities 155; national identity
 28–9, 31; nationalist rivalry 13;
 professionalism 4–5; regional
 rivalry 13; tactics 132–3, 134, 135;
 televised football 91–2; World Cup
 25, 26
English National Investment Company
 (ENIC) 100
epic features of football 172
equity market, football clubs 86, 97–100
ethnicity 146, 164, 170, 171:
 Australia 38; US 36–7
ethno-nationalism, rivalry and 12–13
Europe, East: football clubs 87, 88; *see
 also specific countries*
Europe, South: class 35, 147; *see also
 specific countries*
European Broadcasting Union (EBU)
 94
European Super League 93, 104
Eurosport 88
externalities, negative: football
 grounds 70

family, promotion of 81, 153
family business model, clubs 87
fans *see* supporters
fan projects 63
fantasy football 149
fanzines 149, 150, 165, 168: anti-
 racism 161; rise of 61–3, 64
Far East, gambling 102–3
fascistic political movements, and
 hooligans 41, 42
Fédération Internationale de Football
 Association (FIFA) 27, 60, 74, 79,
 94, 102, 169; FIFA–Adidas World
 League 96; football merchandise 90;
 foundation of 13, 25; offside rules
 130; player agents 103; power in
 27–8; relations with Britain 25;
 safety 113; tactics 134, 143–4;
 videotapes 144
feminization: of the other 155–6
Ferguson, Alex 120, 128
figurations, social: Elias 44–7
finance: equity markets 97–100;
 football 86–106; players 112–13,
 122, (*see also* wage, maximum);
 spectators 144–5
five-a-side football 143
flow: concept of 52–3; global 24
fluidificanti position 134–5
folk football 1–3, 66: women in
 152
football: access to 78–80, 96; cultural
 differences 21–2; direct 133, 135;
 fantasy 149; five-a-side 143; folk
 1–3, 152; global diffusion 6–9;
 history 3–6; meaning of 9–16; and
 religion 17–20; street 78; total
 133–4, 135; *see also specific topics* eg
 grounds
Football Association (FA) 74:
 formation 4; Premier League 92;
 transfers 103
Football Association Cup 4
Football Fans Against the Criminal
 Justice Act (FFACJA) 152
Football League 5
Football Supporters' Association
 (FSA) 62, 149

formations, football: 4–2–4
  formation 132, 135, 137, 168; 4–3–3
  formation 132–3; 4–4–2 formation
  34; sociological research as 171–3;
  WM formation 130–1, 135
Foucault, Michel 108: gaze 80–2
France 33: class 34; club rivalry 12;
  diffusion of football 8; finance 98–9;
  folk football 2; football grounds 67,
  68, 71–2; football prehistory 1;
  masculinities 155; nationalist
  rivalry 13; patronage 88; player
  recruitment 123; racism 163;
  sponsorship 90; televised football 93,
  94; two-club rivalry 11
Frankfurt School 16
freedom of contract principle 108, 112
functionalism, popular culture 128

Gaelic Athletic Association (GAA) 37
gambling 102–3, 104
Garrincha 26, 111, 125, 168
Gascoigne, Paul 117, 140, 156
gate sharing 122
Gaviões da Fiel 59, 64
gaze 80–2: patriarchal 158;
  spectators' 80–2, 111
gender *see* women
Genoa FC 11, 57–8, 77
gentlemen and players' dispute 4–5
geography, and class 150–2
German Football Association
  (DFB) 144
Germany 25: anti-racism campaigns
  161; capitalization 100; class 34;
  club rivalry 12; diffusion of football
  8; fan projects 63; football grounds
  67, 68, 77; hooligans 52;
  masculinities 155; national
  identity 29–30, 31; nationalist
  rivalry 13; patronage 88;
  racism 159, 160; two-club rivalry
  11
Glasgow Celtic 6, 46, 49, 133, 156:
  finance 99; sectarianism 18–19
Glasgow Rangers 7, 46, 49, 115:
  advertisements 89; finance 100;
  football ground 74; sectarianism

  18–19; share prices 99; television
  revenues 93
globalization 24, 35: fan sub-
  cultures 63–5; hooliganism 63–5;
  style 142–5; tactics 138–42
Greece 13, 142: class-based rivalry 12
Greece, Ancient: football 1
Greenland, religion 19
grounds, football 66–85, 167:
  capacities 67–8; disasters 72–8; and
  emotions 69–72; facilities 41–2, 67,
  68; politics of access 78–80; post-
  modernity 82–5; redevelopment
  76–8, 147, 168; and social
  control 80–2

habitus 72: hooligans 51
Havelange, João 28, 86, 168
hermeneutic territory, midfield as
  171–2
heroes, players as 124, 125, 167
heterogeneity, of football 169
Heysel disaster 74
Hilaire, Vince 162
Hillsborough disaster 21–2, 73, 75–8,
  168
Hindus 7, 159
Holland 11: carnival fans 60; diffusion
  of football 8; football grounds 83;
  league sharing with Belgium 94;
  masculinities 155; nationalist
  rivalry 13; racism 160; televised
  football 95; youth recruitment
  114–15
Honduras 13
hooligans and hooliganism 63–4: and
  carnival fans 60; economic and
  cultural capital 51–2; football ground
  disasters 75–6; hierarchy 42–3; at
  internationals 33; Latin America
  57–9; manipulation by 150; market
  for simulation of 53–4; masculinities
  156; psycho-social pleasures of 52–4;
  racism 161; research 39, 40–9; sub-
  cultures 168, 172; and *ultràs* 54–8;
  and women 153–4
hoolivans 82
Hungary 8, 26: corruption 101

hybridity, of football 24, 170
hyperreality 84–5

identity: semantic and syntactic 172; *see also* national identity
imperialism 91
Independent Supporters' Associations (ISAs) 61–3, 64, 149, 150, 165
India, diffusion of football 6–7
individual, collective and 127–8
industrial areas, masculinities and 155
industrial disputes 34
information networks, hooligans 52
injections, pain killing, 110
injuries, player: folk football 2–3; risk of 110, 124
injury time 144
institutionalization, of players 108–9
internationals 166, 167, 169: conflict 139; corruption 102; effect on local economy 77–8; European 93–4; first 4; national identity 23, 33; televising 94; women's 158
Internazionale FC 11, 86, 100, 132: youth recruitment 115
interviews, formal: hooligans 48
Iran 159
Ireland 17, 36: carnival fans 60, 61, 159; folk football 1–2; national identity 37; sponsorship 90; tactics 143; women 164
Ireland, Northern 26: religion 19
irony 150: post-fans 148
Israel 60–1: class-based rivalry 12; club rivalry 13
Istanbul, class-based rivalry 12
Italy 11, 25: anti-racism campaigns 161; capitalization 100; class 34; club rivalry 12–13; corruption 100–1; diffusion of football 8; folk football 2; football grounds 67, 68, 71, 77; gambling 102; industrial conflict 112; patronage 88; racism 159, 160; South American players 32; tactics 131, 132, 134, 135; televised football 93; two-club rivalry 11; *ultràs* 46, 54–6, 56–8; women's

football 158; youth recruitment 115; youth teams 123

Japan 94: merchandising 90–1; and rivalry 14; women 158, 164
joint-stock model, clubs 87
justice, social: televised football 96
Juventus FC 12, 13, 77, 86, 100, 105, 123, 140

Keeling, Peter 115
kick and rush approach 129, 135, 167
Kopa, Raymond 117
kops (ends) 43, 49, 67, 81
Korea, South 94: and rivalry 14
Kuper, Simon 151–2

labour: child 90; developing countries 90
Latin America: feminization of other 136; football clubs 87, football grounds 67, 68; hooliganism 57–9; *see also specific countries*
leagues, football: women's 158
'Leicester School', hooliganism 44–7
Levy, Eleanor 158
Libero! 152
Libya 17–18
liminality 53
Liverpool 6, 21–2, 161–2: Heysel disaster 74
local community, relationship with club 70–1
locality: affective ties to 15; and class 34; club names 33–4
location, geo-political and sports typologies 139–40
London: club rivalry 12; two-club rivalries 10
Low Countries: football grounds 67; hooligans 52; *see also specific countries*

Maguire, Joe 44
Major League Soccer (MLS) 36–7
malandro 140–1
management, club: shielding of young players 120

management by objectives 133
managers 109, 167: as *bricoleurs* 136; social background 128
Manchester United 12, 26, 35, 86: air disaster 118; finance 99: merchandising 89, 105; televised football 93, 95
Mantovani, Paolo 21, 55
Maracanã stadium 68: religious rites 20
Maradona, Diego 58, 117, 120, 135, 138, 140, 172
marginalization, hooligans 41
Marsh, Peter, hooliganism 42–4
Marxism: hooliganism 40–2: labour relations 108; modernization 4
masculinities 154–7, 165
match-fixing 100–1, 104
Matthews, Stanley 111, 117
meaning 9–16, 139
media: and new middle classes 149–50; and players' celebrity status 118, 119; and women 158, 164
Meisl, Willy 133–4: *Soccer Revolution* 26
Mekloufi, Rachid 117
merchandise and merchandising 83, 86, 88–91, 105, 145, 168
Mexico, televised football 96
mezzopunta 135, 137
middle class, new 40, 148–9, 165, 169, 170: and geography 150–2; and media 149–50
migration, labour 122
military leaders, national identity 33
Millwall FC 10, 63: finance 99; relationship with local community 70–1
mobility 24: player 116–17, 121–3
modernity: club finance 103–4; football grounds 83; hooliganism 49–50; and merchandising 88–91; player recruitment 114; tactics 131–4, 135, 143–4
modernity, early 31, 32, 33; Argentina 30; club names 33; England 29; football 28, 167; Germany 29–30; hooliganism 49; player–club relationship 123–4; players 107; tactics 130–1; Uruguay 31
modernity, late 31–2: Argentina 30; England 29; football 28, 168; players 108; Scotland 29
modernization 4, 6: decline of British influence 24–8; lack of in folk football 2–3
Montevideo 10
Moore, Bobby 125
multi-cultural societies, national identity 33, 38
municipalities, football spaces 67, 78
Murphy, Patrick 44
Murray, David 18, 99
museums, football 83, 104
Muslims 159
myth: and death of players 125; players as 118
Nacional FC 9, 12
names: clubs 33–4; *ultras* 54
national boundaries *see* boundaries
National Federation of Football Supporters' Clubs (NFFSC) 62
national identity 23–38, 167: and class 32–5; England 28–9; Germany 29–30; and rivalry 13; Scotland 29: televised football 96–7
national interest, televised football, 96–7
national team, sponsorship 90
neo-functionalism: belief-systems 17; social solidarity 14–16
neo-Nazi groups 161
neo-tribes, urban: casuals as 51
new social movements: football 61–3; single-issue 62–3
Newell's Old Boys 8, 11
Nigeria 159, 163
Nike 89–90
North American Soccer League (NASL) 36, 139
Norway: capitalization 100; carnival fans 60, 61, 159; diffusion of football 8
Oceania Football Confederation 27

officials, club: corruption 103; dugouts 68; racism 162
officials, match: bribery 101–2
offside rules 130–1, 135, 167
opera, and football 35
opposition, binary 10–14
order, social: folk football 3
organization: casuals 51; lack of in folk football 2–3; *ultràs* 55
organized battles, hooligans 52
Orkney, folk football 2
other, the 138–42: feminization of 155–6
Oxford United 42–4

panopticon model of surveillance 81–2, 83
Paraguay: class-based rivalry 11; politics 16; 'third defender' 136–7
Parmalat 88, 90
passing game 129–30
passion, privatization of 81
Patagonia, football prehistory 1
patronage, football clubs 88
Pelé 26, 132, 143, 168, 172
Peñarol FC 8–9, 11–12, 34
Peru, class-based rivalry 11
pitches, football 78: invasions 49
player-club relations 104; 107–10, 123–4
players 107–26, 167: as assets 122; attacks on 57–8; attitudes 136; black 162–4; body capital 108–11, 124; celebrity status 118–20, 124, 125–6, 168; demands on 94, 109; deviance 111, 120, 172; elite 112, 113–14, 169; finances 112–13, 116–17, 122; future employment 120; as heroes 117–18, 124, 125, 167; illegal payments to 101; industrial conflict 112–13; journeyman 112; maximum wage 6, 108, 112, 116, 124; mobility 116–17, 121–3; occupational sub-culture 113–16, 124, 155; poor origins 35, 140–1; recruitment 95, 114–15, 123, 124; retirement 118, 120–1, 124–6; rivalry 10; sale of 32, 91, 105; shielding of young 120;

sponsorship 89–90; transfer market 103; women 157; young black 163
pleasures, psycho-social: of violence 52–4
Poland 142: gender 159
polarization, of support 34–5
police, football ground disasters 73, 75–6
politics: of access 78–80; cultural 146–65; fascistic political movements 41, 42; football as safety valve 15–16; football grounds 67; influence of *barras bravas* 58–9; influence of Britain 9; Italy 56; players 35
Popplewell Report (1986) 74–5
Portugal 11: corruption 101; football clubs 87; football grounds 67; politics 15–16
positions, playing. and body shape 110–11; and racism 163
post-fans 146, 148–9, 165, 169
post-Fordist system 134–6
post-modernity 32, 168–9: Argentina 30, class 34–5; club finance 104–6; club names 33; coaching 115; England 29; equity market 97–100; football grounds 82–5; Germany 30; hooliganism 50–1; market for simulation of hooliganism 53–4; of nation-states 36–8; player mobility 121–3; players 108, 120; Scotland 29; tactics 134–6, 142–5; Uruguay 31; and women 158
post-tourism 148
prices, tickets 78–80
private *see* public
privatization: football clubs 88; football grounds 80–1; passion 81
Professional Footballers' Association (PFA) 112, 161
professionalism 6, 40, 107, 167: conflict over 4–5
public and private: and gender 155, 159; players 119–20
public obscurity, retired players 125

public schools 3–4, 155, 166
publications, football 149
Puskás, Ferenc 117, 137, 168, 172

Raça 59, 64
racism 146, 159–64: anti-racism
  campaigns 160–2, 164;
  normalized 161–2
Ramsey, Alf 132–3
rationalization 3, 4
Real Madrid 57–8, 89
recruitment, player 114–15, 123, 124
referees 6: corruption 101–2, 104; new
  media technology and 144; second
  144
reflexivity 150: post-fans 148
regions: and professionalism 4–5;
  rivalry 12–13
regulator, football: need for 97
religion 17–20: folk football 3
resources, club 136
results, match: influence of television 96
retain and transfer system 108
retirement: players 118, 120–1, 124–6
retro culture 120–1
rites, religious: and football matches 20
rites de passage, folk football as 3
rituals 17–20: mourning 21–2
rivalry 10–14: two-club 10–11
Romania 13: corruption 101: football
  clubs 87–8; politics 16
Romans, Ancient, football 1
Ronaldo 89–90
Rosario Central 8, 11, 34
Rous, Sir Stanley 26, 27–8
rugby 170
rules 166: formulation 4; lack of in folk
  football 2
Russia, diffusion of football 8

Sampdoria FC 11, 21, 35, 55–6, 77
sanctions, players 109–10
satellite television 86, 105; pay-per-
  view 86, 92–4; UK 91–2
Scandinavia: class 34; football
  grounds 67; women's football 158
schools, public 3–4, 155, 166
scientific approach, football 133, 135

Scotland 6, 25, 26: advertisements 89;
  casuals 46, 50–1: defence 130;
  finance 112–13; folk football 2;
  football ground disasters 73–4;
  football grounds 66, 67–8;
  hooliganism 39, 49, 52, 64;
  international conflicts 139;
  masculinities 155; national identity
  29, 31; nationalist rivalry 13; politics
  16; professionalism 4–5; racism 163;
  regional rivalry 13; religion 18–19;
  tactics 135; Tartan Army 60–1, 150;
  televised football 91–2, 93, 94
Scottish Football Association (SFA) 60
season tickets 78–9
secularization, folk football 3
security, football grounds 73
semantics 9–10, 14–16
sexism 146
Sheffield 47: two-club rivalries 11
shirt sponsorship 89–90
Singapore, gambling 102–3
skills: playing 128–9, 137–8;
  appreciation of 156
slow motion action 144
soccerati 151
social complexity 23–4
socialism, state: rivalry and 14
sociological research: fan sub-
  cultures 64: football 169–71; as
  football formation 171–3: football
  grounds 71–2; hooliganism 40–9;
  masculinities 156–7; social
  solidarity 14–16
solidarity, social 14–16: folk football 3
South Africa 28: diffusion of
  football 7–8; politics and football 16
Soviet Union 14: football clubs 87
space: access to 78–80; and emotions
  69–72; and rivalry 10–11; *see also*
  grounds
Spain: capitalization 100; club
  rivalry 12; diffusion of football 8;
  football clubs 87; football grounds
  67, 68; national identity 27; player
  contracts 123; player recruitment
  123; tactics 131; two-club rivalry 11;
  ultras 57

Spartak Moscow 14, 87
spectators *see* supporters
sponsorship 89–91, 104, 117, 168
status crystallization 115–16
stereotypes and stereotyping 138, 140:
   racial 163
steroids, anabolic 110
street football 78
structure, social: action and 127–8
styles, playing 127–45: national 166
sub-cultures: fan 63–5; hooligan 51–2,
   168, 172; player 113–16, 124, 155;
   ultràs 54–6
sublime 173
superstitions 20
support: expressive forms of 147;
   polarization of 34–5
supporter groups: Italy 55; *see also
   barras bravas*; Tartan Army; *ultràs*
supporters 167, 169: commodification
   and 104–5; culture 39–65; effects of
   television 95; and football
   grounds 69–72; ground location
   71–2; growth of 5–6; impact of free
   agentry 122; market exclusion of
   78–80, 96, 106, 145, 164–5; player
   retirement 125; post-fans 146;
   women 152–3, 154
supporters associations:
   independent 61–3; official 62
surveillance, football grounds 81–2
suspensions, match 109–10, 124
Sweden: diffusion of football 8; fan
   projects 63; football style 141–2;
   players 123; racism 160
Swiss Bolt system 131–2
Switzerland, diffusion of football 8
syntax 9–14

tactics 167, 168, 169: analytical
   problems 136–8; modernity 131–4,
   135, 143–4; modernization 130–1;
   post-modernity 134–6, 142–5;
   traditional period 129–30, 135
Tapie, Bernard 98, 100
Tartan Army 60–1, 150
task force, televised football 97
Taylor Report (1990) 76, 79, 99

Taylor, Ian 76: hooliganism 40–2
team kits 89
technology, political impact of 144–5
television 86, 168–9: critical responses
   to 95–7; in dugouts 68; football
   matches 84–5; football programmes
   149; impact of 91–7; pay-per-
   view 86, 92–4; political impact of
   144–5; satellite 105; UK football
   and 91–2; women viewers 154
television revenue 88, 104: players'
   share 95–6, 112; UK 91–2
Televista 96
territoriality, hooligans 43
third defender, notion of 136–7
ticketing policy 78–80
time and motion, in football 143–4
time-outs 144
topophilia and topophobia 69–72, 80–1
Torneos y Competencias (T y C) 96
total football 133–4, 135
tourism 148
traditional period 9, 31: amateurs 107;
   business 103; club finance 103; club
   frameworks 87–8; club names 33;
   England 28–9; football 166–7;
   football grounds 66–7, 83;
   hooligans 49; player recruitment
   114; Scotland 29; tactics 129–30,
   135
trainers 108
training, player 108–9
transfer market 169: corruption 103;
   player mobility 121–3
transgression, authorized: carnival as
   61
Turkey 13

UK: anti-racism campaigns 160–2, 164;
   class 146; decline in influence 24–8;
   fan sub-cultures 63–5; football
   ground disasters 72, 73–5; football
   grounds 66–8; football prehistory
   1–2; gambling 102; government
   policies for televised football 97;
   hooliganism 39–52; players 107–8,
   113–14, 124; racism 163; relations
   with FIFA 25; tactics 134–5;

UK *cont'd.*
   television 91–2; women spectators
   152–3; *see also specific countries*
ultràs 46, 48, 63, 64, 168: ground
   location 71; and hooliganism 56–8;
   names 54; organization 55;
   research 54; sub-culture 54–6
uncertainty of outcome 95–6
Union des Associations Européennes de
   Football (UEFA) 27, 60, 74, 79;
   European League 93; televised
   football 94; transfer system 122;
   videotapes 144
United States 13, 26, 169: national
   identity 36–7; televised sport 91;
   women 146, 158, 164
urban culture, football's centrality to
   5–6
urban deprivation, players 140–1
Urry, John 148
Uruguay 26: class 11–12, 35; diffusion
   of football 8–9; industrial conflict
   113; national identity 30–1, 32, 31;
   nationalist rivalry 13

Valdano, Jorge 120, 135
Vavà 26
videotaped evidence 144
violence: in folk football 2–3; pyscho-
   social pleasures of 52–4; *see also*
   hooligans

Waddington, Ivan 44

wage, maximum 6: abolishment of 108,
   112, 116, 124
Wales 26: folk football 2
Weber, Max: folk football 2, 3;
   rationalization 4
West Ham FC 10, 46–7, 89, 125, 156
Whirl style 133–4
Williams, John 44, 76
Wingless Wonders system 132–3
witchcraft 19–20
women 146, 164, 170, 171:
   attendance 150, 164; carnival
   fans 60; in football culture 157–9;
   historical context 152–4; and
   hooliganism 153–4; players 157;
   private domains 155
women's football 153
World Cups 25, 167–8

young players: black 163;
   recruitment 114–15
youth teams, scrapping of 123
youth training programmes, under
   threat 123
youths, Afro-Caribbean and Asian
   164
Yugoslavia 27: club rivalry 13;
   corruption 101

Zagalo, 26
Zanzibar 159
Zico 110, 138
zona style 134